AUGUSTAN STUDIES

AUGUSTAN STUDIES

GEOFFREY TILLOTSON

UNIVERSITY OF LONDON
THE ATHLONE PRESS
1961

Published by
THE ATHLONE PRESS
UNIVERSITY OF LONDON
at 2 *Gower Street London* WC1
Distributed by Constable & Co Ltd
12 *Orange Street London* WC2
Canada
University of Toronto Press
U.S.A
Oxford University Press Inc
New York

L
C

6001201781
204 804
English

Printed in Great Britain by the
SHENVAL PRESS LTD
LONDON, HERTFORD AND HARLOW

TO MY FRIENDS

WALTER JACKSON BATE

AND

WYNDHAM KETTON-CREMER

BIBLIOGRAPHICAL NOTE AND ACKNOWLEDGMENTS

OF THE PIECES included in this book five are printed for the first time, and the rest, all but one of which are out of print, reappear in revised form. All three essays on poetic diction are occasional pieces, written in response to invitations, and are left as such: I have linked them with cross-references here and there; when they draw on the same material, they use it differently.

The following are the bibliographical particulars for the reprinted pieces, and I am grateful to editors and publishers for allowing their reappearance here, in revised form. 'Augustan Poetic Diction' I and II, originally called 'Eighteenth-Century Poetic Diction', appeared in my *Essays in Criticism and Research*, 1942. Appendix II to 'More about Poetic Diction' is the main part of a notice published in the *Modern Language Review*, XLV, 1950. 'The Manner of Proceeding in Certain Eighteenth- and Early Nineteenth-Century Poems' was delivered as the Warton Lecture of the British Academy for 1948, and was printed in the *Proceedings* of the Academy. The pieces on Pope's minor poems and letters appeared in *The Times Literary Supplement* for 22 October 1954 and 4 January 1957, and 'Pope's Epistle to Harley' in *Pope and His Contemporaries: Essays Presented to George Sherburn*, edited by J. L. Clifford and Louis A. Landa (Oxford, 1949). 'Johnson's Dictionary' served for an address at Stationers' Hall on the occasion of the 'Commemoration of the Bi-Centenary of the Publication of Johnson's Dictionary (Entered at Stationers' Hall 10 April 1755, Published 15 April 1755)', being printed in the *Spectator* of 28 April 1955. 'Time in *Rasselas*' was included in a supplement to *Cairo Studies in English*, collected by Professor Magdi Wahba, and entitled *Bicentenary Essays on 'Rasselas'* (Cairo, 1959).

Much of 'Grongar Hill' was broadcast on the Third Programme of the BBC in 1948.

I wish to thank several of my colleagues in Birkbeck for their kindness in answering questions, and in particular to thank Mr J. F. Jones, Curator of the County Museum, Carmarthen, who checked and enriched my topographical annotations of 'Grongar Hill'. Miss Carol Landon helped with the checking and the proofs, and Dr Frances Mayhew Rippy compiled the index; to both of them I am duly grateful.

G. T.

Birkbeck College
University of London
13 November 1959

CONTENTS

ABBREVIATIONS

Boswell's *Life of Johnson*, ed. G. Birkbeck Hill, revised and enlarged by L. F. Powell, 6 vols., Oxford, 1934–40

Coleridge, *Biographia Literaria*, ed. J. Shawcross, 2 vols., Oxford, 1907

Dryden, *Essays*, selected and ed. W. P. Ker, 2 vols., Oxford, 1900

Gray, *The Correspondence*, ed. Paget Toynbee and Leonard Whibley, 3 vols., Oxford, 1935

Johnson, *Lives of the English Poets*, ed. G. Birkbeck Hill, 3 vols., Oxford, 1905

Keats, *Letters*, ed. Maurice Buxton Forman, 3rd edn., Oxford, 1947

Pope, *The Correspondence*, ed. George Sherburn, 5 vols., Oxford, 1956

Ruskin, *The Works*, ed. E. T. Cook and Alexander Wedderburn, 39 vols., 1903–12

Spence, J., *Anecdotes, Observations, and Characters, of Books and Men*, ed. S. W. Singer, 1820

Spingarn, J. E. (ed.), *Critical Essays of the Seventeenth Century*, 3 vols., Oxford, 1908–9

AUGUSTAN POETIC DICTION: I

In THE greatest poetry of the ages of Dryden and Pope the question of 'poetic diction' scarcely arises:

> When I consider life, 'tis all a cheat;
> Yet, fool'd with hope, men favour the deceit;
> Trust on, and think to-morrow will repay:
> To-morrow's falser than the former day. . . .[1]

> The Dean is dead, (*and what is Trumps?*)[2]

> Yes, I am proud; I must be proud to see
> Men not afraid of God, afraid of me. . . .[3]

> SLOW RISES WORTH BY POVERTY DEPRESS'D:
> But here more slow, where all are slaves to gold,
> Where looks are merchandise and smiles are sold. . . .[4]

> No farther seek his merits to disclose,
> Or draw his frailties from their dread abode,
> (There they alike in trembling hope repose,)
> The bosom of his Father and his God.[5]

In these passages there is no use of prescribed words, nothing in the vocabulary that the subject has not directly and of itself suggested to the poet. These poets wrote their best poetry with man as theme. Whatever else they spoke of, it was with him as stated reference. They stood at the human centre, and saw the horizon and the sky in the sort of way that Ptolemy saw the universe. Man was the centre, however wide the circle described by his stretched compass. Wordsworth thought of the poet as a 'man speaking to men'. Clearly this is the implied view of all poets who publish their poems. Much therefore

---

[1] Dryden, *Aureng-Zebe*, IV. i. 33 ff.
[2] Swift, 'Verses on the Death of Dr Swift', l. 228
[3] Pope, *Imitations of Horace*, 'Epil. to the Satires', ii. 208 f.
[4] Johnson, *London*, ll. 177 ff.   [5] Gray, 'Elegy', ll. 125 ff.

depends on what is meant by 'man' and what by 'men'. If the poets of the late seventeenth and early eighteenth centuries had used this phrase, as they might well have done, they would have meant by 'man' the poet in his capacity as member of a civilized society, and by 'men' those other members of it who resembled him in everything but poetic gifts.

2

For the reception of their discoveries and considerations on the human theme these poets had perfected one metre in particular, a version of the heroic couplet. This version, consciously inaugurated by Waller and steadily improved on by Dryden (at his best) and by Pope, became the most precise metre ever used in English verse. The rules that were evolved for its use have never been fully stated. The ten feet of the couplet were to be kept as closely iambic as possible, the metrical surprises accordingly being of fine gradation. The rimes were to fall on monosyllabic words which therefore received, and could bear to receive, the full terminal accent of the line. Marvell's rime in

> And yonder all before us lye
> Desarts of vast Eternity,

would have been a blemish in one of Pope's poems since -*ty* was a weak syllable. The monosyllabic rime-word, if possible, should have a long vowel, and it was best if one of the two rime-words of the couplet were a verb. Within particular couplets the poet worked out as many contrasts and parallels as he could, providing the maximum number of internal geometrical relationships. Denham's lines on the Thames had fascinated later poets with the possibilities of this kind of configuration. They were frequently imitated—too frequently for Swift's pleasure. Their kind of verbal manipulation was improved on, until in Pope a couplet will often suggest a figure in Euclid, its vowels and consonants, its sense-oppositions and sense-attractions, fitted together like arcs and lines.

> A Fop their Passion, but their Prize a Sot;
> Alive, ridiculous, and dead, forgot![1]

[1] *Moral Essays*, ii. 247 f.

A manner such as this keeps the reader's brain active, fetching and carrying. It is a metre for educated people. No meaning is possible for the 'mind' to review, or for the 'spirit' to kindle at, till the 'brain' has mastered the Euclidean relationships. This manner and metre were evolved to receive the discoveries and observations which these poets made concerning man. They saw man as an oxymoron, a cross-hatching, a contradiction in terms:

> Chaos of Thought and Passion, all confus'd;
> Still by himself abus'd, or disabus'd;
> Created half to rise, and half to fall;
> Great lord of all things, yet a prey to all;
> Sole judge of Truth, in endless Error hurl'd:
> The glory, jest, and riddle of the world![1]

To say what they saw inevitably required the couplet. And the fearlessness of their meaning as inevitably required that they should use words freely.

3

What they saw in external nature was limited and modified in statement by the metre they were finding so perfect for their human materials. A metre of contrasts and concision was un-fitted for rendering the large freedom of landscape. That large freedom they saw and valued, but did not much use, certainly not much in the couplet. When they did use it in the couplet its powerfulness shrank, because of the very 'correctness' of their versification. But if they had felt the large freedom strongly enough, they would have found a right metre for it. John Philips and Thomson found the metre when they wanted it. Dryden and Pope kept to the couplet in their best poems be-cause their matter included nothing to make them reject it. Pope was under no delusions about the beauty of the external world; Dryden and he were under no delusions about its splendour. Pope stated to Spence his belief that a tree was a nobler object than a king in his coronation robes.[2] Yet he has no description of a tree to put beside that of Belinda's exquisite

---

[1] *Essay on Man*, ii. 13 ff. [2] Spence, *Anecdotes*, p. 11.

'petticoat'. He thought that a fine lady would like the stars because they reminded her of candles, and that this would be a pity.[1] Yet in his poems the star he gave most attention to was a fictitious one, the translated lock of Belinda. And the court decoration ('Bare the mean Heart that lurks beneath a Star')[2] was of more value to his work than Hesperus. Even in the superb line

> The sick'ning stars fade off th' ethereal plain,[3]

it is not the actual night he is thinking of, but the night in the mind of man when the curtain of a universal intellectual darkness is being let fall. The poet did not choose to write of external nature in the way Shelley was to, because no man he ever knew, or ever wished to know, so dissolved his 'godlike reason' in ecstasy. Such a man for Dryden and Pope would have been, almost literally, a lunatic, an 'enthusiast'. In so far as man's experience concerned external nature, Dryden, Pope and the rest admit it freely to their verse. And when they admit it they may do one of two things—provide it with words newly chosen for itself, or provide it with 'diction'. If the poet is competent he will bestow or withhold diction as his subject demands. Whether he does one or the other will depend on whether he is looking at external nature for the new experience it adds to his human sum, or whether he is using remembered scraps of it for his own human purpose and pleasure, and for those of his readers. Dryden and Pope most often look on it for what it can give, or, since it is never their main theme, show by the quality of their incidental allusions that they have so looked at it. This is Dryden's description of a storm:

> . . . the hollow sound
> Sung in the Leaves, the Forest shook around,
> Air blacken'd; rowl'd the Thunder; groan'd the Ground. $\Big\}$ 4

This account is obviously individual. (There is something in Dryden's descriptive poetry that recalls Uccello—the heraldic brightness of the colour, the uniform density of the things as

---

[1] Spence, *Anecdotes*, p. 11.
[3] *Dunciad*, iv. 636.
[2] *Imitations of Horace*, Sat. ii. i. 108.
[4] 'Theodore and Honoria', ll. 264 ff.

represented, the ponderous neatness and jolly gravity.) As an example from Pope one might take:

> As to soft gales top-heavy pines bow low
> Their heads, and lift them as they cease to blow.[1]

This is how they saw external nature when they wanted to. But at times they were concerned with seeing it not so much as they knew it deserved to be seen but as they wanted to see it. They superimposed on nature what they considered at certain times to be desirable. They made a selection from nature of elements that suited their interests. This is what all poets do. Dryden, Pope and the rest differ only in what they superimpose and in what they select. They superimposed on nature some of their own humanity. Shakespeare, to take an Elizabethan instance, had superimposed human qualities on nature. He saw waves, for example, as striving, as if they were beasts or men (or, more truly, perhaps, as if they were boys). Romeo even sees the severing clouds as envious—that is, as partaking of a primitive emotion common to men and perhaps to beasts. But the humanity which Dryden and Pope project on to nature is more intellectual and sophisticated, more like the humanity they valued in themselves. In *Windsor Forest* comes:

> O'er sandy wilds were yellow harvests spread,
> The forest wonder'd at th' unusual grain. . . .[2]

Their regard for man made them a little haughty among stars, trees and animals. For them 'man superior walks Amid the glad creation' (the words, surprisingly, are Thomson's).[3] They are interested in nature as it is controlled by man. In this they resembled their hero Virgil, whose *Georgics* rejected the belief of Lucretius that the productiveness of nature was on the wane for the belief that, in Cicero's words, 'the earth, if rightly dealt with, never refuses the "imperium" of man'.[4] Charles II's rigidly controlled garden at St James's, with its Mall, its rectangular

---

[1] *Dunciad*, ii. 391 f.   [2] ll. 88 f.   [3] 'Spring', ll. 170 f.
[4] W. Y. Sellar, *The Roman Poets of the Augustan Age: Virgil*, Oxford, 1897 edn., p. 208.

sheet of water (the 'canal'), its borders of equispaced limes, showed that man's control of nature could be virtually complete within limits, just as for Virgil it could be as complete as Rome's control over a conquered people. They controlled nature perfectly in their gardens. The landscape proved less tractable, though the Kents and 'Capability' Browns did what they could. But their mental control over landscape could be complete at will. And this is what happens in their pastorals, by a kind of wish-fulfilment.

5

The theme of the pastoral was one of man, but it was man at his faintest. An age which valued satire could only amuse itself in pastoral. Man is the theme still, but it is man as a pretty creature, provided with set and toy emotions which last only to the end of the poem. The melodious tear was shed, the lips were silked with a smile, and all this was done out-of-doors. The traditions of pastoral forbad this out-of-doors to be a garden. It had to be landscape. But the landscape, in verse at least, could be perfectly made to own man's imperium.

The pastoralists therefore controlled its appearance in their verse with the same rigid hand that King Charles's gardeners had used on the configuration of St James's Park. They 'methodized' it by taming it in diction, by caging it in a small group of words which satisfied their garden-bred sense of elegance. This sense of elegance required simplification. The landscape, always limited in pastoral, was further limited by being robbed of all characteristics except those which proved its gentleness, its 'tamedness'. The brook could be there but should be a stream. The qualities of the word *stream* cleared away all the pebbles and angles of the brook, canalized it. The stream should purl rather than babble. If the purl of the stream was for some reason undesirable in a line, its purity would be chemically certified as *crystal*. There should be meadows or meads. There should be woods, but not so near that you could see any 'knotty, knarry barren treës old'. The woods should be beheld distantly and seen as a whole, and seen as *waving*. This is how they composed their 'sylvan scenes', a phrase which they borrow from Milton. The imperium of man was further insisted on by the frequent allusion to nature in terms of what man adapted from it for his own use: lawns were *velvet*, sheep *fleecy*. Nature was shown as imitating art—even the fields of heaven for Isaac Watts 'stand *drest* in living green'. The landscapes of Broome and Fenton, both published in the 'Miscellany' of 1712, show with what uniform completeness external nature could be commanded. Broome writes:

> Thee, Shepherd, thee the pleasurable Woods,
> The painted Meadows, and the Crystal Floods,
> Claim, and invite thee to their sweet Abodes.

And a little later he goes on with 'Here Fountains warble . . .'. Fenton, some thirty pages farther on, has the line

> Ye warbling Fountains, and ye Chrystal Floods.

The motto of both these passages is *Everything of the Best*. Broome and Fenton are self-elected Tweedledum and Tweedledee. They are two poets playing for safety. But among the better pastoral poets, though the material is virtually the same, the sense of the ready-made is defeated. The pastorals of Pope, of Ambrose Philips, and of Gay (when he outgrows his wish to parody) employ the recognized diction, but their styles are as distinct as the different flavours of cheese. To amplify one instance: Mr C. V. Deane, in his thoughtful study, shows how the manuscript of Pope's *Pastorals* exhibits the contemporary diction seeking and attaining exactitude of music and statement: 'It cannot be said . . . that in the *Pastorals* Pope's poetic diction becomes a substitute for poetic feeling.'[1] The eighteenth century liked a restriction which operated before the poem was begun, which operated as a condition of the 'inspiration'. Inside that restriction they could keep holiday and the best of them did. And they took advantage of a law which operates in poetry as in everything else, the law of scale, of proportion. They knew that a reader soon scrambles on to the level of the poem and that, when he has reached it, that level becomes his norm. In *Endymion* everything is so exotic that, to provide a surprise, Keats almost has to burst a blood-vessel. In Gray's 'Elegy' the

---

[1] *Aspects of Eighteenth-century Nature Poetry*, Oxford, 1935, p. 116.

even tenor of the style gives a word like 'tinklings' the equivalent of an 'angelic strength', of a 'happy valiancy'. Fenton, small poet as he is, counts on the benefits of this law. A few lines after the line quoted above he introduces the phrase 'living fountains', and with all the more effectiveness after his poetic sleep. Bolder and better poets used this law to the full, especially after the heartening example of Dryden, whose verbs are more habitually energetic than those of any other English poet.

6

The use of diction by these poets offered a major difficulty to nineteenth-century readers, and still offers difficulty. If that use is understood, the poetry made out of it may be seen at least for what it was. Virgil in his *Georgics* had been troubled by the unpoetical frankness of his material. His problem, as Dryden translated it, ran:

> Nor can I doubt what Oyl I must bestow,
> To raise my Subject from a Ground so low:
> And the mean Matter which my Theme affords,
> T' embellish with Magnificence of Words.[1]

The poetic conscience behind that weighed heavily with poets who treated Virgil with awe. Virgil had got over his difficulty partly by ignoring it and writing straight ahead of scabs and footrot, and partly by relying on phrases consecrated to the epic and on the spell of his versification. There is in the georgic poetry of the eighteenth century and in the allied local poetry which began with 'Cooper's Hill' a tendency to be stately as befitted Virgil's conception of poetry. The poets of the eighteenth century attain gracefulness, as Virgil did, by their metre. And more than Virgil needed to do, they attain it by restricting their vocabulary and by preferring phrases like 'fleecy care'. The reasons behind their choice of these phrases are complex. In the work of good poets they are not there simply as a means of avoiding the mention of low material, nor even for the acquisition of full-vowelled music ('fleecy care' is beautiful in this way). The good poets discriminate their use. When a poet like Milton takes up a fashion, he does so because he wants to. He spoke of a

---

[1] iii. 453 ff.

moonlit 'finny drove'[1] because he wanted the reader to be
aware of an exquisite propulsion of fins. In *Windsor Forest*
and the *Seasons*, phrases based on his formula are used only
when the meaning calls for them. This is not as often as the
meaning of *fish* (plural) and *birds* appear, but only when fish
or birds are being thought of as distinct in their appearance
from other groups of creatures. Both Pope and Thomson use
fish and *birds* whenever they want to. And they specify in un-
compromisingly straightforward terms what particular fish or
bird they mean when they mean it—carp, pike, pheasant, lapwing, woodcock. But when they are thinking of fish, as fish are
distinct from birds or beasts, they employ the formula which
embodies their distinction. When Thomson speaks of the
sportsmen with 'gun' and 'spaniel' who

> Distress the footed or the feathered game[2]

he is not merely decorating his poem, but differentiating the
game that is hit flying from the game that is hit running. When
he calls birds 'the glossy kind' it is because he is going on to
show how that glossiness counts in the mating season, when the
male birds

> . . . shiver every feather with desire.[3]

When he speaks of young birds as 'feathered youth',[4] he means
that the birds though young are not too young to have feathers.
He is compressing into two words a long meaning, compressing
it in a way common at the time for other materials than those
of external nature. Pope in *Windsor Forest* speaks of 'the leaden
death' (death by bullet) and 'the iron squadrons' (cavalry).[5]
It is part of the concentration learned from the Roman poets
that often shows itself also in a constricted syntax within the
couplet.

7

These poets knew that the pastoral was a deception. Dryden

---

[1] *Comus*, l. 115.   [2] 'Winter', l. 793.   [3] 'Spring', ll. 617 ff.
[4] id., l. 729.   [5] ll. 132, 363.

knew that even the pastorals of Virgil were playthings, and
vented the denied interests of his mind by translating

> est mihi namque domi pater, est iniusta noverca[1]

by

> A Stepdame too I have, a cursed she,
> Who rules my Hen-peck'd Sire, and orders me.[2]

The gusto even of human triviality was powerful enough to
break into Dryden's pastoral, even into man's chosen holiday
from life. And the force of the tempest was more powerful still.
For all man's forethought, for all his art, there might fall a 'universal darkness', ruining more than his shielded pastoral: Pope's

> The fox obscene to gaping tombs retires,
> And savage howlings fill the sacred quires,[3]

and Gray's adaptation

> Purg'd by the sword and beautifyed by fire,
>   Then had we seen proud London's hated walls,
> Owls might have hooted in St. Peter's Quire,
>   And foxes stunk and litter'd in St Paul's,[4]

and, later, there are Cunningham's lovely lines

> The lizard and the lazy lurking bat
> Inhabit now, perhaps, the painted room. . . .[5]

In passages such as these, in Dryden's and Thomson's storms, in
Gray's dread and courage among mountains, the 'age of reason'
acknowledged the enormous forces of man's environment.

---

[1] *Ecl.* iii. 33.   [2] ll. 48 f.   [3] *Windsor Forest*, ll. 71 f.
[4] 'Impromptu, suggested by a View . . .', ll. 21 ff.
[5] 'Elegy on a Pile of Ruins', ll. 77 f.

AUGUSTAN POETIC DICTION: II

It is still true that most readers of eighteenth-century poetry approach it by way of nineteenth-century poetry. They have been brought up to expect poetry to be written in a certain way, its words to be chosen in accordance with certain principles. They know what Wordsworth said about Pope before they read Pope. And this means that when they read Pope and other eighteenth-century poets, they apply the wrong criteria: criteria which are wrong because irrelevant.

These wrong criteria are often applied to the poetic diction of eighteenth-century poetry. In using the terms 'eighteenth-century' and 'nineteenth-century' I do not intend to imply that they carry any well-defined meanings for the historian or critic of the poetic diction. Blake, who uses almost none of the diction, is an eighteenth-century poet. On the other hand, poets born later are not necessarily immune from the waning infection. The passionate attack on the diction made by Wordsworth and Coleridge, whom we think of as nineteenth-century poets, is all the more passionate because the eighteenth-century is in their blood and will not be expelled. Byron, of course, glories in the ancestral germs. Keats and, to a smaller extent, Shelley use the diction more than is generally seen, and even Tennyson does not cut himself off from it, though he seems to discover it again for himself rather than to use it from habit. Browning appears to be the first poet of the nineteenth century who is not indebted to the diction.

The generalizations made below will apply in various degrees to the poets of the two centuries and also to poets of the seventeenth and the sixteenth, since the methods of forming the diction, and even part of the diction itself, are already found in Spenser, in Sylvester's translation of Du Bartas, and in most succeeding poets except, broadly speaking, the metaphysicals.

2

It is generally true that the vocabulary of nineteenth-century poetry is restricted only in so far as the vocabulary of any poetry is restricted, i.e. only in so far as the subject-matter is restricted. Poems in the nineteenth century tend to be written on what were then considered 'poetical' subjects. The reservation is a serious one when we consider the poetry of other centuries, including our own since 1920; but, barring this, there is no limitation of vocabulary. There still remained, therefore, a great deal of the dictionary out of which the nineteenth-century poet could choose his words. The nineteenth-century poet may be said to provide each poem (whatever the subject, whatever the form) with new diction. He writes almost as if he were the first and the only poet in the world:

> As if he were Earth's first-born birth
> And none had lived before him.[1]

The nineteenth-century poet discovers a new poetic territory and maps it out by himself.

In the eighteenth century the poet was not so free. Then the 'kinds' of poetry were still seen as distinct, and as requiring the use of different kinds of diction. In accordance with this principle Johnson noted a deficiency in two poets of the preceding century: Cowley, he wrote,

makes no selection of words. . . . It seems to follow [sc. merely] from the necessity of the subject, rather than the care of the writer, that the diction of his heroick poem is less familiar than that of his slightest writings. He has given not the same numbers, but the same diction, to the gentle Anacreon and the tempestuous Pindar.[2]

And in the same *Lives* comes this observation on Milton's style, a style in which diction figures prominently:

[1] Wordsworth, 'Expostulation and Reply', ll. 11 f. (adapted).

[2] *Lives of the Poets*, i. 59. This quotation as well as others in my book demonstrates a truth that will come as a surprise to many—that Johnson is a critic both subtle and minute. He is our only substantial critic when it come to rimes—he discovered, for instance, that those of Pope's epitaph on Newton (*night-light*) 'are too nearly allied' (*Lives*, iii. 270). In some respects he is an exquisite among critics. Because he always speaks with force and clarity does not mean that his sense of what is before him, especially when it has to do with poetic technique, is not of a snail-horn sensitiveness.

[it] was not modified by his subject: what is shown with greater extent in *Paradise Lost* may be found in *Comus*.[1]

It follows that much had to be learned from earlier poetry before a poet could write correctly, without offending the rules and distinctions acknowledged by poets and readers. An eighteenth-century poet did not have to create the taste by which he was enjoyed to the same extent as a nineteenth-century poet was conscious of having to.[2] The kinds were ready waiting for him, and, if the rules for the kinds in which he elected to write were properly complied with, the products were recognizable as poems of those kinds. It goes without saying that for the products to be good poems the 'material' to which the rules were applied had itself to be good. The kinds included epic, tragedy in verse, pindaric, elegy, heroic and familiar epistle, pastoral, georgic, occasional verse, translation and imitation. Pope chose to tackle all these kinds in turn. He saw them as distinct:

> After writing a poem, one should correct it all over, with one single view at a time. Thus for language; if an elegy; 'these lines are very good, but are not they of too heroical a strain?' and so *vice versa*. It appears very plainly, from comparing parallel passages touched both in the Iliad and Odyssey, that Homer did this; and it is yet plainer that Virgil did so, from the distinct styles he uses in his three sorts of poems. It always answers in him; and so constant an effect could not be the effect of chance.[3]

This observation is modified later, for when he came to write a poem he did not restrict it to a single kind, any more than did Virgil:

> Though Virgil, in his pastorals, has sometimes six or eight lines together that are epic: I have been so scrupulous as scarce ever to admit above two together, even in the Messiah.[4]

Mixing the kinds, he knew what he was doing and marked off the component parts by the use of different kinds of diction (diction brings with it other linguistic modes such as personification, apostrophe, exclamation). These rules and principles

---

[1] id., i. 190.
[2] See Wordsworth, 'Essay, Supplementary to the Preface [of 1815]'.
[3] Spence, *Anecdotes*, pp. 23 f.   [4] id., p. 312.

may seem curious pedantry after the practice of nineteenth-century poets. But they were based on first-hand scrutiny of good poetry in the past, and so were as unpedantic in the hands of a poet, as, say, the study of Shakespeare was unpedantic in the hands of Keats—or in the hands of Dryden or Pope, for that matter.

For Pope, then, poetic diction would cover all the words used in all the kinds (which meant virtually all the words in the dictionary, except those that nobody knew the meaning of without intense specialization in technical fields). When Pope speaks of words in 'An Essay on Criticism' his criterion of their correct use is appropriateness. He makes no reference to poetic diction.[1]

He does use the term, however, in the 'Preface' to his translation of the *Iliad*, but not in Wordsworth's sense:

> If we descend from hence [i.e. from remarking Homer's descriptions, images and similes] to the *Expression*, we see the bright Imagination of *Homer* shining out in the most enliven'd Forms of it. We acknowledge him the Father of Poetical Diction, the first who taught that *Language of the Gods* to Men. His Expression is like the colouring of some great Masters, which discovers itself to be laid on boldly, and executed with Rapidity. It is indeed the strongest and most glowing imaginable, and touch'd with the greatest Spirit. *Aristotle* had reason to say, He was the only Poet who had found out *Living Words*; there are in him more daring Figures and Metaphors than in any good Author whatever. An Arrow is *impatient* to be on the Wing, a Weapon *thirsts* to drink the Blood of an Enemy, and the like. Yet his Expression is never too big for the Sense, but justly great in proportion to it: 'Tis the Sentiment that Swells and fills out the Diction, which rises with it, and forms itself about it. For in the same degree that a *Thought* is warmer, an *Expression* will be brighter; and as That is more strong, This will become more perspicuous: Like Glass in the Furnace which grows to a greater Magnitude, and refines to a greater Clearness, only as the *Breath* within is more powerful, and the *Heat* more intense.[2]

What follows in the next paragraph must be read in the light of this:

> To throw his Language more out of Prose, *Homer* seems to have

---

[1] For the history of the use of the term see below, p. 46.
[2] Pope, *The Iliad of Homer* (1715: folio edn.), i. D 2ᵛ.

affected the *Compound-Epithets*. This was a sort of Composition peculiarly proper to Poetry, not only as it heighten'd the *Diction*, but as it assisted and fill'd the *Numbers* with greater Sound and Pomp, and likewise conduced in some measure to thicken the *Images*.[1]

This statement about the diction of poetry has a general validity. It would be subscribed to by almost all poets and critics: one exception would be Malherbe. 'In the same degree that a *Thought* is warmer, an *Expression* will be brighter. . . '. Even Wordsworth, despite statements implying the contrary, is found allowing Pope's general position. He seems indeed to be repeating Pope's words—it was to be expected that he should pay attention to Pope's 'Preface' before attacking the diction which he considered to have sprung from the translation that 'Preface' introduced. Wordsworth writes:

The earliest poets of all nations generally wrote from passion excited by real events . . . feeling powerfully as they did, their language was daring and figurative.[2]

Pope's use of the term poetic diction has nothing to do with the narrower sense in which it was used by Wordsworth and others in relation to the poetry of the eighteenth century. He used it to denote expression in poetry that is extraordinary expression. Over most of a poet's verse the diction that is suitable will be diction equally suitable for prose. When, however, his sense becomes more glowingly poetical, he will need a more glowing diction, and this Pope distinguishes as 'poetic'. It is diction in which compound epithets and epithets that are strongly metaphorical find a place.

3

Poetic diction in Wordsworth's sense can only be said to exist in certain kinds of eighteenth-century poetry. As he and Coleridge saw, there is little or no poetic diction in the satires, familiar epistles, and occasional verse. (In the elegy and the heroic epistle the poetic diction is of a kind that has passed

---

[1] Pope, *The Iliad of Homer* (1715: folio edn.), i. E I^r.

[2] 'Appendix' (on poetic diction) added in 1802 to the 'Preface' (1800) to the *Lyrical Ballads* (*Wordsworth's Preface to Lyrical Ballads*, ed. W. J. B. Owen, Copenhagen, 1957, p. 134).

almost unnoticed by the critics: this diction includes such words as *sad, beauteous, trembling, pensive.*) In the satires and familiar epistles the vocabulary is as free in principle as that used in any nineteenth-century poem—*The Ring and the Book,* for example. The vocabulary of all nineteenth-century poetry cowers into a corner when the *Dunciad* walks abroad, seeking whom it may devour. And this applies even to those parts of it where the subject is a favourite one of the nineteenth-century poetry, where the material is external nature. In the same way that the primary human emotions tended to mean for Matthew Arnold only the noble primary human emotions, external nature tended to mean for the nineteenth-century poets only what was 'beautiful' and noble in it. But Pope knew no such distinction. In the *Dunciad* there are the isles of fragrance, the lily-silver'd vales, but also other things:

> So watchful Bruin forms, with plastic care,
> Each growing lump, and brings it to a Bear.[1]

Or

> Next, o'er his Books his eyes began to roll,
> In pleasing memory of all he stole,
> How here he sipp'd, how there he plunder'd snug,
> And suck'd all o'er, like an industrious Bug.[2]

The nineteenth-century poets were squeamish about external nature. So that even on their chosen ground the eighteenth-century poets can beat them in variety of appreciation. There is obviously no poetic diction in the *Dunciad*: except of course where Pope is deliberately mimicking the epic manner. When writing satire the eighteenth-century poet chose his words as freely as any poet. And the same is true when he was writing in several of the other kinds.

But when writing epic, pastoral, and georgic the eighteenth-century poet was not so free.[3] No eighteenth-century poet of much distinction writes an epic (Pope started to write one). But Milton wrote one, and Dryden translated one and part of

---

[1] i. 101 f. Cf. Dryden's inventive translation (ll. 559 ff.) of Ovid's *Metamorphoses,* xv. 379 ff.

[2] i. 127 ff.

[3] I denote by the terms 'pastoral' and 'georgic' not only poems like Pope's *Pastorals,* Thomson's *Seasons,* and Grainger's *Sugar-cane* but local poems like *Windsor Forest,* and Goldsmith's *Traveller.*

another: here the term eighteenth-century extends itself back-ward spiritually as for certain nineteenth-century poets it extends itself forward. Pope follows Dryden's example. There is no need, however, to examine the epic diction here because the nineteenth-century attackers, though they single out Pope's *Homer* as the source of the diction, select for examination that famous passage which could have stood equally in a pastoral or georgic. Coleridge, it seems, was the first to examine the 'popular lines' from Book VIII of the *Iliad*—

> As when the moon, refulgent lamp of night . . . [1]

Southey followed in the *Quarterly Review* (October 1814), and Wordsworth, a year later, in his 'Essay, Supplementary to the Preface' of the *Lyrical Ballads*.

It was in the pastoral and georgic, then, and in pastoral and georgic material intruding into other kinds, that the diction of the eighteenth-century poets came to be most despised. This fate was inevitable, since it was by jealously extending the descriptive elements in these two kinds that the nineteenth-century poets found the form for much of their own best writing. The champion of eighteenth-century diction must take his stand on pastoral and georgic, insisting, of course, that the eighteenth-century poets, unlike those of the nineteenth century, did not do their best work in those kinds. The best poetry of the eighteenth century is generally that of man (any man of a liberal education, of a certain reach of mind) and his fellow-men. The best poetry of the nineteenth century is generally that of man (an individual man of unusual distinction) and external nature: that is, the poet himself in a world of dawns and sunsets, streams and trees, mountains and sea. This difference of favourite subject-matter is at the root of all the differences be-

---

[1] *Biographia Literaria*, ed. J. Shawcross, 1907, i. 26 f. For Southey see the *Review of English Studies*, v (1929), 441 f. The passage, which struck eighteenth-century readers the more forcibly because of the interest in night-pieces shown by Rymer in the preface to his translation of Rapin, had been praised by James Ralph in the preface to his *Night* (1728) and by William Melmoth, who preferred Pope's version to Homer's (*Letters on Several Subjects by the late Sir Thomas Fitzosborne*, 1748, p. 44). Ralph, it may be noted, anticipated Southey in finding certain inconsistencies in the passage which he put down to the tyranny of rime. Arnold cited the passage for dispraise in *On the Study of Celtic Literature*, 1867, p. 164. By that date it was the stalest of chestnuts.

tween the poetry of the two centuries. In discussing poetic diction, therefore, we are comparing the best poetry of the nineteenth century with the less-than-best poetry of the eighteenth.

4

The nineteenth-century poets have a strong sense of the individual quality of each moment of experience. Late in their day the 'Epilogue' to Pater's *Renaissance* enunciated this part of their creed with exquisite finality. The nineteenth-century poets are humble—one is forced to the conclusion—because they see the external world as more startlingly beautiful than anything they have of their own, than anything they themselves can make. When they experience any natural phenomenon, they offer as white a mind as possible to receive it. They tremblingly hold up the mirror to nature. Their business as poets is to prove to their readers that they have been worthy of a unique experience. And so they write of skies, for instance, in the following ways:

> . . . the western sky,
> And its peculiar tint of yellow green.[1]

> The orange sky of evening died away.[2]

> Deep in the orange light of widening morn[3]

> . . . a bed of daffodil sky.[4]

> The orange and pale violet evening-sky.[5]

Coleridge, in the first of these quotations, feels it necessary to excuse his perception of a green sky by allowing that it was 'peculiar'. Later poets (green skies are frequent throughout the nineteenth century, and even survive as late as Empson) make no apology.

The eighteenth-century poets were not so humble. They saw

---

[1] Coleridge, 'Dejection: An Ode', ll. 28 f.
[2] Wordsworth, 'Influence of Natural Objects' (pubd. 1809: *Prelude*, 1850, i. 446).
[3] Shelley, *Prometheus Unbound*, II. i. 18.
[4] Tennyson, *Maud*, I. xxii. ii. 4.   [5] Arnold, 'Thyrsis', xvi. 9.

external nature not as culminating in its own most exquisite moments, but as culminating in man. Thomson, for instance, who looked at external nature as long and as lovingly as any nineteenth-century poet except Wordsworth, considered that

> . . . Man superior walks
> Amid the glad creation.[1]

Thomson forgets this superiority at times and so do many eighteenth-century poets, but this is their attitude in the main. The glad creation provides them with many instances of individual beauty, but they differ from the nineteenth-century poets in being impressed only up to a point. They seldom present a white mind to experience. They present a mind already coloured with all their past experience of all kinds: experience of other past instances of the beauty of external nature (they tend to generalize a description), experience of man, and experience of books (man's record of his experiences). Whereas the nineteenth-century poet is interested in the freshness of his response to experience, the eighteenth-century poet is interested in that response at a later stage: when the new has been welcomed by the old, when it has been accommodated to the existing harmony. It is this presence of a stage intermediary between the fresh response and the written poem that accounts for much of the difference between an eighteenth-century nature-poem and a nineteenth-century one. In every eighteenth-century pastoral and georgic there is something expected, predictable. And it is this element that requires and receives its poetic diction. The poetic diction represents the existing mind, the new words represent the freshness of the response. The poet's worth is measured by the quality of the new, and also by the quality of the new art with which he manipulates the old. Shelley, Newman and Bergson held that fresh experience is itself poetry. The mere fact that there is seen to be an orange and pale violet evening sky is poetry. The art in that phrase is negligible, the fact is everything. But an eighteenth-century nature-poem depends for half its existence on its paper and ink, on its words as words. When you read Arnold's line it is the thing, not the words, that you are given. Arnold—for all his

---

[1] 'Spring', ll. 170 f.

mind—does not exist except as a finger pointing to a unique sky. We praise him for his discovery.

It is another matter when we read the following lines from Pope's juvenile pastoral, 'Spring':

> Soon as the flocks shook off the nightly dews,
> Two swains, whom Love kept wakeful, and the Muse,
> Pour'd o'er the whitening vale their fleecy care . . .[1]

Here in the first and third lines (we must neglect the second because the human element in 'Thyrsis' is unrepresented in the line selected) we find a combination of new and old. Actually there is such a combination in Arnold's line: Wordsworth and Shelley, as my quotations show, had already seen an orange sky. But the combination in Arnold's line is accidental. His line is not, so to speak, built on theirs,[2] and he does not expect us to remember Shelley's 'orange'. He expects us to think both 'orange' and 'pale violet' original and striking. Pope knew of course that the reader would recognize 'fleecy care' as a common phrase in pastorals. And whereas 'fleecy care' is old, a quotation from the diction, there is new and old simultaneously in the preceding phrase: 'Pour'd o'er the whitening vale.' Here *vale* (for *valley*) is old, a quotation from Spenser. *Whitening* is old, but also new. It goes back to Virgil where it is used of the light of dawn (*ut primum albescere lucem Vidit*).[3] Pope expects us to recognize that whitening is a process noted by Virgil and therefore of interest to later poets. But he applied the process to something more surprising than the morning sky. He applied it to the colour of a pasture into which sheep, perhaps newly shorn, are given entry. They appreciably alter the general colour of a field. That this sense was intended is

---

[1] ll. 17 ff.

[2] Keats, and to some extent Shelley, seem to build on the poetic diction of the eighteenth century. Following an age which, for example, delighted in *soft, blooming, sylvan, trembling, purple, blush*, Keats writes with a recognizable variation: 'While barred clouds bloom the soft-dying day' ('To Autumn'), 'Sylvan historian' ('Grecian Urn'), 'trembled blossoms' ('Psyche'), 'a thought . . . in his pained heart Made purple riot' ('Eve of St Agnes'), 'scutcheon blush'd with blood' (ibid.). There are many more instances. In the same way Coleridge's lines in the 'Ancient Mariner': 'As idle as a painted ship Upon a painted ocean' dealt a contemporary shock by using *painted* literally.

[3] *Aeneid*, iv. 586 f.

shown by the use of Pope's verb by later eighteenth-century poets: Shenstone in his 'Pastoral Ballad' writes:

> . . . my hills are white-over with sheep;

and Cowper:

> . . . The sheep-fold here
> Pours out its fleecy tenants o'er the glebe.
> At first, progressive as a stream, they seek
> The middle field; but, scatter'd by degrees,
> Each to his choice, soon whiten all the land;[1]

and even one poet in the nineteenth century:

> Now rings the woodland loud and long . . .
> The flocks are whiter down the vale.[2]

Then again, take *pour'd*. It is startlingly new. Pope seems to have been the first and only poet to observe the effect of sheep bursting out of a fold: they seem to be poured out, like porridge from a pan. (We may note, however, Virgil's fondness for *fundo*.) Then in the first line there is the unpredictable verb, *shook off*.

In summary, then, we can say that Pope has observed something new, as Arnold has. His discoveries are as valuable, though not as spectacular, as those of Arnold. But the record of the discovery is all that there is in Arnold, whereas in Pope the discovery represents only a part of the whole. Pope is using more of his mind.

5

One of the major elements included in the whole mind evident in eighteenth-century pastorals and georgics—what is 'old' in it—may be compendiously stated as Virgil's 'Georgics'. It is the 'Georgics' more than anything else that prepare the mind of the eighteenth-century poet for writing his nature-poem, which are responsible for the element of the old. Virgil helped the eighteenth-century nature-poet in something like the intimate way the Bible helped Bunyan. And the value of eighteenth-century nature-poetry suffered in the nineteenth century, when the reverence for Virgil faded, in the same way as the value of *The Pilgrim's Progress* suffers whenever there is a decline in

---

[1] *The Task*, i. 290 ff. [2] Tennyson, *In Memoriam*, cxv. 5 ff.

Bible reading. Not that the nineteenth century did not honour Virgil. Keats as a boy translated the *Aeneid* into prose. Tennyson saluted Virgil's centenary with a sumptuous ode. In Max Beerbohm's cartoon, the nineteenth-century 'Statesman . . . [makes] without wish for emolument a . . . version of the Georgics, in English hexameters'. That version, however, is confessedly 'flat but faithful'. And we find Hazlitt recording in his 'First Acquaintance with Poets' that on one occasion 'Coleridge spoke of Virgil's "Georgics", but not well. I do not think he had much feeling for the classical or elegant.' Keats as a boy translates the *Aeneid* into prose. But Dryden as an old man translated not only the *Aeneid* but the *Pastorals* and *Georgics*, and not into prose but into splendid verse. The eighteenth century feels Virgil as a divine presence. Hazlitt's 'classical or elegant', even when allowance is made for contemporary usage, were words too cold to describe their reverence for 'the best of the Ancients'.[1] He is Pope's favourite poet, and one of the four busts in his garden is a bust of Virgil. Gray habitually reads him under the beeches at Burnham.[2] Shenstone has his Virgil's Grove at the Leasowes. They arrange part of their very lives about him. Thomson in the first edition of *Winter* cries:

> Maro, the best of poets, and of men!

In the second:

> Maro! the glory of the poet's art!

Later editions read:

> Behold who yonder comes! in sober state,
> Fair, mild, and strong as is a vernal sun:
> 'Tis Phoebus' self, or else the Mantuan swain![3]

The same thing is even true of prose writers: Gilbert White's mind is haunted by the classics. He sounds a Latin phrase now and then as if to tune his English. The echo that was so famous a feature of Selborne seems of its own accord to boom out 'Tityre, tu patulae recubans . . .'. It was with Virgil in his mind that Gilbert White described the women making rush candles at Selborne.[4]

[1] J. Oldmixon, *Amores Britannici*, 1703, A 7ʳ.
[2] Letter to Walpole, Aug. 1736.
[3] Oxford Poets edn., 1906, p. 205
[4] Virginia Woolf, 'White's Selborne' (*New Statesman and Nation*, 30 Sept. 1939, p. 460).

And it is the *Georgics* that for Dryden, and so for most eighteenth-century poets, are 'the divinest part' of Virgil.[1]

Virgil helps the eighteenth-century nature-poets in a dozen ways. He helps them technically. They try to get his 'strength', 'sweetness'[2], and smoothness of tone, to write lines the music of which is as solid, as exquisite, as his. In his translation of Virgil Dryden seems at times to be trying to suggest something of the Latin versification by letting the stress of the lines fall on syllables with long vowels.[3] Virgil also helps them to concentrate their meaning into fewer words, to combine words in new ways. He shows them how subtly meaning may be embodied in appropriate sound (a lesson they usually find too difficult). He furnishes them with many actual words: *liquid, involve, purple,*[4] *irriguous, refulgent, conscious, gelid, crown* (verb), *invade, painted* (used adjectivally). *Care* comes straight from the *Georgics: cura* is Virgil's constant word for the job of the shepherd and farmer. *Fleecy care* itself, in an age of poets who liked adjectives ending in *-y* and invented them by the hundred,[5] springs readily from the juxtaposition: 'superat pars altera *curae, Lanigeros* agitare greges'.[6] The phrase *sylvan scene* comes from another

---

[1] *Essays*, i. 16; cf. i. 259.

[2] Two qualities Dryden insists on as essential in poetry.

[3] Dryden also sometimes appears to be imitating lines like those of Chaucer's 'Knight's Tale', ll. 1747 ff., where the stresses fall on boldly alliterative syllables.

[4] '. . . used in the Latin sense, of the brightest, most vivid colouring in general, not of that peculiar tint so called' (Warburton's note on Pope's 'purple year', 'Spring', l. 28, in his edition, 1751). See below, pp. 205f.

[5] e.g., *calmy, paly, finny, lawny, rushy*. The practice of inventing them begins at least as early as Spenser (see G. S. Gordon, 'Shakespeare's English', S. P. E. Tract xxix, 1928, p. 272). For a list of them from Chapman's *Homer* see de Selincourt's edition of *Keats*, 1907, p. 577, and from William Browne, id. p. 579, and from Dryden, M. Van Doren's *Poetry of John Dryden*, 1931 edn., p. 65. A late invention of this sort is 'stilly'. The *OED* records its use by poets from 1776–1830. No doubt poets formed these words in *-y* because of metrical considerations. Chaucer's verse has what Matthew Arnold phrased as 'a divine liquidity of diction, and a divine fluidity of movement', and that mainly because in his day most of our nouns and adjectives terminated in a syllabic *-e*. When this *-e* became obsolete, poets seem to have sought an occasional compensation by adding an unstressed vowel, as Milton did in the phrase 'heaven-ypointing pyramid' in the lines on Shakespeare, and as Bridges was to do in reverting to the frank medievalism of 'Godës grace'; and also in such phrases as 'a-floating on the sea'. (Hopkins' 'sprung rhythm' was an attempt to make a virtue of the necessity imposed on poets by the disappearance of the *-e*.) The adjective in *-y* served to lighten the run of such lines as were deemed to require it.

[6] *Georgics*, iii. 286 f.

juxtaposition, this time in the *Aeneid*: 'silvis scaena coruscis'.[1]
Dryden spoke for many of these poets when he praised 'the
dictio Virgiliana', adding 'in that I have always endeavoured to
copy him'.[2]

And while Virgil improved the eighteenth-century sense of
metre, the diction which he helped to form was found useful in a
more readily practical way. Many of the nouns in the diction
are monosyllables: *race, tribe, train, gale, vale, swain, tide*, and so
on.[3] They also have long vowels or else diphthongs. And so for
poets who held that rime should have just those qualifications,[4]
here was a body of words suitable for the rime position in
which they usually placed them. It has also been pointed out
that the trochaic adjectives belonging to the diction, when
linked to nouns of one or two syllables, formed convenient
units for getting that balance in a line which was considered
musically valuable.[5] Lines balanced in this way recalled the
'golden' lines of Latin poetry.[6]

By virtue of the words and phrases borrowed or adapted from
Virgil, the nature-poems of the eighteenth century have a
quality which is usually denied them, the quality of 'atmosphere'. The diction is coloured with Virgilian connotation.
Critics have been ready to dismiss the words merely as derived
from Latin, as if their previous life lay only in the multi-
columned pages of the dictionary. But it is because these words
leapt to the eye whenever the poet opened his Virgil that they

---

[1] i. 164.

[2] op. cit., ii. 148. Dryden was writing late in life, in 1695.

[3] Monosyllabic rimes were another means of avoiding burlesque associations:
rimes of two or three syllables formed part of the armoury of burlesque writers—
they were a feature, for instance, of the Hudibrastic measure.

[4] It was by these qualifications that rime escaped Milton's disdainful charge:
'The jingling sound of like endings'. Dryden considered that Milton turned to
blank verse because his own skill in rime was clumsy: 'he had neither the ease of
doing it, nor the graces of it' (op. cit., ii. 30). Cf. G. Sewell, *The Whole Works of
Mr. John Philips*, 1720, p. xxiii. Johnson held that 'every rhyme should be a word
of emphasis, nor can this rule be safely neglected, except where the length of the
poem makes slight inaccuracies excusable, or allows room for beauties sufficient to
overpower the effects of petty faults' (*Lives of the Poets*, iii. 258). He censures
Waller for riming on 'weak words', e.g. *so* (id. i. 294) and Cowley for riming on
'pronouns or particles, or the like unimportant words, which disappoint the ear
and destroy the energy of the line.' (id., i. 60).

[5] T. Quayle, *Poetic Diction: A Study of Eighteenth Century Verse*, 1924, p. 30.

[6] See below, p. 82.

appear whenever he writes nature-poems for himself. Too much attention has been paid to the questionable dictum of Crabbe on Pope: 'actuality of relation, . . . nudity of description, and poetry without an atmosphere'.[1] The dictum only applies to eighteenth-century nature-poems when the reader fails to supply the Virgilian connotation. As the reverence for Virgil faded, the capacity to supply the connotation faded with it. In the eighteenth century the meanings of the favourite Virgilian words are not defined in the dictionaries. They are beyond definition in the same way that Keats's words are, though often for other reasons. They are indefinable because the dictionary cannot assess the Italian light they derive from the *Georgics*. Take, for example, *gelid*. Johnson defines it as 'extremely cold', and this is sometimes its meaning: Professor Sherard Vines, for instance, comments as follows on the use of the word in Thomson's *Winter*:

> The horizontal sun
> Broad o'er the south, hangs at his utmost noon
> And ineffectual strikes the gelid cliff,

tells us in words what Claude would have told us on canvas; he would have seen, not as Ruskin, the tertiary cliff with inclined strata, or glacial curvatures, particular after particular, but in all its essential and generalised dignity, the gelid cliff.[2]

Gelid sometimes has this zero temperature in the *Georgics:* it is applied, for instance, to *antrum*. But it is a warmer word on other occasions, when, for instance, it describes valleys that Virgil longs to idle in.[3] And it has this warmer connotation when Goldsmith writes in *The Traveller:*

> While sea-born gales their gelid wings expand
> To winnow fragrance round the smiling land.

(*Smiling*, a common word in eighteenth-century pastoral, may be considered the equivalent of *laetus*, which Virgil constantly applied to crops.) When Joseph Warton translated *gelidi fontes* (among *mollia prata*)[4] he was right to render it as *cooling fountains*.

---

[1] Preface to 'Tales' (*Works*, 1834, iv. 144).

[2] *The Course of English Classicism*, 1930, p. 98.

[3] i. 488. Addison, not altogether playfully, suggested (*Letters*, ed. W. Graham, 1941, p. 29), that Virgil applied *gelidis* to *convallibus* (*Georgics*, ii. 488) because he was writing in August from Rome and so was sweltering. In other words its use is partly dramatic.

[4] *Ecl.* x. 42.

6

Virgil suits these poets for another reason. The *Georgics* are an exaltation of human control over the stubbornness and fertility of the earth and of the beast. The men of the eighteenth century, like those of any other century, admired this control, but sought more intelligently to refine and enlarge the amount of it which had already been secured: witness their landscape gardening, the improvements in agriculture and in the breeding of stock. But the control that is most worthy of celebration by poets is the control over a stubbornness and fertility which almost have their own way, and which need a ceaseless vigilance. Virgil, therefore, had also celebrated the severe act of labour which is the means to the control. He had experienced the realities of the land on his own farm. And, further, he had laboured like any peasant on the furrows of his poem: the *Georgics*, we are told, cost him seven years to perfect. But it must be confessed that in the georgics of the eighteenth century there is not always much evidence of a struggle. The control which they assume is dry-browed and sometimes almost automatic. A stubbornness which is shown so thoroughly tamed risks the suspicion that it was never stubborn enough. The poets of the eighteenth-century georgics are too much like the absentee gentleman farmer who comes down from town and does his controlling with a straight back and a walking-stick. What Virgil won with pain, they take with a bow. Moreover it is often the same bow: because, whereas you know that minor nineteenth-century poetry will be bad, you know that minor eighteenth-century poetry will be bad in a certain way. And it is partly because of their more facile harvest that the eighteenth-century poets take certain lines in the *Georgics* too seriously. Writing for Augustus and Maecenas, and being himself a poet naturally prone to grandeur rather than to simplicity, Virgil did not always feel that he could write straight ahead as if he were writing merely for farmers. At least he feels the need for an apology before doing so:

> Nec sum animi dubius, verbis ea vincere magnum
> Quam sit, et angustis hunc addere rebus honorem.[1]

[1] iii. 289 f.

But after this apology his words say frankly what he means. It is not because of any abstention that Virgil's poem remains poetical: he uses the words he obviously needs. It is what may compendiously be called the versification that sheds the glory on the poem. By virtue of the richness of the sound, Virgil, in Addison's words, 'breaks the Clods and tosses the Dung about with an Air of Gracefulness'.[1] Some of this glory is present in Dryden's translation, and perhaps it is not without significance that we find Beattie censuring him for 'being less figurative than the original [and] in one place exceedingly filthy, and in another shockingly obscene'.[2] The georgic writers of the eighteenth century may not have been writing for the great of Rome, but no more than Virgil were they writing simply for farmers. They had in mind readers of poetry who had also, actually or potentially, the interests of gentlemen farmers, farmers in a comfortable mood of contemplation. They also, therefore, had their problems of vocabulary, and, of course, they often take the easy path of solving them by glossing. But it must be remembered that their problems were real ones, and that they had at least two strong reasons for being squeamish about using 'low' words in 'serious' poems. Even if they saw that Virgil was often using realistic words, they were conscious that his words were more 'sounding' (to use Dryden's epithet) than their English equivalents. Beside Virgil's Latin, the Saxon and 'low' element in English seemed like human life itself, 'nasty, brutish, and short'. Johnson noted that

Three of [Addison's] Latin poems are upon subjects on which perhaps he would not have ventured to have written in his own language: *The Battle of the Pigmies and Cranes, The Barometer,* and *A Bowling-green.* When the matter is low . . . a dead language, in which nothing is mean because nothing is familiar, affords great convenience . . .[3].

[1] 'Essay on the Georgics' (*Works of Virgil. . . . Translated . . . by . . . Dryden,* 1763 edn., i. 207).
[2] *Essays: on Poetry and Music, as they Affect the Mind,* 1778, p. 257. Dryden (not *mirabile dictu*) certainly heightens the original, but his fiery additions are not made without generous encouragement from Virgil. Virgil may be more 'figurative', but Beattie forgets that the figures are often pictures.
[3] *Lives of the Poets,* ii. 82 f.

And he goes on to speak of 'the sonorous magnificence of Roman syllables'. Another writer, George Sewell, in his Life of John Philips, had put his finger on

the great Difficulty of making our *English* Names of Plants, Soils, Animals and Instruments, shine in Verse: There are hardly any of those, which, in the *Latin* Tongue, are not in themselves beautiful and expressive; and very few in our own which do not rather debase than exalt the Style.[1]

And it was not only the words 'in themselves' which were the trouble. During the latter half of the seventeenth century and the earlier eighteenth century, burlesque was busy blackening the Saxon elements in the English language. These words were being rotted by gross ridicule. None of the 'serious' kinds of

---

[1] op. cit., p. xxv. In the preface to the translation of Virgil by himself and Christopher Pitt, Joseph Warton writes: 'But, alas! . . . what must become of a translator of the Georgics, writing in a language not half so lofty, so sounding, or so elegant as the Latin, incapable of admitting many of its best and boldest figures, and heavily fettered with the Gothick shackles of rhyme! Is not this endeavouring to imitate a palace of porphyry with flints and bricks? A poem whose excellence peculiarly consists in the graces of diction is far more difficult to be translated, than a work where sentiment, or passion, or imagination, is chiefly displayed. . . . Besides, the meanness of terms of husbandry is concealed and lost in a dead language, and they convey no low or despicable image to the mind; but the coarse and common words I was necessitated to use in the following translation, viz. *plough and sow, wheat, dung, ashes, horse and cow*, etc. will, I fear, unconquerably disgust many a delicate reader . . .' (*The Works of Virgil*, 1753, I, vi. f.) This passage introduces another subject. Words in a dead language, even when they are realistic, fasten themselves more lightly than words should to the equivalent objects of the here and now, and may end by making the objects themselves less real. The small poets of the eighteenth century did not guard against this enough. Wordsworth (who is probably speaking of Latin and Greek proses) saw the danger clearly after he had escaped it:

> . . . In general terms,
> I was a better judge of thoughts than words,
> Misled as to these latter, not alone
> By common inexperience of youth
> But by the trade in classic niceties,
> Delusion to young Scholars incident,
> And old ones also, by that overpriz'd
> And dangerous craft of picking phrases out
> From languages that want the living voice
> To make of them a nature to the heart,
> To tell us what is passion, what is truth,
> What reason, what simplicity and sense.
> (*The Prelude*, ed. E. de Selincourt, rev. H. Darbishire, 1959,

p. 180: the version of 1805–6.)

poetry were exempted from brutal parody and to use any of the enemy's words would be to instigate the laugh you dreaded.[1] It is not too much to say that in the eighteenth century part of the English vocabulary was rendered temporarily unusable in 'serious' poetry.[2] Johnson discussing the passage from *Macbeth* (a passage he greatly admires) which includes the words *dun*, *knife*, and *blanket*, finds that he 'can scarce check [his] risibility', and one of the reasons for this lies in his sensitiveness to the occasions when these words or their like have occurred in amusing or offensive contexts which he himself cannot forget:

if, in the most solemn discourse, a phrase happens to occur which has been successfully employed in some ludicrous narrative, the gravest auditor finds it difficult to refrain from laughter. . . .[3]

So that for the 'serious' eighteenth-century poet, a periphrasis was often a means for skirting the company of such parodists as (to name only the greatest) Cotton, Butler, Gay, and Swift.[4] It is inevitable that when there is no other reason for a periphrasis than this strictly temporary one, the periphrasis itself

---

[1] We find Fenton writing as follows: 'I . . . did not like the [word] Homeric; it has a burlesque sound' (*Pope's Correspondence*, ii. 398).

[2] There is an interesting letter from Lady Mary Wortley Montagu to Pope (*Pope's Correspondence*, i. 396 ff.) about some Turkish verses in translation, in the course of which we read: 'I could not forbear retaining the comparison of her eyes with those of a stag, though perhaps the novelty of it may give it a burlesque sound in our language' (p. 402).

[3] *Rambler*, 168. Cf. Beattie, op. cit., pp. 256 ff., for a justification of Pope's translating Homer's 'swine-herd' as 'swain'. Cf. also Wilde, *The Importance of Being Earnest*, Act II:

Cecily: . . . When I see a spade I call it a spade.

Gwendolen (satirically): I am glad to say I have never seen a spade. It is obvious that our social spheres have been widely different.

In the passage from Johnson there is a ready instance of the way words shift their category: we now smile at Johnson's word 'risibility', which was then a 'serious' word: to us it seems ludicrously pompous. In Johnson's parody of Robert Potter's translation of Euripides *dun* and *blood-boltered*, both from *Macbeth*, are prominent words. Wordsworth consciously made the attempt to reclaim for serious poetry words that had been burlesque words in the seventeenth and eighteenth centuries: see Preface to *Lyrical Ballads*, 1800, para. 7 from end.

[4] We can appreciate this linguistic repugnance by examining our own over such a word as *blooming*. It is Saxon, and 'beautiful' (i.e. pleasant to say, having pleasant original associations); it was over-used by eighteenth-century poets and, therefore, vulgarized: it was 'successfully employed in some ludicrous' parody: it even became slang and a euphemistic swear-word; it therefore seems ludicrous whenever it is now met in eighteenth-century poems.

will seem ludicrous to a later, cleaner age. But this does not alter the fact that the periphrasis did once seem preferable. Pope, anticipating ourselves, laughed at the periphrasts.[1] The remedy, he saw, was sometimes worse than the disease. But the disease was a real one.

Some of the poets use the diction as stilts to escape the mud. But not the good poets. It is true to say that the good poets of the eighteenth century use language, including the poetic diction, with a scrupulousness far in advance, say, of Shelley's use of language. Examine, for instance, this excerpt from a snow scene in Thomson's *Winter*:

> . . . The foodless wilds
> Pour forth their brown inhabitants. The hare,
> Though timorous of heart, and hard beset
> By death in various forms, dark snares, and dogs,
> And more unpitying men, the garden seeks,
> Urg'd on by fearless want. The bleating kind
> Eye the bleak heaven, and next the glistening earth,
> With looks of dumb despair; then, sad-dispersed,
> Dig for the withered herb through heaps of snow.[2]

Here the diction is parcel of the meaning. 'Brown inhabitants' is a neat way of grouping creatures which inhabit the scene described and whose brownness is the most evident thing about them in the snow. 'Bleating kind' is anything but an unthinking substitute for 'sheep'. Thomson is saying: we think of sheep as creatures who bleat, but they are silent enough in the snow; it is the dumb eye and not the voice that tells us of their despair.

7

There is at least one more reason why the diction is called for. It helps to express some part of the contemporary interest in the theological and scientific significance of natural phenomena.[3] If external nature was not much regarded for its own sake, it was often regarded for the sake of a straightforward theology and an everyday science. The creatures were a continual proof

---

[1] *Peri Bathous*, xii.   [2] ll. 256 ff.

[3] This interest was of long standing, of course: see, e.g., E. M. W. Tillyard, *The Elizabethan World Picture*, 1943, pp. 9 and 29.

of the wisdom and variety of the mind of the Creator, and a continual invitation for man to marvel and understand. The eighteenth-century theologian and scientist (they were frequently the same man) often see themselves in the position of the writer of Psalms viii and civ, which appear as follows in the version of George Sandys:

> . . . O what is Man, or his frail Race
> That thou shouldst such a Shadow grace!
> Next to thy Angels most renown'd;
> With Majesty and Glory crown'd:
> The King of all thy Creatures made;
> That all beneath his feet hath laid:
> All that on Dales or Mountains feed,
> That shady Woods or Deserts breed:
> What in the Airy Region glide,
> Or through the rowling Ocean slide. . . .

And

> . . . Great God! how manifold, how infinite
> Are all thy Works! with what a clear fore-sight
> Didst thou create and multiply their birth!
> Thy riches fill the far extended Earth.
> The ample Sea; in whose unfathom'd Deep
> Innumerable sorts of Creatures creep:
> Bright scaled Fishes in her Entrails glide,
> And high-built Ships upon her bosome ride. . . .[1]

Like the Psalmist, they are conscious of the separate wonders of the different elements:

> Whate'er of life all-quick'ning æther keeps,
> Or breathes thro' air, or shoots beneath the deeps,
> Or pours profuse on earth . . .
> Not man alone, but all that roam the wood,
> Or wing the sky, or roll along the flood. . . .[2]

And above all they are interested in the adaptation of life to environment. To draw only on one instance. The Rev. William Derham in 1713 published his Boyle lectures with the title *Physico-Theology: or, a Demonstration of the Being and Attributes of God, from his Works of Creation.* The book went into many

---

[1] *A Paraphrase upon the Psalms,* 1676 edn., pp. 14 and 178.
[2] Pope, *Essay on Man,* iii. 115 ff.

editions. One chapter concerns the *Clothing of Animals* 'in which we have plain Tokens of the Creator's Art, manifested in these two Particulars; the *Suitableness of Animals Cloathing to their Place and Occasions,* and the *Garniture and Beauty thereof*'.[1] The poetic diction is obviously a means of differentiating the creatures in this way: *the scaly breed, the feather'd race,* and so on. It is not surprising to find it cropping up in brief descriptions of the genesis of the world: see, for instance, Sylvester's *Du Bartas*;[2] John Hanson's *Time is a Turne-Coate*:

> The winged-people of the various Skie,
> The scalie Troupe which in the Surges lie;[3]

Davenant's *Gondibert*;[4] Dryden's *State of Innocence,* where the newly created Eve, seeking to distinguish what she is, sees

> from each Tree
> The feather'd Kind peep down, to look on me;[5]

and Blackmore's *Creation*.[6] The notion of the great Scale of Being, which Professor Lovejoy has so thoroughly interpreted for us,[7] provided for an infinite scale of creatures, ranging from angels, whom Dryden calls 'Th' Etherial people'[8] to

> . . . the green myraids in the peopled grass.[9]

All these 'people' were variously adapted to their place in the sublime chain. Life manifested itself on every link, and the grouped bearers of that life (*people, inhabitants, race, train, troop, drove, breed*) are clothed in appropriate bodies. Derham, for

---

[1] 9th edn. 1737, p. 215. Cf. Montaigne, 'Of the use of apparel': 'My opinion is, that even as all plants, trees, living creatures, and whatsoever hath life, is naturally seen furnished with sufficient furniture to defend itself from the injury of all weathers:

> *Proptereaque fere res omnes, aut corio sunt,*
> *Aut seta, aut conchis, aut callo, aut cortice tectae.*
> (Lucan, iv. 935)
> Therefore all things almost we cover'd mark,
> With hide, or hair, or shells, or brawn, or bark.

Even so were we.'
[2] I. v. 33.   [3] 1604, p. 33.   [4] II. vi. 57.
[5] 1677, p. 13.   [6] ii. 150.
[7] Arthur O. Lovejoy, *The Great Chain of Being,* 1936.
[8] *State of Innocence,* 1677, p. 37.
[9] Pope, *Essay on Man,* i. 210.

example, uses terms such as *vegetable race, winged tribes, watery inhabitants*.[1] The diction, then, is not simply 'poetic' diction: it is also 'physico-theological' nomenclature. All this tells against Owen Barfield's suggestion in his brilliant book *Poetic Diction*:

No one would have dreamed of employing the stale Miltonics [Barfield followed Sir Walter Raleigh in deriving the poetic diction from Milton], which lay at the bottom of so much eighteenth-century 'poetic diction', *in prose*, however imaginative.[2]

The evidence, however, runs the other way, and we must allow for this in estimating the degree to which the poetic diction was poetic to contemporary eyes. Among Derham's terms for dividing the creation into groups of creatures is the term 'heavenly bodies'. This term alone has survived into the scientific usage of our own century. We should not suspect any poet who dared to use this term of attempting decoration. And with this as evidence we may believe that those terms of the poetic diction which were also the terms of the moralists and scientists had an intellectual toughness about them as well as a neatness and fashionable grace. It is possible to argue that the poets ceased to use the diction only when the scientists did.

Enough has been said of the poetic diction of the eighteenth-century to indicate that when it comes to be examined as thoroughly as it never yet has been, much of eighteenth-century poetry will be seen more clearly. The reasons why eighteenth-century poets use the diction are among the main reasons why they write poetry at all.

[1] op. cit., p. 9.
[2] *Poetic Diction: A Study in Meaning*, 1928, p. 177.

III

MORE ABOUT POETIC DICTION

THE TERM 'poetic diction' does not appear in the *OED*, and
it seems that even the term 'diction' was not admitted into any
diction-ary until Johnson's in 1755. No doubt both terms were
considered too specialized—they were terms used solely by
critics. To critics the concept of poetic diction had been familiar
from the first—in his *Art of Poetry* Aristotle had discussed the
diction of tragedy. As to the English term for it, Dryden preferred one that for us covers the whole of which diction is a part.
In 1685 he almost adopted the new word, actually writing
'diction', but proceeding with a preferred alternative—'or (to
speak English) . . . expressions'.[1] And ten years later he fell
back more decisively on the familiar seventeenth-century term,
speaking of the '*dictio Virgiliana*', and translating the noun by
'expression'.[2] Accordingly it was John Dennis who gave us our
term: in the preface to his *Remarks on a Book entituled, Prince
Arthur, an Heroick Poem. With some general critical Observations, and
several new Remarks upon Virgil* he announces: 'I design'd particularly to have examin'd the difference between a Poetick and a
Prosaick Diction. . . .'[3] Unfortunately, as his editor tells us,
that design remained unfulfilled. Something of his conclusions,
however, may be gathered from his requiring 'expression',
when it is that of an epic poem, to be 'pure, clear, easie, strong,
noble, poetick, harmonious',[4] even though some of these
desirable qualities can now be properly discerned only by
scholars versed in the civilization of the late seventeenth century, and even though the term 'poetick' unashamedly begs
the question. In the Preface to his *Iliad* in 1715, Pope also used
the term, or a form of it, in describing Homer as 'the Father of

[1] *Essays*, i. 266.
[2] id., ii. 148.
[3] *Critical Works*, ed. E. N. Hooker, Baltimore, 1939–43, i. 47.
[4] ibid.

Poetical Diction, the first who taught the *Language of the Gods* to Men'.[1] But of all writers writing expressly on the diction of poetry it is Wordsworth who is best remembered. In the third edition of the *Lyrical Ballads* in 1802 he included an appendix enlarging on 'poetic diction', a term he had used in his preface in its 1800 and later form. In some respects this appendix is a perverse piece of criticism, and I shall look at it later on.

Before we attend to what 'poetic diction' meant to these writers, we may ask what it would mean to ourselves if we were to use it.

In its narrowest sense it might mean for us (i) the sum of the words used in poetry but not in prose—by 'poetry' I mean verse and by 'prose' I mean prosaic prose, not partly poetical prose like, say, Sir Thomas Browne's. If we did give it this meaning, we should use it mainly of the verse of the past, whether poetical or not, for modern verse makes no use of a special vocabulary of this kind. We should mean by it such words as 'ope' or 'morn', shortened forms that were found convenient because of the local claims of metre, and which, in addition, may have once been felt to be delightful. That would be as strict a use of the term as possible, and it would imply nothing as to the status of the 'poetry' concerned, being applicable to words used in metre, whether or not by a poet. When we use the term otherwise the distinction between words of verse and words of prose gives way before the law that whatever words are used in verse are poetical when—to be obvious—the verse attains to poetry, even though most of the words are prosaic (if I may use that word without pejorative sense) when used in prose. No critic, I think, has improved on Saintsbury's simple account of this sublimation:

The highest poetry can be written in what is, literally speaking, the vocabulary of the most ordinary prose; but when it is—for instance, 'The rest is silence', or 'To-morrow and to-morrow and to-morrow', or 'Put out the light',—there is always some *additional*

---

[1] 1715, folio edn., i. D2ᵛ. The italic phrase refers to the ancient idea that the first poets were divinely inspired.

meaning which, in ordinary prose use, the words would not bear.[1]

It goes without saying that words in metre not only 'ought to attract . . . notice',[2] but cannot escape doing so, and that they attract it with varying force—plainly nouns, verbs, (apart from the commonest) adjectives and adverbs, when used in verse usually strike us more forcibly than particles.

Another meaning of 'poetic diction' is (ii) the sum of the words used by any single poet, or single set of poets. Wordsworth spoke of Gray's 'own' poetic diction,[3] i.e. he saw how individual is the sum of the diction of one great poet, whose diction, as it happens, is unusually striking—it is as rich as Shakespeare's proportionately to quantity of writing. All great, or merely good poets will strike us as having their own set and sum of words. We imply this meaning of the term when we say that Shakespeare used 21,000 words, and Milton (in his poems) 7,500.[4]

Then again 'poetic diction' might mean (iii) the sum of the favourite words used by a single poet or a single set of poets. These, which may well figure in prose, strike us with particular

---

[1] *The Peace of the Augustans*, 'World's Classics' edn., p. 10n. 'And, further,' he proceeds, 'this vocabulary, in the vast majority of instances, requires supplementing by words and combinations of words which would seldom or never be used in prose.'
The instances Saintsbury gives are all from near the end of tragedies. That is why the meaning additional to that they would bear if taken out of their context is so weighty. One of the best instances of the accumulated sense that a few monosyllables can carry occurs in *Macbeth*, though the result, being a sense appropriate for Banquo, is not poetical. To begin Act III, Banquo says in soliloquy 'Thou hast it now'—'thou' is Macbeth, 'it' is the crown, and 'now' looks back to the meeting with the witches, the short intervening spell being crammed with the horror we have witnessed and which Banquo is beginning to suspect. And perhaps Saintsbury missed the pun that exists in that first instance, the pun on 'rest', which can mean 'the ceasing of musical sound' as well as 'remainder' (which refers back to Hamlet's first soliloquy). The musical term is recorded as first used in 1579. To use words wittily is characteristic of Hamlet, and Horatio follows it up when, a few words later, he prays that 'flights of angels [may] sing thee to thy rest'. Another instance comes from the end of *Lear*, whose 'Prithee undo this button' is emitted by a human creature who began by issuing commands in martinet style, and dividing a kingdom, and who now has to beg for the meanest kindness.

[2] Coleridge's *Table Talk and Omniana*, Oxford, 1917, p. 256.

[3] *Wordsworth's Preface to Lyrical Ballads*, ed. W. J. B. Owen, Copenhagen, 1957, p. 119.

[4] See the calculations quoted by Otto Jespersen, *Growth and Structure of the English Language*, 1940 edn., pp. 199 f.

force in the writings of the poets concerned because they appear frequently. They are necessary because the poets rely on them for the effects they wish to make and to make often. While reading the poetry (which I shall here for convenience call Augustan, i.e., poetry written by most poets from Elizabethan times till into the nineteenth century, with a concentration in, say, the years 1650–1750), while reading this poetry I have noticed some of the recurrent favourites, some of which I have mentioned above,[1]—*sad, pensive, anxious, purple,* (usually in the sense it has in Latin poetry of 'very bright'), *various, refulgent* (sometimes in its literal sense: when Pope spoke of the moon as 'the refulgent lamp of night', he was partly engaged in reminding his readers of the recently discovered fact that the light of the moon reflected that of the sun), *num'rous, glitt'ring, beauteous, promiscuous, trembling, pale, British* (a glorious word in the eighteenth century), *harmonious, easy, opening, emulate, yielding, conscious* (usually with some taint of its Latin sense of 'guiltily conscious'). These words and others recur at frequent intervals in eighteenth-century poetry. The poetry of every age has its favourite words; most poets of the 1930's, for instance, liked the word 'history'—and also the generalizing word 'the', as Sir George Rostrevor Hamilton perceived and widely investigated in his thoughtful book, *The Tell-tale Article.* Most poets of the nineteenth century liked to use *shadowy, violet* (adjective), *wild, light* (adjective), *breathe;*[2] and recognizably favourite words were common enough in poetry to prompt Charles Kingsley, when writing on the new poet Alexander Smith and on the old poet Alexander Pope, to speak of

this new poetic diction into which we have now fallen, after all our abuse of the far more manly and sincere 'poetic diction' of the eighteenth century.[3]

This sort of diction is sometimes dubbed 'stock', but it is only that for poets who fail to rise to occasions. Each time a word is used by a good poet it is a partly new thing; the good poet is a

---

[1] See above, p. 35.

[2] For an account of the use of 'breathe' in English poetry see my *Criticism and the Nineteenth Century,* 1951, pp. 163ff.

[3] *Literary and General Lectures and Essays,* edn. 1890, p. 97. Kingsley's vigorous essay first appeared in 1853.

D

voice, and only the bad poet that mindless thing, an echo—to adapt Goethe's useful distinction between genius and talent. To take a few obvious instances. Tennyson begins his 'fragment' on the eagle with

> He clasps the crag with crooked hands.

The sense of *crooked* here is scarcely the dictionary sense, the word being applied, as only a poet dare, to 'hands'. So applied, it means gnarled, sharply knobbled, the sharpness being partly due to the incisiveness of the two *k* sounds. In Shakespeare's day *crooked* was not infrequently used in a metaphorical sense; even so, we are not prepared for his use of it in Sonnet 60:

> Nativity once in the maine of light
> Crawls to maturity, wherewith being crown'd,
> Crooked eclipses gainst his glory fight.

And the same sort of remark applies to *main* in this passage. Two lines later in the same short poem of Tennyson *ringed* is used so as to suggest a new meaning:

> Ringed with the azure world, he stands.

In another sonnet of Shakespeare, the sixth, we find 'winters wragged hand', on which the Variorum edition has the note:

wragged Schmidt (1875): Metaphorically, =rough.—Pooler (ed. 1918): Rough, or perhaps, roughening, but no instance of the active sense is given in *New Eng. Dict.* 1903.

Plainly *wragged*, i.e., *ragged*, is here used in a sense met with nowhere else, and it is a test of a reader's competence to discover its meaning from the context, and from his own experience of winter.[1] The reading of poetry imposes a continuous series of such tests.[2]

---

[1] It is possible that Shakespeare is using a dialect word here: *rag*, which is still found as far south as Derby, and possibly Devon, means hoar-frost, and also mist and fog. It is also possible that he gave the word the initial *w* in order to mark it off from *ragged* in the more familiar sense.

[2] There is still another possible modern meaning for 'poetic diction'. It might mean (iv) the sum of words used in poetry as a whole, whatever their status in the dictionary, whether they are words of plainest prose or words sacred to expression in metre. We can scarcely suffer this possible sense, however, the materials it covers being too unwieldy for any practical purpose.

To the literary student the examination of diction is a favourite duty because, in some at least of the senses of the term, it takes him near the heart of his subject.

2

In practice we study only a part of the total diction of poetry, usually only a part of the diction of a few poets. And a further limitation is sometimes called for. Words are less significant as items of diction as they are more significant as items of plot or theme. If, in an age before paper money had ousted gold, a poet wrote a poem about a miser, he could not avoid references to the thing gold. Accordingly when his poem refers to it by its straightforward name, *gold* has little or no significance from the point of view of diction in the stricter sense. Only such words as deliberately avoid *gold* will contribute significantly to diction —words, for instance, like Pope's 'yellow dirt' or Milton's 'precious bane' (which I shall mention again later). Various writers on Shakespeare have not, I think, allowed for this distinction. I can do no more than touch on this big topic here, saying only that words when used in literature are less prominent as words in proportion as they lead the mind towards the things they signify. If I say 'the gold is on the table', all that matters is the thing gold and the thing table. If I say 'the precious bane is on the table', my words are attended to for their own sake and for the sake of the moral criticism they convey, and so to the detriment of the things denoted. Something like the same distinction would apply if these spoken remarks were to occur in writing.

And so to a limitation I am myself proposing in this essay. In certain sections of it I am concerned with diction that fulfils the condition of being recognizably preferred to other diction. It may be objected that this condition is too general, choice always being recognizably deliberate. We shall agree, however, that there are degrees of this deliberation, that in seeing words as having been chosen we are more conscious of their avoided alternatives in some cases than in others. To take a simple instance. The word *spoke* (verb) has little interest to the student of the diction of modern poetry because it would not occur to one of our poets to avoid it, or rather it would not occur to him on ordinary occasions not to use it. On the other hand, if we find *spake* in a poem written after the time at which it dropped out of common speech or prose, it is a significant item of poetic diction as I am at present concerned with it. If a modern poet were to use *spake* it would be because of a deliberate choice to write archaically, diction playing an important part in any archaic effect. An obvious avoidance is one of the principles at stake in Johnson's notorious passage about Shakespeare's diction in *Macbeth*:

When Macbeth [Johnson may have quoted from memory for he mistakes the speaker, who is Lady Macbeth] is confirming himself in the horrid purpose of stabbing his king, he breaks out amidst his emotions into a wish natural to a murderer:

> —Come, thick night!
> And pall thee in the dunnest smoke of hell,
> That my keen knife see not the wound it makes;
> Nor heav'n peep through the blanket of the dark,
> To cry, Hold, hold!

In this passage is exerted all the force of poetry; that force which calls new powers into being, which embodies sentiment, and animates matter; yet, perhaps, scarce any man now peruses it without some disturbance of his attention from the counteraction of the words to the ideas. What can be more dreadful than to implore the presence of night, invested, not in common obscurity, but in the smoke of hell? Yet the efficacy of this invocation is destroyed by the insertion of an epithet now seldom heard but in the stable, and *dun* night may come or go without any other notice than contempt.[1]

And he goes on to expose the offensiveness of *knife* ('an instrument used by butchers and cooks in the meanest employments'), and *peeping through the blanket* (which he finds ludicrously homely when applied to supernatural 'avengers of guilt').[2] The

---

[1] *Rambler*, no. 168.

[2] The words that offended Johnson had ceased to be acceptable as early as the late seventeenth century. In Davenant's *Macbeth, a Tragedy. With all the Alterations, Amendments, Additions, and New Songs. As it's now Acted at the Dukes Theatre*, 1674, p. 12, the ending of Lady Macbeth's speech had become:

> . . . make haste dark night,
> And hide me in a smoak as black as hell,
> That my keen steel see not the wound it makes:
> Nor Heav'n peep through the Curtains of the dark,
> To cry hold! hold!

words Johnson found offensive were chosen by Shakespeare deliberately, and this implies the equally deliberate avoidance of others. In Johnson's time as well as in Shakespeare's, people spoke freely of knives, of dun horses and cows, and of blankets, and writers of prose were at liberty to follow suit. But for the climax of a tragedy—the murder of a king by a noble person—Shakespeare should, according to Johnson, have used words of a different status. The words that readers or spectators looked to find were *sword* or *dagger*, *darkest*, and *cloak*, and they had been deliberately avoided by Shakespeare in preference to words so far insulting, it seemed, to decorum as to be words of the butcher, the ostler and the housewife. To a deeper view, however, *knife*, *dun* and *blanket* are words of poetic diction just because they avoid the words we should expect to be used in prose. They are poetic diction because deliberately chosen by a writer who was conscious (not wholly conscious, it might be, in the heat of writing, but ready to approve when fully so) of what he was avoiding. The reason for the avoidance was not discerned by Johnson, nor would it have been even if he had correctly re-membered the speaker of the lines. Lady Macbeth is praying to be filled 'top-full' (like a flagon or tumbler—another 'low' household phrase) of 'direst cruelty', and the whole speech is her attempt to incite herself to savagery. She knows other sorts of words than those that offended Johnson, and uses them when there is no call to avoid them: she speaks later of having left the *daggers* of the drugged grooms ready to Macbeth's hand, and repeats the word soon afterwards; and this is the word Macbeth himself had used when he thought he saw a lethal weapon floating in the air before him. *Dagger* is the word we expect, because it is the plain word for the plain thing that Macbeth and the grooms carry about them. Lady Macbeth avoids the word on the occasion in question because though a queen would take a dagger if she wanted a lethal weapon, she is here forcing herself to be the fiercest of brutes—all the fiercer in words because when deeds are called for savagery is to fail her ('Had he not resembled my father . . .')—and *knife*, especially when prefixed by 'keen', is a more savage word than *dagger*, having no military or courtly dignity about it, the best word for a weapon at its most nakedly and brutally instrumental, and suitable for

53

all occasions including, in Johnson's words, 'the meanest employment', which is exactly the employment Lady Macbeth is proposing for it. The same sort of principle of verbal selection explains the diction of the rest of her speech, including *dunnest* and *blanket*. More dignified words would have been suitable for a murderer who wished to claim dignity, but not for a murderess who wanted to be supremely base and cruel.

The diction, then, that I shall be mainly concerned with is that where words are recognized as words of avoidance. One of the interests of the diction of Augustan poetry springs from this condition: when some of the words used in poetry are seen to be chosen deliberately, the words they have avoided, if and when such are used, strike all the more forcibly. I have said elsewhere that Pope, whose vocabulary is dictionary-wide, called fish by one sort of group word when the sense called for it (*finny prey* and so on); and, when occasions changed, used another sort of group word, the plain *fish;* and, occasions changing again, named the separate fishes as *carp, flounder, gudgeon, pike* and so on.[1] Accordingly the maximum force is given to all three kinds of word by contrast with each other. In the Augustan age Gray's line,

> What cat's averse to fish?

was all the sharper because of the presence of 'tabby kind' in the same poem (which, though a joke, is founded on a serious formula of nomenclature),[2] and the presence in other Augustan poems of similar group names for fish.

3

Nowadays English poets do not need to make any acts of verbal avoidance: in theory at least, they can use any words whatever. It is sometimes thought that certain poets at certain earlier times were equally free. Looking back to the time before

---

[1] See above, p. 21.

[2] At this date *tabby* meant 'of a brownish, tawny or grey colour, marked with darker parallel stripes or streaks'. Gray himself glosses *tabby* in the line:

> Her coat, that with the tortoise vies.

The word had borne that sense from the last years of the seventeenth century. *Tabby* in the sense of female cat was a nineteenth-century development.

Dryden and the seventeenth-century reformers, Johnson saw the available diction as a chaos:

if we except a few minds, the favourites of nature, to whom their own original rectitude was in the place of rules [he was probably thinking mainly of Milton], this delicacy of selection was little known to [English] authors: our speech lay before them in a heap of confusion, and every man took for every purpose what chance might offer him.[1]

This account is grossly unfair to the Elizabethans, who were as fully conscious of rules for choosing diction as Johnson himself was.[2] But though a modern poet does not think of English words as lying before him in a heap of confusion, he is otherwise very much like the Elizabethans as Johnson represented them. Writing one word rather than another, he selects, but from the whole wide dictionary, and without a thought that words may once have had a defined status. To him, in theory at least, words are all on the same footing, all equally ready to serve his single purpose—that of expressing his thought and contributing to the sort of general effect he is in process of creating, an effect that owes something also to metre and perhaps (though this is an aid not much available nowadays) to unusual word-order. But though the poet of today is free in theory, he is not quite free in practice, for the general effect he is aiming at, being a modern effect, is limited to modern means, and so is limited to words, or sorts of words, that are already fashionable, or that do not offend against fashion, or that are in process of creating fashion. It is doubtful if he could use *influence* as Wordsworth and George Eliot used it in such a phrase as 'an influence for good', or *glee* (a word as 'good' as *joy* in Wordsworth's day), or *visage*, or *breathes* (as in 'breathes a fragrance') or *wrought* (a word that found a frequent place in prose as well as poetry in the nineteenth century), or *thou* (with its verbs in -est, or -edst) or *dreamful* or *awanting* (a word which like *wrought* was at home in prose as well as poetry in the nineteenth century[3]), or *athwart* or *higher* (as in 'higher influences')

---

[1] *Lives of the Poets*, i. 420.
[2] Cf. Marjorie Latta Barstow, *Wordsworth's Theory of Poetic Diction*, New Haven, 1917, p. 11.
[3] See E. S. Dallas, *Poetics*, 1852, p. 16.

—the reader can extend the list for himself. All poets of whatever age wish to achieve a modern effect even if a modern archaic effect. The difference between the modern effect aimed at nowadays and the then modern effect aimed at in some earlier ages including the Augustan, lies in this, that the former does not include any specific admixture of the old. The poetry of today has little of the past in it, and the modern poetry of some, perhaps all, earlier ages had much of it, without in any way seeming archaic.

There are complex reasons for the way a modern poet regards the English language, and for his no doubt fallacious sense of being 'free of its four corners'. Weighty among them is the reason that nowadays English is fully 'accepted' as a language.

It was not fully accepted two hundred years ago and earlier, when it was thought to be miserably inferior to Latin—so miserably that some of our writers abandoned it altogether on occasion, and wrote poems and epitaphs in Latin. It was also thought inferior to Greek: Pope, introducing his translation of the *Iliad*, speaks of Homer as providing 'an excellent Original in a superior Language'.[1] And inevitably, when writing English, at least for purposes more or less formal, Augustan writers wrote a version of English nearer to Latin than the English written today. It is sometimes too near for our modern taste. That is why in reading Augustan English we have to use the historical imagination, and acquire the sense of the superiority of Latin that Englishmen have long outgrown, and the close knowledge and awful love of it that were common two and three hundred years ago. Otherwise we cannot but misjudge the writings of this earlier time.[2]

Because it never now crosses our minds to wish that English were different (for, besides having great richness in itself, it can rise to new occasions by its power of absorbing foreign words and creating new ones), our poets are able to feel free. And their enfranchisement has been accompanied by a change in the way they regard the dictionary. They feel it now to be more of a republic of words, and less of a hierarchy giving

[1] 1715, folio edn., i. H 1ʳ.
[2] For more on the subject see Appendix I below, pp. 98f.

preference to words derived from Latin. Actually it is a hierarchy still, however blunted: rank is inseparable from words not
because words have different linguistic ancestors but because
they are inseparable from things. The difference is that the
'high' words are no longer as high as they were, that they are
nearer the 'lower'. For various obvious reasons, a word like
channel ranks higher than *gutter, phial* than *bottle, smile* than
smirk, burn than *fry, wainscot* than *picture-rail*. In prose there is
the high status of words derived from Greek, words denoting
intellectual processes that not everybody can rise to, words
like *criticism, logic, analysis* and the adjectives derived from them.
Our poetry cannot readily take them in because their sense and
associations are too purely intellectual: Gray even thought that
poets ought to avoid *philosophy*, though he himself used *philosophical* once in his verse.[1] These differences in rank are always of
importance to literature, and especially to poetry where words
have to create an æsthetic effect over and above the effect they
create for the intellect.

The changes I have noted as having come about since
the Augustan age mean loss to literature as well as gain. At
any one time the effects possible to literature cannot but depend,
to a large extent, on the condition of language at the time, and
so it is obvious that today, when the ranks of words are not
widely disparate, writers are debarred from achieving certain
effects that were possible in an age when the ranks of words
were well marked. We cannot produce the same degree of effect
when we produce bathos—for us no words are as high as for
Augustan readers, and therefore cannot fall as far. Nor can
we so readily produce effects of significant variation (of which
more later). Nor what may be called effects of 'culmination' (of
which, again, more later). In judging the literature of an age
we are concerned to some extent with the way that writers
avail themselves of the linguistic conditions around them, and
improve their occasions.

4

To go back in time only a little way is to see that, for poets,

---

[1] See *Correspondence*, ii. 606, and 'Hymn to Adversity', l. 43.

words have not always been quite so much on a level as they are at present. Mr Eliot's *Waste Land* is now about forty years old. In that poem he felt himself free to use any word, but he also felt bound to show that he was free. The 'shocking' words—not only those in quoted popular songs but those like *gashouse*, introduced in passages otherwise 'beautiful'—these words Mr Eliot not only used but flourished. Employing them, he was proclaiming his freedom from the ban on such words in Tennyson's poetry— or rather the ban on words such as those for poems of Tennyson that flew as high as *The Waste Land*. Tennyson did use words as low and whilom-modern as *gashouse:* he has phrases like 'to trifle with the cruet', 'go fetch a pint of port', 'with the napkin dally', and

> Thy care is, under polish'd tins,
> To serve the hot-and-hot.

(The 'hot and hot' were dishes of food served in succession as soon as cooked, and as it happens the word and the thing have their counterpart in *The Waste Land* with its 'get the beauty of it hot'.) They are all from 'Will Waterproof's Lyrical Monologue', which is one of the poems where Tennyson came close to Dickens. And then there are his frankly dialect poems, in which occur expressions like the 'poor in a loomp is bad'.[1] In other words Tennyson marked off certain poems for certain sorts of diction. This is one way of putting it, but a better, of course, would indicate that the subject and mood decide, the 'kinds' being themselves a traditional expression on the largest scale of subject and mood. There is no place for the word *hot-and-hot* in the *Idylls of the King* because there is no place for the thing. And the matter is sometimes more complicated, for it does not follow, when a thing is in place, that it can be called by its plain name. The light in which the thing is seen, the mood in which it is being regarded, may proscribe its plain name, in favour of a kenning or what not. In 'Morte D'Arthur' Tennyson wished to bring in icebergs, but did not feel like calling them in by name: speaking of Excalibur, which Sir Bedivere is hurling into the lake, he writes:

[1] 'Northern Farmer. New Style', xii. 4.

The great brand
Made lightnings in the splendour of the moon,
And flashing round and round, and whirled in an arch
Shot like a streamer of the northern morn,
Seen where the moving isles of winter shock
By night, with noises of the northern sea.[1]

Tennyson was not afraid of the word *iceberg*, new as it was—it had been introduced into English towards the end of the eighteenth century, and was associated mainly with exploration and scientific enquiry, and therefore with newspapers. Indeed he used the word in 'The Lover's Tale', quite without fuss:

Thus had the earth beneath me yawning cloven
With such a sound as when an iceberg splits
From cope to base.[2]

The use here was possible because the matter of the lover's tale was modern matter, and accordingly not epical, as in the *Idylls of the King*. Matter, then, and mood decide, and also the purposes of the moment. Which word to choose of several for denoting a certain sort of thing calls for a nice decision. No doubt if the word is suitable in poetry of any sort—say *crown* or *rose*—it will be used almost automatically: such words are always welcome. But if the plain name of the thing suits only with a single mood, then it must be called by a name that does not spoil the mood favoured by the poet on this occasion. Furthermore, a word may occasionally be avoided not as unsuitable but because a substitute is preferable. We cannot believe that Tennyson avoided giving a frank beard to Arthur— *beard* is a word used more than once in the *Idylls of the King*. On the occasion in question, however, he saw that *beard* could be bettered—in the interests of the finest dignity as death approached. And so the hero of 'Morte D'Arthur' is furnished with 'the knightly growth that fringed his lips'.[3] Kennings are often

---

[1] ll. 135 ff.   [2] i. 602 ff.

[3] l. 119. In his interesting and little known book, *Some Aspects of the Diction of English Poetry*, Oxford, 1933, H. C. Wyld erred in thinking this a periphrasis for *moustache* (a quite impossible word of course in epic, having so strong a sophistication about it): the plural 'lips' is decisive on the point. At some stage in the history of the word, the hair denoted by *beard* came to exclude that on the upper lip, but the *OED* offers no help as to the date of the change.

used positively—as much for the purpose of enrichment, or of pointing the expression of the mood of the poem, as for the purpose of avoidance. They are often thick with the particular sort of poetry the poet is prizing for the time being. To put the matter in the way that had become obsolete by Tennyson's time, he was aware of the 'kinds', to some extent at least, and of the diction appropriate to them. Nor does he write in any kind such as Byron invented for *Don Juan*, which mixed the Keatsian sumptuous (or as near that as Byron could come) with the vulgarest everyday—the kind to which *The Waste Land* belongs.

From this generalization, however, *In Memoriam* stands a little apart. In places it achieves, what Tennyson could achieve so readily, the Keatsian sumptuous, but does not avoid the everyday—'the dewy deck', 'I hear a [ship's] bell strike in the night', 'Stepping lightly down the plank'. The reason for this mixture is that the series of elegies of which the poem consists are frankly of their time, as 'Lycidas', 'Adonais' and even 'Thyrsis' are not. They are as much of their time as a diary is. The death of Arthur Hallam affected Tennyson's daily life more than the death of Edward King and Arthur Hugh Clough affected the daily life of Milton and Arnold, and the poem is the contemporaneous record of Tennyson's grief, and thinking, and turning away. Accordingly *In Memoriam* has almost everything in it (as anybody's daily life has), and almost every sort of diction accordingly—'plank', and, on the other hand, the 'still perfume' of sycamores, and the material that invited the richest of kennings:

> Or where the kneeling hamlet drains
> The chalice of the grapes of God.

The range of Tennyson's diction over all the poems is wide, but to some extent he thinks of diction as falling into groups, unlike a modern poet who sees it whole as the dictionary is one thing bibliographically. I have defined Augustan as stretching from the age of Elizabeth until into the nineteenth century, but it could be seen as stretching further still, for the diction of a poet so late as Tennyson includes several items that belong to it. In 'Aylmer's Field' he calls his hero's hair 'a manelike mass of rolling gold'.[1] Again, in 'The Gardener's Daughter', the securing of a blown-down rose-bush is called 'fragrant toil'.[2] These are items of Augustan poetic diction. A present participle + 'gold' had helped earlier poets to the sort of effect they wanted. When Sandys encountered Ovid's 'aurumque volubile' as a kenning for one of the apples in the Atalanta story, he translated it as 'rowling gold',[3] which Gray had in mind in speaking of 'the rolling circle's speed'[4]—that is, the hoop's. And Milton had placed 'blooming gold' instead of 'golden apples' on the tree in the garden of the Hesperides.[5] 'Fragrant toil' also had its history in English poetry. Lucan's description of bees used the phrase 'laboris floriferi',[6] which Thomas May in the seventeenth century translated by 'flowery tasks'. A few years later Milton spoke of the bees' 'flowery work'.[7] In his turn Pope has occasion for a simile about bees which opens with

> Thick as the Bees, that with the Spring renew
> Their flow'ry Toils, and sip the fragrant Dew. . . .[8]

On another occasion Tennyson calls the hair of the Persian girl 'redolent ebony',[9] where the adjective, though not in English a present participle, was so in origin. Among the many debts of Tennyson, then, is a debt to Augustan diction, and it is a mutual compliment that this is so. Moreover, the use of this sort of formula does not die out with him, for it has continued to exercise an attraction for English writers. The other day I found a writer of Travel Notes in the *Observer* newspaper speaking of 'the fishy harvest' brought in by Ulster fishermen. A recent letter in the same newspaper dealt with the infections carried by racing pigeons, and was given the title 'Feathered Risks'. Phrases built on these lines are current throughout our society. Other phrases on the same pattern have a currency limited to the vulgar. There is much liking for the formula in the less-than-grand context. Antony was described by Shakespeare as the 'noble ruin' of Cleopatra's magic, but we also hear

[1] l. 69.   [2] l. 142.
[3] Ovid's *Metamorphoses*, x. 667.
[4] 'Ode on a Distant Prospect of Eton College', l. 29.
[5] *Comus*, l. 394.   [6] *Pharsalia*, ix. 289 f.
[7] 'Il Penseroso', l. 143.   [8] *Temple of Fame*, ll. 282 f.
[9] 'Recollections of the Arabian Nights', l. 138.

of 'blue ruin' as a synonym for gin. Tennyson himself spoke of 'bristled grunters' in *The Princess*,[1] but Miss Braddon brandished the formula much more directly in *Just as I am* (1880): 'Even the pigs were the aristocracy of the porker kind.'[2] Another sort of Augustan formula has fallen to the would-be cultured: the American fashionable hostess in *Daisy Miller* (1877) speaks of a girl as a 'dangerous attraction' just as Johnson had described Aspasia as 'beauteous Plunder', 'glitt'ring Bribe' and 'bright Temptation', all in the course of a few lines.[3] Over the years I have collected instances of this formula from our classics. Here are some of them: Sidney's 'inky tribute' in *An Apology for Poetry;* Shakespeare's 'shady stealth' (of the stealthy shadow of the dial), 'iron indignation' for cannon-fire, and 'wooden slavery' for Ferdinand's log-bearing; Webster's 'frail reward' for a drink of water;[4] Dryden's 'liquid gold' for honey[5] and 'little seether' for kettle;[6] Cowper's 'golden hopes', beautifully apt for birds' eggs;[7] Yeats's 'feathered glory', in 'Leda and the Swan';[8] and Blunden's 'silver death' for that inflicted by a pike on its prey, which is an adaptation of Pope's 'leaden death' for the death of lapwings by gunshot.[9] William Browne's 'iron shower' for spears reminds us how close this formula and sometimes its application are to the usage of the Latin poets—'ferreus imber' comes in Ennius and Virgil;[10] Milton's 'precious bane' is a translation of Boethius's 'pretiosa pericula', and 'the dangerous attraction' in *Daisy Miller* echoes Horace's 'dulce periculum'.[11] Not all these instances are formed on the same principle: though all of them are metaphors, some mix concrete and abstract ('leaden death'), some two concretes ('iron shower'),

[1] v. 27. [2] See *OED*, s.v. 'porker'.
[3] *Irene*, I. ii. 96, 102, 125.
[4] *White Devil*, III. i. 50.
[5] *Virgil's Pastorals*, iv. 36.
[6] 'Baucis and Philemon', ll. 56 f:
    The Fire thus form'd, she sets the Kettle on,
    (Like burnished Gold the little Seether shone).
[7] 'A Fable', *Works*, 1836, viii. 311.
[8] Cf. Hazlitt 'Of Persons one would wish to have seen': 'Garrick mimicking a turkey-cock . . . a seeming flutter of feathered rage and pride'.
[9] *English Poems*, 1925, p. 45, ('Water Moment'); and *Windsor Forest*, l. 132.
[10] *Britannia's Pastorals*, II. iv. 56.
[11] See the *Review of English Studies*, xviii (1942), p. 318: and *Daisy Miller* in Macmillan's Collected Edition, p. 46.

some two abstracts ('dangerous attraction'). But they hang sufficiently together to form a group.[1]

It is clear from my haphazard list that this particular group of related formulas for 'poetic' diction is felt to belong not to poetry as a whole but to certain kinds of it—to verse tragedy, to epic (in the early seventeenth century *Britannia's Pastorals* was thought to be as much epic as pastoral) and to the georgic (which I expand for convenience to cover country poems other than those about farming). Their origin in the kinds seems to cling to them even when they are used by twentieth-century poets—in 'Leda and the Swan' Yeats was writing on a subject treated in Ovid's *Metamorphoses* (which in the Augustan age was considered an epic), and Mr Blunden and the writer of the *Observer* Travel Notes were writing in the long georgic tradition. No doubt our sense of the 'kinds' has now almost dissolved away. Pope, as I shall come to show, helped to dissolve it by making *The Rape of the Lock* so much more than a mock-heroic poem, and Wordsworth and Coleridge when they called the volume of 1798 not *Ballads* nor *Lyrics* but *Lyrical Ballads*. During the nineteenth century kinds ceased to exist as the strict things they had been felt to be, and the various groups of diction began to coalesce into one vast whole. The sense of the kinds and the diction proper to them was a keen sense in the Augustan age. For Pope they were sharply individual: he told Spence that, when correcting a poem, he went over it several times, each time with a particular matter in mind:

Thus for language; if an elegy; 'these lines are very good, but are they not of too heroical a strain?' and so *vice versa*.[2]

---

[1] It seems characteristic of English, or at least of literary English, to like a juxtaposing of abstract and concrete: Shakespeare likes phrases such as 'expectancy and rose'; Milton has 'flown with insolence and wine' (cf. Virgil below, p. 75); A. H. Clough has 'their idleness horrid and dog-cart' (*Poetical Works*, ed. H. F. Lowry, F. Mulhauser, and A. L. P. Norrington, 1951, Oxford, p. 135) Henry James 'a spectacled German, with his coat-collar up [in Venice], partook publicly of food and philosophy' (*Wings of the Dove*, IX. ii), and E. M. Forster 'telegrams and anger'. The juxtaposition is often evident when the figure zeugma is used: '. . . sometimes counsel take, and sometimes tea'. A similar brace of words is used by George Herbert as a means for the construction of a poem: see 'Affliction' ('When first thou didst entice me . . .'). Vulgar usage has paid the formula the compliment of imitation, as when an aircraft pilot is said to have returned home 'on a wing and a prayer'. [2] *Anecdotes*, pp. 23 f.

This attempt at purity of kind was impossible in practice, and he confessed that it did break down, though only for short spells. His instance was 'The Messiah'. This poem was a pastoral, and he claimed that, even in a pastoral so closely bordering on the splendours proper to epic poetry, he had not admitted 'above two lines together' of epic 'language'. He was thinking no doubt of these lines:

> No more shall nation against nation rise,
> And ardent warriors meet with hateful eyes,
> Nor fields with gleaming steel be cover'd o'er,
> The brazen trumpet kindle rage no more. . . .[1]

where there seem three lines together offending against the quieter diction of pastoral. A good instance of intrusive heroic diction occurs in 'An Elegy on the Death of an Unfortunate Lady', where we get the couplet:

> On all the line a sudden vengeance waits,
> And frequent herses shall besiege your gates.[2]

The question of diction, I repeat, was secondary, though it was often discussed by itself, to the question of matter. It was the need they felt to keep kinds of matter apart that led them to keep kinds of words apart. The matter of the heroic was ancient warfare and royalty; of elegy, love with or without sadness;[3] of pastoral and georgic, the countryside and its farmer, animals and husbandry; of tragedy, again royalty (and in Pope's time tragedy did not brook the admixture of a drunken porter or of a 'rural fellow' bringing in a basket of figs complete with its 'pretty worm of Nilus'). The matter determined the diction according to the literary law of decorum.

We must also allow for the way matter was classified. I have said that the status of things determines to some extent the status of words, and the Augustan status of things differed from that of today. For the Augustans things in general were more thoroughly departmentalized than for us, and this was partly

---

[1] ll. 57 ff.   [2] ll. 37 f.

[3] 'His conception of an elegy [Shenstone] has in his Preface very judiciously and discriminately explained. It is, according to his account, the effusion of a contemplative mind, sometimes plaintive, and always serious . . .' (Johnson, *Lives of the Poets*, iii. 355).

because of the deeper divisions among the social classes. In particular it greatly mattered to the poets that the reading public included aristocrats as their first patrons. At that time aristocrats were not the 'barbarians' Matthew Arnold was to find them. Most of them were learned men or men trying to appear so. And they encouraged, in public at least, the fiction that they lived completely apart from the 'low' and commonplace, that they were indeed truthfully represented in the fulsome dedications of the time. For such people the poems that came to be called 'primitive' epics were not august enough. The manners of the ancient heroes had to be apologized for to a politer age. Indeed it seems that the process of finding matter for apology helped to create the historical sense which by the nineteenth century had grown so strong. In Homer, Rapin had said flatly, 'Kings and Princes . . . talk to one another with all the Scurrility imaginable',[1] but Pope was at pains to excuse all such lowness as having been high in its day. One of Homer's similes and its application he had translated in this way:

> As on some ample Barn's well-harden'd Floor,
> (The Winds collected at each open Door)
> While the broad Fan with Force is whirl'd around,
> Light leaps the golden grain, resulting from the ground:
> So from the Steel that guards *Atrides*' Heart,
> Repell'd to distance flies the bounding Dart.[2]

And to this passage he appended a note:

We ought not to be shock'd at the Frequency of these Similes taken from the Ideas of a rural Life. In early Times, before Politeness had rais'd the Esteem of Arts subservient to Luxury, above those necessary to the Subsistence of Mankind, Agriculture was the Employment of Persons of the greatest Esteem and Distinction: We see in sacred History Princes busy at Sheep-shearing; and in the middle Times of the *Roman* Common-wealth, a Dictator taken from the Plough. Wherefore it ought not to be wonder'd that Allusions and Comparisons of this kind are frequently used by ancient heroick Writers, as well to raise, as illustrate their Descriptions. But since these Arts are fallen from their ancient Dignity, and become

---

[1] *The Whole Critical Works of Monsieur Rapin . . . Newly Translated into English by several Hands*, 1706, i. 153.

[2] *Iliad*, xiii. 739 ff.

the Drudgery of the lowest People, the Images of them are likewise sunk into Meanness, and without this Consideration, must appear to common Readers[1] unworthy to have place in Epic Poems. It was perhaps thro' too much Deference to such Tastes, that *Chapman* omitted this Simile in his Translation.

Those who believed Homer to be unassailably sublime—he was the great object of contention in the Battle of the Books—had to show that his heroes were essentially the kings and princes to whom modern poems were dedicated, giants of splendour who did not blush when they were called 'Godlike',[2] 'Roi Soleil', 'my Genius', 'guide, philosopher and friend'.[3]

The epic diction was a means of keeping Homer up to his grand Augustan rôle. And as we shall see from Dryden's discussion about 'village words', a similarly heightened diction was felt to be necessary when translating Virgil's *Georgics*.[4] The heightening of village stuff was partly to please 'the thoroughbred lady' (in Pope's phrase), who preferred 'a prince in his coronation robes' to a tree, and a candelabra to the stars in the firmament,[5] and the 'modish lady' whom Johnson went on to speak of after discussing *dun, knife* and *blanket*:

These imperfections of diction are less obvious to the reader, as he is less acquainted with common usages; they are therefore wholly imperceptible to a foreigner, who learns our language from books, and will strike a solitary academic less forcibly than a modish lady.

And he goes on to justify the right of modish ladies to have a say in how literature should be written. They are a part of the general reading public, and literature addressed to them—and much literature was coming to be so addressed—could not but respect their tastes, or what men felt ought to be their tastes.

5

This principle of heightening so as to keep up the fiction of grandeur and politeness does not explain what came to be

[1] The earliest instance of this Johnsonian term I have come across.
[2] *Absalom and Achitophel*, i. 14.
[3] Pope, *Essay on Man*, iv. 373, 390.
[4] See below, p. 100.
[5] Spence, *Anecdotes*, p. 11.

thought particularly notorious in Augustan poetic diction—the formula by which birds were referred to as the 'feathered tribe', fishes as 'the scaly breed', and so on. It has now been amply shown by Mr Arthos in his *Language of Natural Description in Eighteenth-Century Poetry* that though this formula had been used throughout Latin poetry—by Ennius and Lucretius and later poets—it was not a formula confined to use in metre, but was in accordance with the regular terminology of what we should now call science.[1] Because of its use by prose-writers the phrases produced by its application cannot be placed where most nineteenth- and twentieth-century critics have placed them, in my first category of poetic diction, that occupied by words used only in verse. The assumption that this diction was exclusively 'poetic' diction was a nineteenth- and twentieth-century misjudgment depending on a larger misjudgment—that Augustan poetry was poetry grimly determined to be 'poetical'. I shall say more about this later. Certainly the Augustan age had a sense of its own dignity, but it also had as strong a sense of its own elegant freedom from stiffness and empty pomp. It loved gracefulness and ease as well as splendour. And the same preference is discernible among the ideals that guided the poets in their use of words and in the general formation of their style. As far as words went, they preferred those that were at home in the prose they were trying to write well. Most of the words I have listed as favourites of theirs could have been used in their prose without looking self-conscious. Indeed, these writers were engaged in expelling from the diction of poetry all words that were items of poetic diction according to my first category. If they continued to use words only to be found in verse, they usually had a particular reason for doing so. Pope, for instance, used 'ope' in the *Rape of the Lock*:

> *Sol* thro' white Curtains shot a tim'rous Ray,
> And op'd those Eyes that must eclipse the day;[2]

and in the *Dunciad:*

> Next Smedley div'd; slow circles dimpled o'er
> The quaking mud, that clos'd, and op'd no more.[3]

[1] For a note on Mr Arthos's book, originally published as a review of it, see below pp. 108 ff.

[2] i. 13 f.   [3] ii. 291 f.

But in his other poems he used the verb in its unabbreviated form:

> But grant, in Public Men sometimes are shown,
> A Woman's seen in Private Life alone:
> Our bolder Talents in full light display'd;
> Your Virtues open fairest in the shade.[1]

and

> You too proceed! make falling Arts your care,
> Erect new wonders, and the old repair,
> Jones and Palladio to themselves restore,
> And be whate'er Vitruvius was before:
> Till Kings call forth th' Idea's of your mind,
> Proud to accomplish what such hands design'd,
> Bid Harbors open, public Ways extend . . .[2]

and also

> While You, great Patron of Mankind, sustain
> The balanc'd World, and open all the Main . . .[3]

The distinction is plain. 'Ope' is welcome in (mock) epic, but not in epistle and essay. It is in place in epic, and so in mock-epic, because those forms aim at grandeur, or mock grandeur, according to an archaic mode. It is out of place in epistle and essay because these are forms that deal frankly with up-to-date matter, or age-old matter viewed in a strong modern light, and though formal are formal according to the easy elegant manner of Pope's day. In working according to this principle, Pope is carrying on a late seventeenth-century tradition that had received lively expression in a preface to Rochester's *Valentinian* (1685), where Robert Wolseley defends Rochester's memory against an attack from Mulgrave. In the course of his argument he examines the diction of some lines of Mulgrave's:

However, let us take a view of this his legitimate Sence in his own Dresse; the lines are these:

> But obscene Words, too grosse to move Desire,
> Like heaps of Fuel do but choak the Fire.
> That Author's Name has undeserved Praise
> Who pall'd the Appetite he meant to raise.

[1] *Moral Essays*, ii ('Of the Characters of Women'), 199 ff.
[2] op. cit., iv ('To Burlington'), 191 ff.
[3] *Imitations of Horace*, Ep. ii. i. ('To Augustus'), 1 f.

In the first place, What does that *ed* in *undeserved* do there? I know no businesse it has, unless it be to crutch a lame Verse and each out a scanty Sence, for the Word that is now us'd is *undeserv'd*. I shou'd not take notice of so trivial a thing as this, but that I have to do with a Giver of Rules and a magisterial Corrector of other men, tho' upon the observing of such little Niceties does all the Musick of Numbers depend; but the Refinement of our Versification is a sort of Criticism which the *Essayer* (if we may judge of his Knowledge by his Practice) seems yet to learn, for never was there such a Pack of still ill-sounding Rhimes put together as his *Essay* is stuff'd with; to add therefore to his other Collections, let him remember hereafter that Verses have Feet given 'em, either to walk graceful and smooth, and sometimes with Majesty and State, like *Virgil*'s, or to run light and easie, like *Ovid*'s, not to stand stock-still, like *Dr. Donne*'s, or to hobble like indigested Prose; that the counting of the Syllables is the least part of the Poet's Work, in the turning either of a soft or a sonorous Line; that the *eds* went away with the *forto's* and the *untils*, in that general Rout that fell on the whole Body of the *thereons*, the *thereins*, and the *therebys*, when those useful *Expletives*, the *althos* and the *untos*, and those most convenient *Synalæphas*, '*midst*, '*mongst*, '*gainst*, and '*twixt*, were every one cut off; which dismal slaughter was follow'd with the utter extirpation of the ancient House of the *hereofs* and the *therefroms*, &c. Nor is this Reformation the arbitrary Fancy of a few who wou'd impose their own private Opinions and Practice upon the rest of their Countreymen, but grounded on the Authority of *Horace*, who tells us in his Epistle *de Arte Poeticâ*, That present Use is the final Judge of Language (the Verse is too well known to need quoting), and on the common Reason of Mankind, which forbids us those antiquated Words and obsolete Idioms of Speech whose Worth time has worn out, how well soever they may seem to stop a Gap in Verse and suit our shapelesse immature Conceptions; for what is grown pedantick and unbecoming when 'tis spoke, will not have a jot the better grace for being writ down.[1]

As Spingarn notes: 'The later seventeenth century insisted more and more that the language of poetry should conform to that of cultivated conversation and prose.'[2] And not only cultivated conversation, but conversation between men in most of the social ranks.

The poets of the time did not see themselves otherwise than as

[1] Spingarn, iii. 26 f. [2] op. cit., iii. 302.

'men speaking to men'—where 'speaking' must be given its full force, and divided off from 'chanting' or 'singing'. Literature was the one category that contained prose and verse, and within that category came the various 'kinds', some of which properly demanded more formal and splendid diction than others, but none, except for comic purposes, demanding a diction too far removed from the norm that existed in *An Essay on Criticism*, *Gulliver's Travels* and *Robinson Crusoe*. When in 1742 Gray made his famous remark that 'The language of the age is never the language of poetry'[1] he was kindling a rebellion —what Gray says is generally true, of course; but to say it so sharply shows that, unlike Waller, he wished to widen a gap instead of narrowing it.

Where the Augustan diction is of the 'scaly breed' kind, it is common alike to prose and poetry. As I have said, we still use the term 'heavenly bodies' and use it only in prose.[2] It is a survival from the ancient means of keeping distinct the different groups of created things by referring to the element in which they exist, or to their covering, which came to be seen as designed to suit the conditions under which the Creator had chosen to place them. This sort of diction was involved in the way human beings looked out of themselves at the external creation. It was sacred to their philosophy. And only when this philosophy began to change into another was it seen as old-fashioned and tawdry. Coleridge was to remark that Augustan poetry 'may, notwithstanding some illustrious exceptions, be too faithfully characterized, as claiming to be poetical for no better reason, than that it would be intolerable in conversation or in prose'.[3] We are familiar with this idea through Mr Eliot's remark that Augustan poetry, far from being unpoetical, is too much the reverse—i.e., is determinedly poetical, and according to a debased standard.[4] Coleridge followed up his remark with a qualification:

Though, alas! even our prose writings, nay even the style of our

---

[1] *Correspondence*, i. 192.   [2] See above, p. 45.

[3] *Biographia Literaria*, ii. 21.

[4] 'One does not need to examine a great deal of the inferior verse of the eighteenth century to realize that the trouble with it is that it is not prosaic enough' (Introductory Essay to edn. of Johnson's *London*, 1930, p. 12.)

more set discourses, strive to be in the fashion and trick themselves out in the soiled and over-worn finery of the meretricious muse.

This was written when the Augustan philosophy was passing away. Coleridge was thinking mainly of diction. The clause 'strive to be in the fashion' evinces that much of the diction still lingered, and that it was still vital; but since it was a fashion that had remained unchanged from the beginning of literature, the act of striving must by Coleridge's time have become second nature. New terms were on the way, and the poets were to leave off using the sort of diction Coleridge had in mind; but only when the scientists did. To quarrel with 'scaly breed' and so on is to quarrel with an age-long period of intellectual history rather than with poetry itself.

The intellectual interests of any period in the past have a weighty claim on the attention of any successive period, and triviality should be the last shortcoming attributed to them, if only to stave off a retort from a later age on our own. In the light of this principle we may examine the view of Miss Barstow in *Wordsworth's Theory of Poetic Diction*, a book I have already noticed—the examination will serve to summarise what I have been saying.

In the course of her book Miss Barstow quotes a passage from Miss Myra Reynolds about Dryden's use of the part of the diction that pertains to the external world:

the ocean is a 'watery desert', a 'watery deep', a 'watery plain', a 'watery way', a 'watery reign'. The shore is a 'watery brink', or a 'watery strand'. Fish are a 'watery line', or a 'watery race'. Sea-birds are a 'watery fowl'. The launching of ships is a 'watery war'. Streams are 'watery floods'. Waves are 'watery ranks'. The word occurs with wearisome iteration in succeeding poets.[1]

With this as starting point Miss Barstow continues:

Such mannerisms seem to be due to the heedlessness of a man writing with great facility, but ignorant of, or indifferent to, the phenomena he mentions. He seizes upon the most obvious, and, at the same time, the most matter-of-fact and uninteresting detail, and then, when he perceives the necessity for varying his expression, he acts like the clever writer that he is rather than the sympathetic

[1] op. cit., p. 44.

observer that he is not: instead of mentioning a new detail, he merely thinks of a synonym for the expression that he has already used. In this way all the tiresome array of stock phrases that mean nothing came into being. Most of them ring monotonous changes upon the most obvious features of things, such as the fact that the ocean is composed of water, that birds have feathers and fish have fins. To call fish the 'finny race' is not to say anything new or interesting about them; to vary the expression to the 'scaly tribe' is only to make matters worse. Yet it is easy to see that all these atrocities might be produced, with no intention of thus distinguishing poetry from prose, by any man who was trying to write well without knowing what he was talking about. In fact, the same kind of diction occurs in prose which attempts to deal with the same kind of subject-matter.

Dryden is charged with heedlessness. Miss Barstow does not see what this charge brings with it. For if Dryden is heedless, so by and large are all the Augustan poets. Far from being heedless, however, they are intent on heedfulness for aspects of things Miss Barstow overlooks. In the first place they respect tradition. They know that epic poetry descends from Homer. What Miss Barstow ascribes to Dryden fits Homer remarkably well: certainly he 'seizes upon the most obvious, and, at the same time, the most matter-of-fact and uninteresting detail'. This being so, the epithets Miss Barstow sees as applied heedlessly are applied with heed of the literary kinds. The literary kinds in question are the epic and georgic, which call for the sort of epithet listed by Miss Reynolds as much as for the 'heroic' line (the line of five beats). I have also argued that their use satisfied the poets' need to honour, or to be seen to be honouring, the work of the Supreme Artificer, whom Sylvester apostrophized with the line

O King of grassie and of glassie Plains.[1]

Sylvester is here the happy theologian and poet, remarking a likeness between English words that matches a likeness between two great items in the creation. Similarly when Dryden speaks of waves as 'watery ranks', he is noticing a marvel of the natural world which, it goes without saying, has always been of

[1] *Devine Weekes* [of Du Bartas], i. iii, 1605, p. 76. The line caught Benlowes' fancy: see *Theophila* xii. 109: 'LORD of all grassie and all glassie Plains'.

interest to all who have to accommodate themselves to it, or who have the chance to note it,[1] and which in Dryden's day was of particular interest because of the work of Newton, who explored the subject of the tides in the light of the law of universal gravitation. Such phrases do not 'mean nothing'; and this might have been sufficiently gathered from their use, which Miss Barstow notices, by prose-writers.

Further, the nouns that accompany the epithets combine with them euphoniously. None of the phrases Miss Reynolds quotes is, to say the least, cacophonous. The accompanying nouns, as I have shown, were euphonious in the way that qualified them for use as rimes.[2] The Latin language had made Latin poetry so 'harmonious'[3] that it did not need to rime, but to Johnson, in theory and practice, and to most of these poets in practice, English poetry could not dispense with rime and remain shapely and forceful;

'Rhyme,' [Milton] says, and says truly, 'is no necessary adjunct of true poetry.' But perhaps of poetry as a mental operation metre or musick is no necessary adjunct; it is however by the musick of metre that poetry has been discriminated in all languages, and in languages melodiously constructed with a due proportion of long and short syllables metre is sufficient. But one language cannot communicate its rules to another; where metre is scanty and imperfect some help is necessary. The musick of the English heroick line strikes the ear so faintly that it is easily lost, unless all the syllables of every line co-operate together; this co-operation can be only obtained by the preservation of every verse unmingled with another as a distinct system of sounds, and this distinctness is obtained and preserved by the artifice of rhyme. The variety of pauses, so much boasted by the lovers of blank verse, changes the measures of an English poet to the periods of a declaimer; and

---

[1] Dryden's interest in the sea goes without question. It is well evinced in his translation of Horace, *Odes*, i. 3, which contains a couplet also making use of *ranks:*

> What form of death cou'd him affright,
> Who unconcern'd with stedfast sight,
> Cou'd view the Surges mounting steep,
> And monsters rolling in the deep?
> Cou'd thro' the ranks of ruin go,
> With Storms above, and Rocks below!

[2] See above, p. 36.   [3] See below, p. 99.

there are only a few skilful and happy readers of Milton who enable their audience to perceive where the lines end or begin. 'Blank verse,' said an ingenious critick, 'seems to be verse only to the eye.'

Poetry may subsist without rhyme, but English poetry will not often please [without its aid]. . . .[1]

These poets, unless determined to try their mimic hand at blank verse in the manner of Milton or, if they wrote plays, in the manner developed from that of Beaumont and Fletcher, strongly felt the necessity of rime, and the sort of rime that they could approve, with Latin in mind, as harmonious.[2] The diction provided many such words—e.g. *race, breed, reign* (cf. Virgil's use in a phrase like 'inania regna' of Avernus); and the words related to the elements, or the species of the animal kingdom—e.g., *care* (of the country-man's relation to his stock) and *prey* (of the relation of an animal to a hunter, whether man or beast). All such words are usually found occupying the rime-position. All told, we see the reasonableness of the poets' use of this diction. And to allow that is to be free to credit them with any stirring they may care to make in the direction of the sort of observation we prize as modern. To confine ourselves to the items on Miss Reynolds's list, 'watery ranks' is not the phrase of a poet who had never troubled to look at the sea for himself.

6

To some extent the formula 'covering+group word' provided a norm, and whenever that exists in literature, or out of it, the liveliness that is inseparable from the human intelligence shows itself in departing from it—it is this principle that makes metre so engaging. Poetic diction, in its turn, encouraged departures from the norm.

First in the direction of amusement. Dryden departs from phrases like 'scaly breed', and laughs at frogs as 'the loquacious Race',[3] and dubs the creatures on a lower rank still 'the tadpole train'.[4] Another comic departure of his is best considered along with one of Pope's. In *On the Poetry of Pope* I instanced this sort of laughable culmination by referring to Pope's use of the

---

[1] *Lives of the Poets*, i. 192 f.   [2] *Virgil's Georgics*, i. 521.   [4] *The Medall*, l. 304.
[3] id., iii. 654. The laugh is improved when we grasp that Milton invented the word, and put it in *Paradise Lost*.

word *dissolved*. It had been used, as Ovid had used its Latin equivalent, for the relaxed state of sleep or ease, and Pope added to that sense a sense plainly English:

> And Alma Mater lie[s] dissolv'd in port![1]

A reviewer of my book[2] supplied an intermediary stage I had overlooked; he showed that Dryden had gone some way towards the laugh of the *Dunciad*: in his *State of Innocence* he told how

> Seraph and cherub, careless of their charge,
> And wanton, in full ease now live at large:
> Unguarded leave the passes of the sky,
> And all dissolved in hallelujahs lie.

In his Preface, written as a defence against likely fault-finding, Dryden claimed these lines as the best 'example' his piece affords of 'excellent imaging', and went on to discuss the application of the particular word in question:

I have heard (says one of [my well-natured censors]) of anchovies *dissolved* in sauce; but never of an angel *in hallelujahs*. A mighty witticism! (if you will pardon a new word), but there is some difference between a laugher and a critic. He might have burlesqued Virgil too, from whom I took the image. *Invadunt urbem, somno vinoque sepultam.* A city's being buried, is just as proper on occasion, as an angel's being dissolved in ease, and songs of triumph . . .

Dryden was aware of a single source for his way of using the word, and that not the obvious one. Pope's awareness, we may be sure, was complete. And he used Dryden's remarks as a reminder to add another source to the obvious one found in Ovid's description of the cave of Sleep. Ovid's description of the god has the phrase 'membris languore solutis', which his delightful seventeenth-century translator Sandys had interpreted as meaning 'dissolved in rest'.[3] Virgil had spoken of a town as *buried* in *sleep* and *wine*, and Ovid of limbs *dissolved* in *ease*, so why not take *dissolved*, which Ovid and many poets after him had employed as a metaphor, and affix it to that item of Virgil's metaphorical phrase, *vinum*, which can literally be said

---

[1] *Dunciad*, iii. 338.
[2] Professor V. de S. Pinto in *English*, ii (1938), vii. 48.
[3] See my *On the Poetry of Pope*, 1938, p. 153.

75

to act as a solvent? In doing so, he improved *wine* to *port* (and so collected another joke—to 'lie in port' is a nautical phrase beautifully apt for the final, placid and vinous slumbers of the *alma mater*). As usual Pope has the wit to benefit from the sweat of others' brows.

Then there is Pope's use of *vocal* in the *Dunciad*. Milton used it beautifully and surprisingly of reeds; Dryden and Pope were to use it as beautifully of echoing hills.[1] But Pope also made it the occasion of a surprise of another sort:

> . . . Ass intones to Ass,
> Harmonic twang! of leather, horn, and brass;
> Such as from lab'ring lungs th' Enthusiast blows,
> High Sound, attemp'red to the vocal nose . . .[2]

The Dissenters are laughed at for their abuse of the human head—in normal men it is the mouth and throat that are vocal —and the laugh is the sharper because up to this point in the history of English language *vocal* has been a word of high status.

Gray in his turn is quite as brilliant as Pope. His triumphs come in the 'Ode on the Death of a Favourite Cat', a poem that for all its title is partly a mock epic. At certain points in that poem, which I shall discuss later on, Gray completes a long process.[3] Dryden had introduced a panther into his great Æsopian satire, and had praised her as the 'fairest creature of the spotted kind';[4] and Pope had referred to Helen on the walls of Troy (looking down on the armed warriors as Gray's cat looks down on the fishes complete with their 'scaly armour') as 'the brightest of the Female Kind'.[5] (This particular formula comes to be widely regarded as a butt: we learn that Carlyle's young sister Jane referred to a particular letter as 'the meanest of the letter kind', a phrase that became current in the Carlyle household'.)[6] Dryden's 'spotted' was itself an amusing departure, but not so amusing as when the cat Selima is described as 'Demurest of the tabby kind'. Gray's comic 'ode' also illustrates the same practice in so far as it concerns single words. One of

---

[1] See below, p. 107. Dryden, *Virgil's Pastorals*, iv. 4, and below, p. 90.
[2] *Dunciad*, ii. 253 ff.   [3] See below, p. 220.
[4] *Hind and the Panther*, i. 328.   [5] *Iliad*, iii. 473.
[6] J. A. Froude, *Early Life of Thomas Carlyle*, 1890 edn., i. 181.

the epithets prominent in Augustan poetic diction is *conscious*, which, as I have said, was often used with a colouring of the original sense of guilt. After usages like that in *Ovid's Epistles, Translated by Several Hands* (1680):

> The night, and we are conscious of the rest;

it was a pleasant literary shock to meet, in a description of a cat,

> Her conscious tail her joy declar'd.

No better word than *conscious* could be applied to the stealthy expressiveness of a cat's tail, but the word was enriched for the reader of 1748 because of the status and colouring of *conscious* amid the poetic diction of a great deal of the world's poetry. Its status had been of the highest, and its colour of the darkest.

So much for the comic departures. The 'serious' ones were made quite as consciously. In the *Temple of Fame* Pope brings an item of the diction to its intellectual culmination in a poem that had already used it three times innocently, in lines like

> The figur'd Games of *Greece* the Column grace.

On its last appearance it adds to its mild stateliness an ironic sting:

> When thus ripe Lyes are to perfection sprung,
> Full grown, and fit to grace a mortal Tongue . . .[1]

Then again, there is an interesting passage in his translation of the *Odyssey* where he demonstrates how far from idle the old periphrases can be, or rather how various and full of sense can be new applications of the old formula for making them. Menelaus is recounting his adventures after the destruction of Troy. He had been unable to sail, the winds not being favourable, until advised by the goddess Eidothea to seek the help of her father, Proteus, the prophet-god who can assume any shape. The passage quoted begins where Eidothea is instructing Menelaus how to supplicate a god who requires to be approached with caution: I italicize the phrases that are of interest for my present purpose (and accordingly romanize what is italic in the original text).

[1] op. cit., ll. 216 and 479 f.

77

. . . Obedient to my rule, attend:
When thro' the Zone of heav'n the mounted sun
Hath journey'd half, and half remains to run;
The Seer[1], while Zephyrs curl the swelling deep,
Basks on the breezy shore, in grateful sleep,
His oozy limbs. Emerging from the wave,
The Phocæ[2] swift surround his rocky cave,
Frequent and full; the consecrated train
Of her[3], whose azure trident awes the main:
There wallowing warm, th' enormous herd exhales
An oily steam, and taints the noon-tide gales.
To that recess, commodious for surprize,
When purple light shall next suffuse the skies,
With me repair; and from thy warrior band
Three chosen chiefs of dauntless soul command:
Let their auxiliar force befriend the toil,
For strong the God, and perfected in guile.
Stretch'd on the shelly shore, he first surveys
The flouncing herd ascending from the seas;
Their number summ'd, repos'd in sleep profound
The *scaly charge* their guardian God surround:
So with his batt'ring flocks the careful swain
Abides, pavilion'd on the grassy plain.
With pow'rs united, obstinately bold
Invade him, couch'd amid the *scaly fold*:
Instant he wears, elusive of the rape,
The mimic force of every savage shape:
Or glides with liquid lapse a murm'ring stream,
Or wrapt in flame, he glows at every limb.
Yet still retentive, with redoubled might
Thro' each vain passive form constrain his flight.
But when, his native shape resum'd, he stands
Patient of conquest, and your cause demands;
The cause that urg'd the bold attempt declare,
And sooth the vanquish'd with a victor's pray'r.
The bands relax'd, implore the Seer to say
What Godhead interdicts the *wat'ry way?*
Who strait propitious, in prophetic strain
Will teach you to repass th' unmeasur'd main.
She ceas'd, and bounding from the shelfy shore,
Round the descending nymph the waves redounding roar.

[1] i.e. Proteus.   [2] i.e. sea-calves.   [3] Amphitrite.

> High rapt in wonder of the future deed,
> With joy impetuous, to the port I speed:
> The wants of nature with repast suffice,
> 'Till night with grateful shade involv'd the skies,
> And shed ambrosial dews. Fast by the deep,
> Along the tented shore, in balmy sleep
> Our cares were lost. When o'er the eastern lawn,
> In saffron robes the Daughter of the dawn
> Advanc'd her rosy steps; before the bay,
> Due ritual honours to the Gods I pay:
> Then seek the place the sea-born nymph assign'd,
> With three associates of undaunted mind.
> Arriv'd, to form along th' appointed strand
> For each a bed, she scoops the hilly sand:
> Then from her azure car, the *finny spoils*
> Of four vast Phocæ takes, to veil her wiles;
> Beneath the *finny spoils* extended prone,
> Hard toil! the prophet's piercing eye to shun;
> New from the corse, the *scaly frauds* diffuse
> Unsavoury stench of oil, and brackish ooze:
> But the bright sea-maid's gentle pow'r implor'd,
> With nectar'd drops the sick'ning sense restor'd.[1]

And so, in the end, the god is brought to speaking terms. Meanwhile we have seen the various applications of the formula which, when most simply applied, gives us *scaly breed*. It is a long way from that to such a variation as *scaly frauds*.

Finally, another eighteenth-century instance of the use of this principle from Gray. I have noted that *anxious* was a favourite Augustan epithet. So was *pleasing*. Gray brought them together, and for the purpose of describing what in those times was the subject of subjects, the proper study of mankind:

> For who to dumb Forgetfulness a prey,
> This pleasing anxious being e'er resign'd . . .?[2]

The principle, of which Gray is master as well as Pope, is to take what is tediously under everybody's nose and make it suddenly delightful and startling.

To complete the picture we may look at those nineteenth-century poets who followed the same principle because they saw

[1] op. cit., iv. 538 ff.
[2] 'Elegy wrote in a Country Churchyard', ll. 85 f.

the advantage of building on the poetry of the past, instead of cutting away from as much of it as possible, as Browning did. An Augustan term for sea or lake was *liquid plain,* but Wordsworth used it so as to make us see how accurately:

> While Grasmere smoothed her liquid plain
> The moving image to detain.[1]

In the famous skating scene in *The Prelude* we get a further instance:

> Not seldom from the uproar I retired
> Into a silent bay, or sportively
> Glanced sideway, leaving the tumultuous throng,
> To cut across the reflex of a star
> That fled, and, flying still before me, gleamed
> Upon the glassy plain . . .[2]

When Sylvester had apostrophized the king of the grassy and the glassy plains, he was using *glassy,* as so many poets had done, as a metaphorical epithet applied to water in its liquid form. Wordsworth applied it to a substance to which it is still more applicable, for ice has the smoothness and shine of glass, and also its hard solidity. A further step, consciously taken, comes in *In Memoriam* where Tennyson imagines the voyage of the ship carrying home the corpse of his friend, and pictures it as proceeding gently

> Athwart a plane of molten glass.[3]

Here is the glassy plain with additions—with the addition of a complete horizontality, for a plane is levelness itself, and with the addition also of liquid in a new and intenser form—molten glass is glass at its most shiningly liquid, and it is Italian seas that the ship is sailing.

In Wordsworth there is an instance of something different—the conscious *avoidance* of an expected item of the diction. The Augustan epithet for 'woods' is *waving;* but compare

> The woods, my Friends, are round you roaring,
> Rocking and roaring like a sea . . .[4]

This is all the more superb for our being conscious of what it

---

[1] *The Waggoner,* iv. 232 f: the image is that of the waggon.
[2] I. 447 ff.　　　[3] xv. 10.　　　[4] *Peter Bell,* ll. 11 f.

avoids. It is true that *waving* would not have done for Wordsworth here, because the sense required a livelier motion—he is speaking of windy weather—but he purposely goes beyond what is strictly necessary, and, as it were, shows the more timid among the Augustan poets what woods can do when they really try.

These instances show that the old diction was not a static thing for the Augustans It was a medium for recognized variations. The best of the poets did not use it as if they were half asleep.

7

I have made use of two expressions, 'words' and 'phrases'. We usually think of diction as composed of single words, but it is already obvious that the Augustans paid much attention to phrases. Diction was a matter of both. It is almost inevitable that phrases taken from poetry should be phrases in which adjectives are included. Poetry affords a place for the adjective where prose does not. Adjectives are functional as other words are, but their functions vary as they are used in poetry or prose. In prose the usual function of words is to indicate a sense that means business, as it were, that is looking ahead, not having leisure also to look about it. If in prose we use the words 'the fair man' we mean to distinguish him from the dark man, so as to push ahead and say something about his actions. In poetry the epithet functions in order to adorn, or, to speak more exactly, in order to express a sense that is partly aesthetic. There are consequently many more adjectives in poetry than in prose, and because of this a phrase quoted from poetry usually contains an adjective, that adjective often being its most striking item. Phrases are words in combination, and poetry depends on combination more than on single words—that is why words that singly are words of prose become words of poetry when combined. Wordsworth had both single words and phrases in mind when he discussed Augustan diction: he used both the terms 'diction' and 'phraseology'. Unless we understand the importance of phrases, we shall mistake Augustan poetry. We shall also mistake some contemporary writings on it. These poet-critics were interested in Virgil more than in any other poet, and one of Virgil's characteristics is his frequent use of adjectives. The 'golden line', particularly associated with him, was made up of two units, each having an adjective-and-noun—it is familiar to us in the pattern of such frequently recurring English lines as Sidney's

> A rosy garland and a weary head.

The list of favourite words I gave at the outset[1] consisted almost entirely of adjectives, and adjectives presuppose a phrase—they cannot exist without nouns. I should have represented Augustan poetry more faithfully if I had given them alongside nouns, though this would be unfair in another way, since the nouns vary. Gray had phrases in mind when he wrote his famous letter to West about the language of the age. The phrases he instances are not examples of the diction—Gray quotes them as unusual because revived or invented—but many are of the adjective-noun kind. Johnson also had phrases in mind when he named Dryden as the great originator of our poetic diction:

> Every language of a learned nation necessarily divides itself into diction scholastick and popular, grave and familiar, elegant and gross; and from a nice distinction of these different parts, arises a great part of the beauty of style . . .
>
> There was . . . before the time of Dryden no poetical diction: no system of words at once refined from the grossness of domestick use and free from the harshness of terms appropriated to particular arts. Words too familiar or too remote defeat the purpose of a poet. From those sounds which we hear on small or on coarse occasions, we do not easily receive strong impressions or delightful images; and words to which we are nearly strangers, whenever they occur, draw that attention on themselves which they should transmit to things.
>
> Those happy combinations of words which distinguished poetry from prose had been rarely attempted; we had few elegances or flowers of speech: the roses had not yet been plucked from the bramble or different colours had not been joined to enliven one another.
>
> It may be doubted whether Waller and Denham could have overborne the prejudices which had long prevailed, and which even then were sheltered by the protection of Cowley. The new versification, as it was called, may be considered as owing its establish-

[1] See above, p. 49.

ment to Dryden; from whose time it is apparent that English poetry has had no tendency to relapse to its former savageness.

The affluence and comprehension of our language is very illustriously displayed in our poetical translations of ancient writers . . .[1]

Prompted by Johnson and also by general principles, we ought, when reading Augustan poetry, to be aware of phrases as more important than single words. On this point one may cite an amusing document from the newspapers of Pope's day. *A Compleat Collection of all the Verses, Essays . . . occasioned by the Publication of Three Volumes of Miscellanies by Pope and Company* (1728) reprints a mock bill of sale from the *Daily Journal*. In form it resembles Pope's bill of sale for the shaped yew-trees he disliked in old-fashioned formal gardens, a parody with which he concluded an essay published as *Guardian* 173.[2] The interest here is that this amusing literary form is turned against phrases from his translations of Homer:

From the Daily Journal, *April* 5, 1728.

Notice is hereby given,

To all Lovers of Art and Ingenuity,

That the following Collection of such uncommon Curiosities as never were yet exhibited in any publick Auction belonging to a noted Person at *Twickenham*, who has been long since advised to leave off his Business, may be view'd there any Day in the Month of *April* Instant, Qui non credit Hodie, Cras credat. *Ex Auto* T.R.

1.	Curling Spire	*freely toucht.*
2.	A frighted Sky	*copy from the great* Blackmore.
3.	A Silver Sound	*harmoniously sketch'd.*
4.	An awkward Grace	*after the manner of* Settle.
5.	An ambrosial Curl	*Entire.*
6.	A nectar'd Urn	*Historical.*
7.	Adamantine Lungs	*as good as New.*
8.	A Vermilion Prore	*Dutch.*
9.	A many-colour'd Maid	*Flemish.*
10.	A Triple Dog	*The Romish School.*
11.	A singing Spear	*a Copy from* Blackmore.

[1] *Lives of the Poets*, i. 420 f.

[2] Pope may have taken his cue from Shakespeare—Olivia (*Twelfth Night*, i. v. 250 ff.) proposes to 'give out divers schedules of my beauty . . . as, *Item*, Two lips, indifferent red; *Item*, Two grey eyes with lids to them . . .'.

12. A quivering Shade	*somewhat shook in stretching.*
13. A dancing Cork	*with great Spirit.*
14. A sequestred Scene	*Still Life.*
15. A Velvet Plain	*after* Brughell.
16. An Oozy Bed	*Water Colours.*
17. A Liquid Road	*perfectly New.*
18. A Branching Deer	*Capital.*
19. A Feather'd Fate	⎫ *These two go together.*
20. A Leaden Death	⎭
21. A Pensive Steed	*an undoubted Original.*
22. A winged Wonder	*from the Dutch* Gabriel.
23. A living Cloud	*after the Life.*
24. A brown Horror	⎫ *both very Capital.*
25. A blue Languish	⎭
26. A self-mov'd Tripod.	*after the Blacksmith of* Antwerp.

N.B. The Gentleman's Nurse, who us'd to show the above-mention'd Collection, being lately deceased, Attendance will be given only in a Morning.[1]

The interest of the list for my present purposes is that it shows us phrases being considered as units. The parodist's purpose was to single out what could be laughably annotated as *objets d'art*, and it was only by accident, therefore, that his items belong to one of the large group of words and formulas that make up the Augustan poetic diction—that of the epics. But items 2, 11, 15, 19, 20 and 22 do plainly belong to that group.

To see that phrases rather than single words are commonly the unit in Augustan diction is to become less impatient with an offending word—*scaly* or *reign* or whatever—and to look to

---

[1] I have made no special search in Pope's *Homer* for these phrases, but have lighted on some of them accidentally. The most remarkable item is no. 25. *Iliad* xviii. 50 reads:

> And the blue Languish of soft *Alia's* Eye.

Pope here uses *languish* in a strangely new sense, which the *OED* defines as 'a tender look or glance'. He passed on the use to Thomson: cf. 'Spring', l. 1038 (of the moon):

> Beneath the trembling languish of her beam;

and to Collins; cf. *Persian Eclogues*, iv. 53 ff:

> In vain *Circassia* boasts her spicy Groves,
> For ever fam'd for pure and happy Loves:
> In vain she boasts her fairest of the Fair,
> Their Eyes' blue languish, and their golden Hair!

see what contribution it makes to its phrase, and beyond the phrase to the context. When we do not automatically dismiss these phrases because of our dislike of one of their constituents, more of them than we used to suppose are seen to be unique. Even when both the joined words are 'stock', the phrase they make may nevertheless be original, and not, to use Wordsworth's word, 'mechanical'.

8

For the analysis of these phrases we need a finer instrument than that used by Wordsworth in his various examinations of the diction, or more generally the language, of Augustan poetry. He did not see what Lascelles Abercrombie came to see, that

whenever the eighteenth century succeeded in its poetry it did so not because it had established an authorized poetic diction but because its poets had found some way—and they found a good many ways—of using this diction poetically; that is, of using it in precisely the same way as *low*, *mean*, or *vulgar* words may be used poetically.[1]

Wordsworth's standard was wrong to start with, for he was claiming that the 'language' of poetry could and should be the language of prose. It can never be that, if what is meant by 'language' is the whole of which diction is a part. 'Language' in this total sense includes—to mention one constituent other than diction—rhythm; and poetry, because of its stricter rhythm has a different language from prose, even though it uses the same words. For instance, at this point of writing my MS, I note that the first six words of the preceding sentence could figure as a five-beat line in a poem; that alternative use for them passed unnoticed—both by me and, I hope, my reader— for being read in its prose context it was read in a different tone of voice, at a different pace, and with a different sort of critical attention than if it had occurred in, say, a dramatic monologue by the ageing Browning. In his preface and related writings, Wordsworth used 'language' without giving a clear indication of his meaning, and I shall assume for my present

[1] *The Art of Wordsworth*, Oxford, 1952, p. 91.

purposes that he included under the term nothing more than single words and those phrases that are made up of a noun and adjective.

When engaged in writing much of his poetry, Wordsworth ignored the standard of 'diction' (the single word) and 'phraseology' (the phrase consisting of adjective and noun) which he set up in 1800 and thereabouts. He ignored it in his early poems, and in the *Excursion* and most of his later poems, where by and large it is in place. He practised it in the first printed version, if not always in the later, of 'Goody Blake and Harry Gill', 'Simon Lee', and a few other poems, though the first of these contains such 'poetical' phrases as 'ruddy clover' (which in the twentieth century might be only too accurately the language of men!), and 'lightsome summer-day', 'lusty splinter', and 'crisp with frost' and 'cold moon'; and the latter poem such 'poetical' phrases as 'sweet shire', 'the chiming hounds' and 'thanks and praises seemed to run/So fast out of his heart', where the word *run*—a favourite of Dryden and Pope as a metaphor—is not the word as it is used in prose. I call these phrases 'poetical' because though some of their words, when separate, are as much at home in prose as poetry, they produce, when combined, an effect proper only to poetry. Otherwise the poems I have named not only use words that are, by and large, as much at home in prose as in poetry, but combine them as prose-writers would, except where the metre demands an inversion. Apart from these clumsy inversions, the words fit the metre well, and help to produce a poetical effect when in addition to the pleasantly used metre, the sense is poetical. This it often is, though its poetical sense is one that many readers have found too bleak. But in any event Wordsworth's 'experiment' cannot be said to be wholly successful if only because he himself kept tinkering at it, and, in the second place, because readers have differed about it too much, and have gone on doing so for too long. My present task is not to discuss Wordsworth's poetry— even the *Lyrical Ballads* would need a book to itself—but to discuss his dismissal of Augustan poetry in 1800 and thereabouts. But before doing so, I should like to demonstrate that Wordsworth's sense of words was sometimes exquisite in a way that is not always credited to him, and to do so by means of an unfamiliar quotation. In the 'Memoir', signed 'E.H.P.', which was prefixed to later editions of *Guesses at Truth*, we read:

"I recollect", writes Dr Whewell, "a very interesting conversation, mainly between Wordsworth and Hare. The question was the relative value of the Saxon and the Latin portions of the English language. Hare was at that time disposed, as much as possible, to reject the latter. Wordsworth held that the mixture of the two elements made the language richer, and often modified a thought or image in a way that Saxon could not have done. 'Thus,' he said, quoting his own poetry, where he describes himself and his schoolfellows as skating by moonlight, in the line which says that their movements

'Into the woodland sent an alien sound,'

'the word "alien" conveys a feeling which no more familiar word could have expressed.' Hare replied, still quoting from the poet, 'No; I like an accumulation of short Saxon words, such as in those lines,

'The world is too much with us; morn and eve,
Getting and spending we lay waste our powers.'

Wordsworth replied, by quoting a strong example of style being elevated by the introduction of words of Latin origin—

'It would
The multitudinous sea incarnadine!' "[1]

At its best Wordsworth's sense of diction was so exquisite that he used many of the words of Augustan poetic diction when occasion called for just them and no other, demonstrating, as Tennyson was to, how useful to a poet they are. But in the years when he was writing and commenting on the *Lyrical Ballads*, he felt it necessary to denounce the diction. He had no alternative at that juncture in his career, for, like certain other great poets, he wished at this time to write poetry that should be strikingly new, denunciation of what he saw as strikingly old following inevitably from that. And, of course, his contemptuous criticism is sound in so far as he invokes what he calls 'bad poets'. His error was that his denunciation included some good poets, or, to be more exact, some poems and pieces of poems of good poets.

To take his three main instances. Of Gray's sonnet on the death of West he can accept only the lines which, at that date,

---

[1] A. W. Hare and J. C. Hare, *Guesses at Truth*, 1871 edn., pp. xxii f. Wordsworth, or his recorder, miswords two of the quotations, though not fatally.

he himself might have written, and quite fails to see the point of the rest. The point, as it happens, is sharp. When Gray begins his poem with

> In vain to me the smileing Mornings shine,
>   And redning[1] Phœbus lifts his golden Fire:
> The Birds in vain their amorous Descant joyn;
>   Or cheerful Fields resume their green Attire;
> These Ears, alas! for other Notes repine . . .

he means us to take the 'poetic diction' as dramatic—for though it is himself who is speaking, he speaks by means of quotations from others. With grief like his he has no use for the spring-time things that his fellow poets, quite properly on their less heavy occasions, have taken delight in, and have described in the sort of phrases he recalls—most pointedly of all, 'amorous descant' is ironically lifted from the famous passage in the fourth book of *Paradise Lost* ('Now came still evening on . . .'), which prepares us for Adam's amorous address to Eve. These things are stock-in-trade, and that is the point of Gray's rejection of them. For grief so sincere as his—

> I fruitless mourn to him, that cannot hear,
>   And weep the more because I weep in vain

—for the expression of such grief Gray rejects the sights and sounds of the spring, which poets less stricken have described in the stock terms he quotes. Wordsworth does not see the principle prompting this part of the poem: he thinks that the lines in question embody Gray's own account—his own competitive account—of the external world. The truth is that, like Wordsworth himself, Gray used the diction when and where it was in place, speaking as occasion served here of a 'broader browner shade' (where *browner* is 'stock') and there of the particular sort of beech

> That wreathes its old fantastic roots so high.

---

[1] The meaning of *redning* cannot be wholly detached from colour—Virgil and Ovid used *rubesco* with *Aurora* (*Æneid*, iii. 521, and *Metamorphoses*, iii. 60.)—but here the word means, first of all, becoming more healthy, vigorous, glowing. Something like this is its meaning in Pope's lines:

> Thro' his young Woods how pleas'd Sabinus stray'd,
>   Or sad delighted in the thick'ning shade,
> With annual joy the red'ning shoots to greet . . .
>   (*Moral Essays*, iv. 89 ff.)

There is the same degree of justification for what offended Wordsworth in the second of his exhibits, Pope's 'Messiah'. No poet has made a freer selection of words than Pope as occasion prompted—it would be superfluous at this time of day to argue the point. In certain of his poems, accordingly, the Augustan diction is beautifully in place. Wordsworth finds the 'Messiah' offensive 'throughout'. It is one of those instances figuring in the 'Appendix' that he added in the 1802 edition of the *Lyrical Ballads*, and is included in the group of 'metrical paraphrases . . . of passages in the old and new Testament'. Wordsworth prefers the diction used in 'our common Translation'—i.e. in the Authorized Version. The quarrel here is simply on a matter of taste—Wordsworth's single taste as against the twofold taste of other people, including Pope—and is therefore proverbially futile. For Pope does not offer his 'Messiah' as an improvement on any other version of the same material—Vulgate, or Douai, or Authorized—and his diction is not in competition with theirs. To dismiss it is to dismiss the whole meaning and tone of the thing. And much hangs on the dismissal, for if the 'Messiah' goes, so also does a great deal of religious art, the religious music (to go no further back into the past) of Bach and Handel, Haydn and Mozart, and Wren's churches, and all those baroque ones that Mr Bourke and Dr Finkenstaedt have recently made so vivid to us:

> though I revelled in the beauties of line and form, of colour and statue and painting, the attraction that [the Bavarian baroque] churches had for me remained something of a puzzle to me until one day I heard a rendering of 'Messiah' in one of the greatest of them whose architect was born in the same year as Handel. An inner relationship then opened up between what I saw all around me and what I was listening to. That a church such as that in which I was sitting should awaken the response it did in anyone as devoted as I had always been to the music of Corelli and Handel and Bach, I saw to be natural and inevitable. It was as if the epoch had spoken with *all* its voices, as if only through their concerted harmony it could breathe its fervour and rekindle its vision.[1]

[1] John Bourke [and Thomas Finkenstaedt], *Baroque Churches of Central Europe*, 1958, p. 9.

All these things would have to be dismissed—and, for that matter, Gothic churches, too. For the 'Messiah' contains such a passage as this—to single out what Wordsworth may have disapproved of most, though he instanced the poem entire:

> Swift fly the years, and rise th' expected morn!
> Oh spring to light, auspicious[1] Babe, be born!
> See Nature hastes her earliest wreaths to bring,
> With all the incense of the breathing spring:
> See lofty Lebanon his head advance,
> See nodding forests on the mountains dance:
> See spicy clouds from lowly Saron rise,
> And Carmel's flow'ry top perfumes the skies!
> Hark! a glad voice the lonely desert cheers;
> Prepare the way! a God, a God appears:
> A God, a God! the vocal hills reply,
> The rocks proclaim th' approaching Deity.
> Lo, earth receives him from the bending skies!
> Sink down ye mountains, and ye valleys rise,
> With heads declin'd, ye cedars homage pay;
> Be smooth ye rocks, ye rapid floods give way!
> The Saviour comes! by ancient bards foretold:
> Hear him, ye deaf, and all ye blind, behold!
> He from thick films shall purge the visual ray,
> And on the sightless eye-ball pour the day:
> 'Tis he th' obstructed paths of sound shall clear,
> And bid new music charm th' unfolding ear:
> The dumb shall sing, the lame his crutch forego,
> And leap exulting like the bounding roe.
> No sigh, no murmur the wide world shall hear,
> From ev'ry face he wipes off ev'ry tear.
> In adamantine chains shall Death be bound,
> And Hell's grim Tyrant feel th' eternal wound.[2]

The loud-sounding glory of such poetry is a fit expression of the

---

[1] Dryden had twice used the word *auspicious* in translating the Pollio eclogue of Virgil, but he failed to make the word tell as it does in Pope:
> The lovely Boy, with his auspicious Face
> Shall *Pollio*'s Consulship and Triumph grace . . .
> Begin, auspicious Boy, to cast about
> Thy Infant Eyes, and with a smile, thy Mother single out . . .

[2] ll. 21 ff.

glory that worship creates in some minds at some times, and is nicely in place on so august a theme.[1]

Finally, Wordsworth's other instances of offensive translations of Biblical passages include Johnson's version of a famous passage from Proverbs. Wordsworth quotes this in full, and contrasts its 'hubbub of words' with what exists in the original Authorized Version:

> Go to the ant, thou sluggard; consider her ways, and be wise: which having no guide, overseer, or ruler, provideth her meat in the summer, and gathereth her food in the harvest. How long wilt thou sleep, O sluggard? when wilt thou arise out of thy sleep? Yet a little sleep, a little slumber, a little folding of the hands to sleep: so shall thy poverty come as one that travelleth, and thy want as an armed man.[2]

Putting the contrast aside as irrelevant—as if anyone 'could imagine, either waking or dreaming', that Johnson intended his version to compete with that of the Authorized Version!—we can look at his lines for what they are:

> Turn on the prudent Ant, thy heedful eyes,
> Observe her labours, Sluggard, and be wise.
> No stern command, no monitory voice
> Prescribes her duties, or directs her choice,

---

[1] In this same appendix Cowper is blamed for his epithet 'church-going' in 'Alexander Selkirk':

> But the sound of the church-going bell
> These vallies and rocks never heard . . .

Wordsworth writes: 'The epithet "church-going", applied to a bell, and that by so chaste a writer as Cowper, is an instance of the strange abuses which poets have introduced into their language till they and their readers take them as a matter of course, if they do not single them out expressly as objects of admiration.' Wordsworth is being perverse, according to the literal-mindedness that is the occasional disadvantage of his reverence for the concrete. He takes 'church-going' as a compound participle used attributively (cf. 'life-giving') and ludicrously makes Cowper's phrase mean 'the bell that goes to church' in the same way as 'life-giving food' means 'food that gives life'. Cowper's 'church-going' is a gerund in origin, and 'church-going bell' means 'bell for church-going' just as 'drinking water' means water for drinking and 'cooking egg' egg for cooking. There is a passage in Trollope's *Mr Scarborough's Family* (chr. xviii) that takes comic advantage of the possible ambiguity in the epithet: 'Then Mr Grey, with a loud long sign, allowed his boots and his gloves, and his church-going hat, and his church-going umbrella to be brought to him.' Here the compound 'church-going' may be either participial or gerundial in nature, and so means both 'for church-going', and 'which goes to church'. In Cowper's poem the meaning of 'church-going' is obvious.

[2] Proverbs, vi. 6 ff.

Yet timely provident, she hastes away
To snatch the blessings of the plenteous day;
When fruitful summer loads the teeming plain,
She gleans the harvest, and she stores the grain.
   How long shall sloth usurp thy useless hours,
Dissolve thy vigour, and enchain thy powers?
While artful shades thy downy couch enclose,
And soft solicitation courts repose,
Amidst the drousy charms of dull delight,
Year chases year, with unremitted flight,
Till want, now following fraudulent and slow,
Shall spring to seize thee like an ambush'd foe.

Is it not true that these lines, especially the later ones, have qualities that no other poet could give us—the masculine vigour of Dryden joined to the fine discretion of Milton. And as for diction, I can see no trace in them of anything 'stock', and accordingly see no need to defend them. As for the phrase 'gaudy and inane phraseology,' which Wordsworth used elsewhere—in the 'Advertisement' to the first edition of the *Lyrical Ballads* (1798)—where is any trace of it in Johnson's weighty and splendid lines?

If it comes to that, gaudiness exists in plenty in Wordsworth's first two published volumes—*An Evening Walk* and the *Descriptive Sketches*—and very fine it is, if we can accept the kind, as, some five years later, Wordsworth himself could not. Emile Legouis has an excellent chapter in his *Early Life of William Wordsworth*, demonstrating the remarkable process of enrichment employed by Wordsworth in making more gorgeous the diction of his then beloved Augustan poets—a process by which a phrase like Collins's 'the lily peace' becomes Wordsworth's 'the redbreast peace'.[1] The gaudiness of those early poems—the *Evening Walk* and *Descriptive Sketches*—was aptly characterized when Coleridge recalled the impact they made on him as a young man:

During the last year of my residence at Cambridge, I became acquainted with Mr Wordsworth's first publication entitled "Descriptive Sketches"; and seldom, if ever, was the emergence of an original poetic genius above the literary horizon more evidently

---

[1] *La Jeunesse de William Wordsworth*, trans. by J. W. Matthews, 1921, pp. 140 f.

announced. In the form, style, and manner of the whole poem, and in the structure of the particular lines and periods, there is an harshness and acerbity connected and combined with words and images all a-glow, which might recall those products of the vegetable world, where gorgeous blossoms rise out of the hard and thorny rind and shell, within which the rich fruit was elaborating. The language was not only peculiar and strong, but at times knotty and contorted, as by its own impatient strength; while the novelty and struggling crowd of images, acting in conjunction with the difficulties of the style, demanded always a greater closeness of attention than poetry (at all events, than descriptive poetry) has a right to claim. It not seldom therefore justified the complaint of obscurity. In the following extract I have sometimes fancied, that I saw an emblem of the poem itself, and of the author's genius as it was then dis-played.

> " 'Tis storm; and hid in mist from hour to hour,
> All day the floods a deepening murmur pour;
> The sky is veiled, and every cheerful sight:
> Dark is the region as with coming night;
> And yet what frequent bursts of overpowering light!
> Triumphant on the bosom of the storm,
> Glances the fire-clad eagle's wheeling form;
> Eastward, in long perspective glittering, shine
> The wood-crowned cliffs that o'er the lake recline;
> Wide o'er the Alps a hundred streams unfold,
> At once to pillars turn'd that flame with gold;
> Behind his sail the peasant strives to shun,
> The West, that burns like one dilated sun,
> Where in a mighty crucible expire
> The mountains, glowing hot, like coals of fire."[1]

Whether we call the diction of these two early poems glorious or gaudy it falls under the strictures of 1798 and after.

It is in Erasmus Darwin, rather than in the first published poems of Wordsworth, that we find gaudiness without glory. Wordsworth may have had him in mind in coining his phrase, for there is no gaudiness in Pope (not even in the night piece from the *Iliad*) or in Gray. But if Darwin is gaudy, he is not inane. Nor is the gaudiness wanton, for it is that of bits and pieces of the natural world itself. Darwin is a scientist who writes accu-

---

[1] *Biographia Literaria*, i. 56 f. Coleridge errs in thinking that *Descriptive Sketches* was published earlier than *An Evening Walk*.

rately. His poem *The Botanic Garden* is furnished, as its title page announces, 'With Philosophical [i.e. scientific] Notes'. These alone would be sufficient to show his interests, and the factual basis of his gaudy poetry. In the second canto of the first book of the *Botanic Garden* we read:

> . . . glows [*sic*], refulgent Tin! thy chrystal grains,
> And tawny Copper shoots her azure veins;
> Zinc lines his fretted vault with sable ore,
> And dull Galena[1] tessellates the floor;
> On vermil beds in Idria's mighty caves
> The living Silver rolls its ponderous waves;[2]
> With gay refractions bright Platina[3] shines,
> And studs with squander'd stars his dusky mines;
> Long threads of netted gold, and silvery darts,
> Inlay the Lazuli, and pierce the Quartz;—
> —Whence roof'd with silver beam'd PERU, of old,
> And hapless MEXICO was paved with gold.

The detailed geology of this passage is, I am assured, at all points accurate, except perhaps in the penultimate couplet, where threads of gold would not seem correctly placed in lapis lazuli. Of course, when it comes to gaudiness, Darwin is sophisticating to the extent of cleaning up his metals and polishing them before describing them: the most precious contents of the soily earth are usually dirty to start with. But the process of cleaning is surely legitimate enough, since it merely allows the metals to show themselves for what they are. If Darwin is inane and gaudy, then geology itself is, and science generally. But in truth Wordsworth might have been expected to repress any criticism on the score of inanity. I myself do not think that 'Goody Blake and Harry Gill' is inane but it does contain the lines:

> . . . evermore his teeth they chatter,
> Chatter, chatter, chatter still.

Wordsworth was enough of a geologist not to dub Darwin inane. In making the charge he may have had in mind, as Miss

[1] Common lead ore.

[2] Idria, in Italy, is a source of mercury. *Living silver* is an excellent item of diction, framed by analogy from Virgil's phrase for statuary *spirantia aera* (*Æneid*, vi. 847). Pliny's name for mercury, *vivum argentum*, lacks the engaging presnt participle.

[3] *Platina* was the name for platinum until into the nineteenth century.

Barstow suggests, the verses in the magazines of the time—
verses such as these, which appeared over the signature 'Agenor',
and under the overweening title of 'The Plunderer', in the
Carlton-House Magazine: or, Annals of Taste, Fashion, and Politeness,
for March 1792.

> Fair, soft, and young, one tender flower
>   I rear'd, with fond, peculiar care—
> I watch'd it ev'ry passing hour,
>   And joy'd to see it, soft and fair.
>
> My eager hand could scarcely wait
>   In patience the appointed day,
> Appointed both by love and fate,
>   To bear my blooming prize away.
>
> To absence forc'd, one little week,
>   I left my darling, tender flow'r:
> Ah! Why must pale misfortune wreak
>   On my sad head her heaviest show'r?
>
> Some bolder hand, alas! than mine,
>   Pluck'd the fair blossom I had rear'd,
> And dar'd invade that sacred shrine,
>   Through all my trembling frame endear'd;
>
> And spoil'd me of the only stay
>   To which each bright'ning prospect hung,
> And bade me ever weep the day,
>   I left my flower, fair, soft and young.

If Wordsworth has this magazine verse in mind, then his attack
is in this respect an attack on inanity pure and simple. There is
no gaudiness in such poems, but plain sense plainly set down
with as little variation from prose as verse allows. What they
lack is strength of sense, a lack deplored from the dawn of
literary criticism.

9

As time went on the parcels of poetic diction came loose and
dispersed. Pope, as we have seen, was keenly aware of the groups
that words fell into, but his fine sense of them must always have
been unusual, and the cult of the sense by others slackened off
in the later eighteenth and nineteenth centuries. I have spoken

of the mixing of the formal kinds in a single poem, and it is perhaps because of this mixing that the kinds of diction came to be confounded. Pope was aware when one sort of diction gave place to another, but because the changes happened so often the grouping of the words came to lose distinctness. For this change, then, Pope himself had some responsibility. The *Rape of the Lock* was described by its author as 'an heroic-comical poem', but he had placed within its closely packed limits such a rainbow-variety of sorts of poetry, other than epic and comic, each sort occupying only a line or two, that it came to be thought of as poetry in general. As time went on its colours seemed to run into each other, and when Keats wrote his own sort of epic in *Endymion*, all he thought of in the way of 'kind' was something so general as scarcely to exist: 'I must make 4,000 Lines of one bare circumstance and fill them with "Poetry"';[1] and he justified the length of the poem in these words:

Do not the Lovers of Poetry like to have a little Region to wander in where they may pick and choose, and in which the images are so numerous that many are forgotten and found new in a second Reading: which may be food for a Week's stroll in the Summer?[2]

He saw his poem as one thing, one kind, one length from the one loom. That was not how Pope saw the *Rape of the Lock*, which for him resembled a grotto carefully packed with distinct stones and jewels gathered from many known sources, all contributing to form a single thing because of the controlling skill of the poet. As time went on readers of the *Rape of the Lock* ceased to be aware of diversity in all its clear divisions, and retained only their sense of its unity. The other important contributor to this dispersion of the kinds is Gray. I have spoken of the Shakespearean variety of his diction. The variety is observable in single poems—in the 'Elegy' and particularly in the 'Progress of Poesy' and 'The Bard'. In the former of these two great odes, we move from

> . . . verdant vales, and Ceres' golden reign,

to

> Enchanting shell! the sullen Cares
> And frantic Passions hear thy soft control,

[1] *Letters*, p. 52.   [2] ibid.

to this recollection of the entry of the ballerina:

> With arms sublime, that float upon the air,
> In gliding state she wins her easy way,

to

> Night, and all her sickly dews,

to

> Woods, that wave o'er Delphi's steep,
> Isles, that crown th' Egæan deep,

to

> . . . The dauntless Child
> Stretched forth his little arms, and smiled,

to

> He saw; but blasted with excess of light,
> Closed his eyes in endless night,

to

> Nor the pride, nor ample pinion
>   That the Theban Eagle bear,
> Sailing with supreme dominion
>   Thro' the azure deep of air.

To do some of one's finest work in a kind that allowed the intrusion of so much variety was to help dissolve the idea of kinds altogether. And, a *Rape of the Lock* on a gigantic scale, there came *Don Juan*, which I have already mentioned as a poem playing havoc with the kinds. Poets were coming to delight more in poetry, and less in divisions of poetry. This meant of course that those kinds that had always been allowed to be less full of obvious poeticalness than others, essays and satires, were pushed outside the bounds of poetry altogether—an *Essay on Criticism* and even an *Essay on Man* and the *Imitations of Horace*. The diction of Pope and Gray came to seem to belong to poetry as a whole, and even when to later readers it seemed dated, it was not avoided. Keats used, as I have shown, many Augustan words, and found them capable of fresh applications.[1] And if certain *combinations* of them were avoided with repulsion, that was because of a change that had happened outside poetry —a change in the way the common man, who moves in the train of the scientists, thinks of the external world.

[1] See above, p. 32.

APPENDIX I

ENGLISH AND LATIN

In the seventeenth and eighteenth centuries there were many testimonies to the advantages of Latin, but we have only to read them to see how often the witnesses were critical of the degree to which words of Latin origin were admitted into English. Dryden thought that Ben Jonson had gone too far over towards Latinization: he 'did a little too much Romanize our tongue'.[1] And here is another passage showing that, as far as diction went, Dryden was out to write English that would be recognized as good by Englishmen, however much he admired the sources from which he was enriching it:

I will not excuse, but justify myself, for one pretended crime, with which I am liable to be charged by false critics, not only in this translation, but in many of my original poems; that I latinize too much. 'Tis true, that, when I find an English word significant and sounding, I neither borrow from the Latin nor any other language; but, when I want at home, I must seek abroad.

If sounding words are not of our growth and manufacture, who shall hinder me to import them from a foreign country? I carry not out the treasure of the nation, which is never to return; but what I bring from Italy, I spend in England: here it remains, and here it circulates; for, if the coin be good, it will pass from one hand to another. I trade both with the living and the dead, for the enrichment of our native language. We have enough in England to supply our necessity; but, if we will have things of magnificence and splendour, we must get them by commerce. Poetry requires ornament; and that is not to be had from our old Teuton monosyllables; therefore, if I find any elegant word in a classic author, I propose it to be naturalized, by using it myself; and, if the public approves of it, the bill passes. But every man cannot distinguish between pedantry and poetry: every man, therefore, is not fit to innovate. Upon the whole matter, a poet must first be certain that the word he would introduce is beautiful in the Latin, and is to consider, in the next place, whether it will agree with the English idiom: after this, he ought to take the opinion of judicious friends, such as are learned in both languages: and, lastly, since no man is infallible, let him use this licence very sparingly; for if too many foreign words are poured in upon us, it

[1] *Essays*, i. 82.

98

looks as if they were designed not to assist the natives, but to conquer them.[1]

Dryden reassures us partly because of the reasonableness of his attitude, and partly because of the quality of the English in which he expresses it.

On another occasion he hoped that in translating the *Æneid* he had

in some sort . . . copied the clearness, the purity, the easiness, and the magnificence of [Virgil's] style;[2]

in other words, achieved the epic style that Dennis had desiderated in the previous year. One quality that these poets admired in Latin, and particularly in the Latin of Virgil, was its musicalness. 'Harmonious' is a word that recurs, and Johnson added another:

He dwelt upon Buchanan's elegant verses to Mary Queen of Scots, *Nympha Caledoniæ*, &c. and spoke with enthusiasm of the beauty of Latin verse. 'All the modern languages (said he) cannot furnish so melodious a line as

'Formosam resonare doces Amarillida silvas'.[3]

On another occasion he singled out a line from his own Latin version of Pope's 'Messiah':

As we were leaving the College [Pembroke], he said 'Here I translated Pope's Messiah. Which do you think is the best line in it?— My own favourite is,

"Vallis aromaticas fundit Saronica nubes." '
I told him, I thought it a very sonorous hexameter.[4]

It is Thomas Warton who is recording the incident, and he adds 'I did not tell him, that it was not in the Virgilian style', which of course Johnson knew very well for himself. Johnson indeed had his own Latin style, De Quincey remarking of him that

He wrote [Latin] genially, and not as one translating into it painfully from English, but as one using it for his original organ of thinking. And in Latin verse he expressed himself at times with the energy and freedom of a Roman.

One thing they envied in Latin was its spacing of consonants and vowels:

[1] *Essays*, ii. 234 f. [2] *Essays*, ii. 228.
[3] Boswell's *Life*, i. 460. [4] id., 272.

There is a beauty of sound, as Segrais has observed, in some Latin words, which is wholly lost in any modern language. He instances in that *mollis amaracus*, on which Venus lays Cupid, in the First Æneid. If I should translate it *sweet marjoram*, as the word signifies, the reader would think I had mistaken Virgil: for those village words, as I may call them, give us a mean idea of the thing; but the sound of the Latin is so much more pleasing, by the just mixture of the vowels with the consonants, that it raises our fancies to conceive somewhat more noble than a common herb, and to spread roses under him, and strew lilies over him; a bed not unworthy the grandson of the goddess.[1]

Obviously the conformation of many English words, that of *strength*, for instance, was strangely unlike the conformation of any Latin word—unlike and therefore plainly, it was assumed, inferior. And so they were not wholly free to appraise the peculiar worth of words of this English sort—words that go to make English the fine language that we, in our freer condition, know it to be. There is a passage in Johnson's 'Grammar of the English Tongue', one of the essays prefacing the Dictionary, where he is impressed with strong English monosyllables against his will. He is engaged in characterizing English as a language, and devotes half a page—half a long folio page in small print—to quotations from the *Grammatica Linguæ Anglicanæ* of Dr John Wallis. The 'learned and sagacious' Wallis, to whom 'every English grammarian owes a tribute of reverence', published the first edition of his grammar in 1653—we may note that it was written, as its title implies, in Latin—and its sixth and last edition appeared ten years after Johnson's praise of it in the Preface. Wallis claimed that many of the commonest words in English, other than those that are as frankly onomatopoetic as *bump* or *splash*, convey their sense or a quality of it partly by their sound, that they have what we might call a discreet onomatopoeia. Here is a sample paragraph from those quoted in Johnson's translation:

words that begin with *str* intimate the force and effect of the thing signified, as if probably derived from σρόννυμι, or *strenuus*; as *strong, strength, strew, strike, streak, stroke, stripe, strive, strife, struggle, strout, strut, stretch, strait, strict, streight*, that is, narrow, *distrain, stress, distress,*

[1] Dryden, *Essays*, ii. 233.

string, strap, stream, streamer, strand, strip, stray, struggle, strange, stride,
straddle.

Johnson dismisses Wallis's contention as 'ingenious, but of
more subtlety than solidity', and adds that it is 'such as perhaps
might in every language be enlarged without end'. But to quote
at length proves, I think, that he felt there was more in the
theory than he was consciously prepared to allow, and that in
consequence English monosyllables had much to be said for
them as bringing words nearer to things. Admittedly some of
Wallis's items weaken his case, but at its strongest it is supported
where support is firmest—by the use made of these words by
poets, and also by prose-writers. For they use them as though
they subscribed to his view, satisfied that words like these have
more to them than their dictionary sense,[1] and that the addition,
which at its most concrete is sonoral, is in keeping with that
sense. Johnson always staunchly supported the view that words
are no more than arbitrary signs, except where they are clearly
onomatopoetic, that they are, as he put it, only the 'daughters
of earth' and so lack a parity with things, which are the 'sons
of heaven'. Pope came nearer to suggesting the mysterious truth
when, in that phrase I have already quoted, he called poetry
'the language of the gods'. And when Johnson himself was engaged in writing he found, like any other great writer, that
words are more than signs; he wrote as if he were aware of
the latent onomatopoeia of much of the English language; he
wrote as if he were on the side of Wallis, whom he quoted at
so bemused a length. We might examine the word *strength* in
this connection. If the English word denoting strength had been
lool, it would surely have been avoided by poets as not expressive enough. We cannot imagine Tennyson writing:

My lool is as the lool of ten,

even if the word had meant strength so long that Englishmen
other than poets had grown dull to its lack of sinew; for words
in poetry show themselves as words, and rouse us to look at
them as if for the first time, and in this imaginary instance to
see them as inadequate. Again, if words are merely signs, why

[1] Cf. Otto Jespersen, *Language, its Nature, Development and Origin*, 1922, p. 397:
'there is something like sound symbolism in *some* words'—i.e., in some words not
obviously onomatopoetic.

was Milton able to build a line having so particular a quality of contemptuous sound as

> Grate on their scrannel Pipes of wretched straw,

where one word only is onomatopoetic according to the ordinary way of reckoning? Except for *Pipes*, which he either could not avoid, or welcomed so as not to seem too carefully complete, these words were chosen and placed by Milton because they have a latent power, which is partly sonoral, of enforcing the contemptuous meaning.[1] I know how easily one can come to seem fantastic on this subject, but that, I think, is because it is 'subtle' rather than because it lacks 'solidity'.

I have called this quality in our words their 'discreet onomatopoeia'. In the most part of our ordinary speech and writing it remains latent. But it is revealed when words are used in the way that good poets use them, making us aware of them as meaning more than we guessed, or rather than we cared, or had occasion, to guess. All that can be said in general about the characteristics of this or that language is mainly irrelevant when we are confronted with the use of it by the poets, and also prose-writers, who know how to write it according, as we say, to its genius. Then from a language that is supposedly harsh melodiousness can be forthcoming when wanted, and from a language supposedly melodious, sonority. Languages

---

[1] 'Lycidas', l. 124. It is relevant to my argument to quote Thomas Newton's mid-eighteenth-century note on this line: 'No sound of words can be more expressive of the sense; and how finely has he imitated, or rather improved, a passage in Virgil! *Ecl.* iii. 26.

> —"non tu in triviis, indocte, solebas
> "*Stridenti miserum stipula disperdere carmen?*"

I remember not to have seen the word *scrannel* in any other author; nor can I find it in any dictionary or glossary that I have consulted; but I presume it answers to the *stridenti* of Virgil.' *Scrannel*, as Thomas Warton was soon to discover, meant 'thin, lean, meagre', and according to the *OED* Milton is the first to write it. These lines of Virgil were instanced by Dryden in support of his contention that Virgil could have written 'sharper satires than either Horace or Juvenal, if he would have employed his talent that way'. (*Essays*, ii. 86). He holds that in these lines Virgil gives 'almost as many lashes as he has written syllables'. It is plain, however, that the English language allows Milton to lay on more fiercely. But the language needs a supreme master to help it to its supreme effects. When Dryden translated those admired lines he scarcely 'imitated' Virgil, let alone 'improved' on him; he produces an effect completely his own:

> Dunce at the best; in Streets but scarce allow'd
> To tickle, on thy Straw, the stupid Crowd.

shed their defects in the hands of poets, and for the nonce assume qualities that come more easily to other languages. Look for instance at the despised monosyllable. Dryden, who was repeating an old complaint, spoke of 'monosyllables . . . clogged with consonants, which are the dead weight of our mother tongue;'[1] and soon afterwards Pope was to warn English poets that

> Ten low words oft creep in one dull line.[2]

The most interesting contemporary discussion of the charge that monosyllables are the bane of English is Elizabeth Elstob's, and what she says is the last word on the subject. The twofold question, as she puts it, is 'whether or not the Copiousness and Variety of *Monosyllables* may be always justly reputed a fault, and may not as justly be thought, to be very useful and ornamental', and she begins from the beginning by justifying monosyllables in general, there being monosyllables in every language. But she sees that it is a question of proportions, and admits that the only passages in Greek and Latin that show a notable preponderance of monosyllables are the pedagogic rimes in Lilly's 'Rules concerning Nouns'! ('I mention' [this school grammarian], she adds, 'not as a Classick, but because the Words are Classical and Monosyllables'.) It is another matter when she comes to the use of them by the English poets, and she assembles a remarkable catena of verse passages wholly or mainly in monosyllables from Chaucer to Lady Winchilsea. As we read the passages, however, we see only too well why Dryden and Pope criticised such things—many of them ignore the opportunities offered by metre; their rhythm is merely a plod. Miss Elstob does not seem fully to see this; but she rises to the occasion when she comes to interpret some of Dryden's remarks on the subject. She approaches Dryden from the direction of classical writers:

Now if these [partly monosyllabic lines from Homer, Virgil and Horace] are Beauties, as I doubt not but the *politer Criticks* will allow, I cannot see why our Language may not now and then be tolerated in using *Monosyllables*, when it is done discreetly, and sparingly; and as I do not commend any of our Moderns who contract words into *Monosyllables* to botch up their Verses, much less such as do it

[1] *Essays*, ii. 226.   [2] *Essay on Criticism*, l. 347.

out of Affectation;[1] yet certainly the use of *Monosyllables* may be made to produce a charming and harmonious Effect, where they fall under a Judgment that can rightly dispose and order them. And indeed, if a Variety and Copiousness of Feet, and a Latitude of shifting and transposing Words either in Prose or Poetical Compositions, be of any use, towards the rendering such Compositions sweet, or nervous, or harmonious, according to the Exigencies of the several sorts of Stile, one wou'd think *Monosyllables* to be best accommodated to all these Purposes, and according to the Skill of those who know how to manage them, to answer all the Ends, either of masculine Force, or female Tenderness; for being single you have a Liberty of placing them where, and as you please; whereas in Words of many Syllables you are more confined, and must take them as you find them, or be put upon the cruel necessity of mangling and tearing them asunder. Mr. *Dryden*, it is true, wou'd make us believe he had a great Aversion to *Monosyllables*. Yet he cannot help making use of them sometimes in entire Verses, nor conceal his having a sort of Pride, even where he tells us he was forc'd to do it. For to have done otherwise would have been a Force on Nature, which would have been unworthy of so great a Genius, whose Care it was to study Nature, and to imitate and copy it to the Life; and it is not improbable, that there might be somewhat of a latent Delicacy and Niceness in this Matter, which he chose rather to dissemble, than to expose, to the indiscreet Management of meaner Writers. For in the first Line of his great Work the *Æneis*, every word is a *Monosyllable*; and tho' he makes a seeming kind of Apology, yet he cannot forbear owning a secret Pleasure in what he had done.

My first Line in the *Æneis*, says he, is not harsh.
> *Arms and the Man I sing, who forc'd by Fate.*

But a much better Instance may be given from the last line of *Manilius*, made *English* by our learned and judicious Mr. *Creech:*
> *Nor could the World have born so fierce a Flame.*

Where the many liquid Consonants are placed so artfully, that they give a pleasing Sound to the Words, tho' they are all of one Syllable.

It is plain from these last Words, that the Subject matter, *Monosyllables*, is not so much to be complain'd of; what is chiefly

---

[1] She is alluding to the growing practice, often deprecated at the time, of shedding the syllabic ending of the preterite and past participle of weak verbs, as in *walk'd* for *walk-ed*, of contracting *not* as in *can't*, and for curtailing certain words —e.g. *vulgus mobile* to *mob* and *positive* to *pos*.

to be requir'd, is of the Poet, that he be a good Workman, in forming them aright, and that he *place them artfully*: and, however Mr. *Dryden* may desire to disguise himself, yet, as he some where says, Nature will prevail. For see with how much Passion he has exprest himself towards these two Verses, in which the Poet [*Denham*] has not been sparing of *Monosyllables*:

> I am sure, says he, there are few who make Verses, have observ'd the Sweetness of these two Lines in *Coopers Hill*;
> *Tho deep yet clear, tho gentle, yet not dull;*
> *Strong without Rage, without o'erflowing full.*

And there are yet fewer that can find the reason of that Sweetness. I have given it to some of my Friends in Conversation, and they have allow'd the Criticism to be just.

You see, Sir [she is speaking to Thomas Hickes, to whom her preface is addressed], this great Master had his Reserves, and this was one of the *Arcana*, to which every Novice was not admitted to aspire; this was an Entertainment only for his best Friends, such as he thought worthy of his Conversation. . . .[1]

The English language is clogged with the consonants of monosyllables only when not written felicitously. It is clogged when Arnold begins a line with 'Who prop, thou ask'st . . .'. But Dryden's poetry (and prose), for all its monosyllables, is free from inert weight, and Pope wrote monosyllabic lines that triumphantly escape 'dullness'. Indeed, though it is often thought that among English words those taken from the Latin are weightiest, there is no lack of weight in

> He that is down needs fear no fall,
> He that is low, no pride;[2]

or when Watts imitating a psalm of David writes:

> Our God, our Help in Ages past,
> Our Hope for Years to come;

[1] Elizabeth Elstob, *The Rudiments of Grammar for the English-Saxon Tongue* . . ., 1715, pp. xiv ff. I have partly modernized the method of indicating a quotation. I owe my knowledge of Miss Elstob's remarks to Miss Helen Donaldson's thesis, *Opinions of the English Language as a Medium of Literary Expression*, awarded the degree of M.A. in the University of London, 1959.

[2] Bunyan, *Pilgrim's Progress*, ed. J. B. Wharey, Oxford, 1928, p. 250. Some of my instances are taken from Mr Walter Shewring's 'Notes on Greek Literature', an excellent series of papers that appeared in the *Ampleforth Journal* between 1936 and 1940, and which because of the interruption of war lack their concluding instalment.

or when Ruskin ends a paragraph with 'Now, as he was sinking
—had he the gold? or had the gold him?'[1] Moreover, our
greatest poets have rejoiced in the monosyllables of English
partly because a Latin polysyllable can achieve among them an
effect of which Latin itself, being unable to provide a wide monosyllabic context, is incapable:

> Now hast thou but one bare hower to liue,
> And then thou must be damnd perpetually . . .
> O Ile leape vp to my God: who pulles me downe?
> See see where Christs blood streames in the firmament,
> One drop would saue my soule, halfe a drop, ah my Christ . . .[2]

(which also shows that consonantal monosyllables can make
strong emphasis possible, as occasionally in Latin, e.g., 'stat
crux dum volvitur orbis');[3]

> What though the field be lost?
> All is not lost; th'unconquerable Will
> And study of revenge, immortal hate. . . .[4]

> Oh spring to light, auspicious babe, be born![5]

> Rolled round in earth's diurnal course;[6]

> But she is in her grave, and oh!
> The difference to me.[7]

Or again, take the question of 'smoothness'. Johnson was
greatly pleased by the smoothness of those lines from Latin
poetry, one Virgil's and one his own.[8] As it happened, he had
translated Virgil's line as a boy, and mainly because of the
loose start to the line, had not made much of it in the English:

> And the wood rings with Amarillis' name.

---

[1] *Works*, xvii. 86.

[2] Marlowe, *Doctor Faustus*, ed. W. W. Greg, Oxford, 1950, p. 288.

[3] The first half of the motto of the Carthusians from at least 1239, apparently
composed by Dom Martin, the Prior General of the Order, who in that year
designed the arms of the order.

[4] Milton, *Paradise Lost*, i. 105 ff.

[5] Pope, 'Messiah', l. 22.

[6] Wordsworth, 'A slumber did my spirit seal . . .'

[7] Wordsworth, 'She dwelt among the untrodden ways . . .'

[8] See above, p. 99.

English poetry could achieve a melodiousness superior to that, sometimes at the hands of Johnson himself, often of Milton, as in:

> Smooth-sliding *Mincius*, crown'd with vocall reeds;[1]

And there were the two lines of Pope's that most pleased his ear:

> Lo! where Maeotis sleeps, and hardly flows
> The freezing Tanais thro' a waste of snows:[2]

and many more.

Indeed, at several other points, these Augustan critics could not have failed to see—had their minds been free to see it— that English is superior to Latin as a language expressive word by word. Look at one particular sound. Dowson considered, and some of us would agree, that [v] is the loveliest sound among our consonants, and superior to the Latin [w]. He chose as his favourite in English that line of Poe's:

> The viol, the violet, and the vine.

And some years earlier the delightful small poet, Thomas Julian Henry Marzials, had rivalled it with his

> Bronze and rainbow, rose and blues,
> Velvet, violet, vermilly,
> Ruby, peach, and pink, and pea. . . .[3]

This particular sound is quite lacking from classical Latin. And so the English *sylvan*, a favourite Augustan adjective, is superior in point of melodiousness to the Latin from which it is derived. If, as I have suggested elsewhere,[4] the 'sylvan scene' of Milton, and others after him, comes from the juxtaposed words of Virgil, 'silvis scaena coruscis,' it is bettered in the borrowing because [silv] is more melodious than [silw] (as [si:n] is more melodious than [skain] or [skaen]). I am suggesting that the presence of the sound *v* makes for melodiousness in lines such as Pope's

> The mossy fountains, and the sylvan shades;[5]

---

[1] 'Lycidas', l. 86. [2] *Dunciad*, iii. 87 f. [3] *A Gallery of Pigeons*, 1873, p. 16.
[4] See above, pp. 35f. [5] Messiah, l. 3.

or his

The youth rush eager to the sylvan war;[1]

or Keats's

Sylvan historian, who canst thus express[2]

—a line that would be hideous indeed without its 'sylvan', for it shows English monosyllables to be as clogging as Dryden alleged, and demonstrates Keats's failure, on this brief occasion, to circumvent the shortcomings of the language. We may also notice that one of the cacophonous words in Keats's line is a dissyllable from the Latin.

Clearly, then, English had little to fear from comparison with other languages, ancient or modern, for melodiousness, sonorousness, magnificence or what not, when in the hands of those who could humour it. These Augustan critics and poets knew all this in their heads and hearts—how could they miss knowing it with the poems of Milton, not to mention Herrick and some others, before them? They also knew it from the evidence of their vocal chords. But they revered and admired Latin so much that they were not free to glory in the knowledge and to act on it freely.

APPENDIX II

Readers of Augustan poetry have welcomed Mr Arthos's careful work on what he has called the 'language' of natural description in 'eighteenth-century poetry'.[3] And others also, though the title modestly did not invite them. If eighteenth-century poetry has the first claim on his interest, that of earlier centuries comes closely second. Students of the poetry of the sixteenth and seventeenth centuries in particular, and not merely of the English poetry of these centuries, have found as much for them in this book as have the students of the poetry of the century named. Nor is this all. There is much of interest for students of earlier poetry, since Mr Arthos, more comprehensively and systematically than any previous writer, has

[1] *Windsor Forest*, l. 148.
[2] 'Ode on a Grecian Urn', l. 3.
[3] J. Arthos, *The Language of Natural Description in Eighteenth-century Poetry*, Ann Arbor, 1949.

found much of the diction already formed in the ancient poets and also in writings where diction that has reached us as 'poetic' has not often been suspected to exist, in writings of ancient and later 'scientists'. The great value of his book, therefore, lies in its first appendix which lists words of this diction along with samples of their use down the ages in the verse and prose of poets and scientists. This appendix contains many surprises. For instance, in reading *The Dunciad* one comes across this couplet:

> No meagre, muse-rid mope, adust and thin,
> In a dun night-gown of his own loose skin.

The latest editor of the poem has had the curiosity to consult the *OED* s.v. *adust* (= scorched, dried up) and so has understood the word. What he found in the *OED* is now amply supplemented (and complicated) by the quotations given by Mr Arthos, quotations which start with those from Ovid, Lucan and Pliny. Speaking for myself, I have always lazily approached Pope's word by way of the English *dust* as if it were a coinage of Pope's (as it was to be of George Eliot's when she spoke of one 'tired and adust with long riding'), rather than by way of the Latin *adurere*, or the Elizabethan *to adure*, or *to adust*—the latter of which verbs is found in *Paradise Lost*. A further instance. In *Windsor Forest* comes this couplet:

> Thy shady empire shall retain no trace
> Of war or blood, but in the sylvan chase.

Few modern readers can have suspected that 'empire' is as much of the poetic diction as is 'sylvan'. Besides demonstrating that diction it is, Mr Arthos adds the illuminating footnote: 'See also Climate and Clime, Kingdom, Region, Reign.' Such are the surprises of Mr Arthos's first appendix, which, stretching to almost three hundred pages, forms the bulk of his book.

Besides his concern with diction word by word, Mr Arthos is interested in accounting for the use of it by reference to intellectual beliefs. Briefly, he sees it as the inevitable terminology of poets for whom the universe was a completed thing:

A large number of poets formed and exploited a stable language because they believed that the design of the world was stable. (p. vii.)

So much in undiluted praise.

The weakness of the book is that Mr Arthos is not enough a critic either of language or of the use made of it by poets. He does not distinguish finely enough between the workings of the sub-divisions of what he has lumped together as 'language'. He is mainly concerned with diction, though he calls it 'language'— see for instance the above quotation. Diction is a well-defined subdivision of language, especially when it is 'stock diction': he is dealing for much of the time with technical terms. But even in this part of his book he misses the opportunity to show how some poets use even technical terms in a way one can call 'creative'. (I have given ample instances above.) But Mr Arthos's book ranges further than diction: it ranges into peri-phrasis. Periphrasis is a much more subtle and lively subdivision of language. Whereas diction is a collection, periphrasis is a formula. And a formula bids writers compete in its appli-cation. It is one thing to be the last person to call air 'liquid', it is another to be the first to call a hive 'a straw-built citadel'. In the first instance, you select, in the second you select and then invent—that is, you select the formula of periphrasis and find new matter to feed it with. Mr Arthos's subject bristles with problems with which he is not concerned. What he has chosen to demonstrate, he demonstrates well, but he gives us material for further thought.

IV

THE MANNER OF PROCEEDING IN CERTAIN EIGHTEENTH- AND EARLY NINETEENTH-CENTURY POEMS

ONE OF the main differences between the way we experience a piece of writing and the way we experience a picture is the order in which we experience their constituent parts. We look at a picture, and see it as a whole straight off; we continue to look at it and spend the minutes in exploring its square inches, relating its particulars a few at a time, testing how much of our suspended indifference or eager pleasure they can be trusted not to betray. The eye fingers its details: however well the painter may have managed his construction in the hope that the spectator will play with his details in a certain order, the spectator goes his own way among them, more or less. The writer, on the other hand, not only arranges his particulars, but controls the order in which we receive them—unless, of course, we defeat his plan by dipping or skipping. Both the painter and the writer give us wholes—the painter gives us the whole twice over, once at first sight, and again as a reward for our having investigated the details. But the whole that we get from a piece of writing on our first and crucial experience of it is built up as word follows word in fixed order.

As word follows word. You see at once that I am proposing to slow down the speed at which most of us read literature. For some centuries now, readers have read literature fast. Fast reading is right for literature written carelessly, or designed for fast reading. It is probable that the slow reader gets no more out of the novels of, say, Defoe, than the fast reader. Most novels should be read fast, and certain poems also: those of Swinburne and William Morris, for instance. But what can a fast reader get from 'Lycidas', or *The Dunciad*, or *The Vanity of Human Wishes*, or the 'Ode on a Grecian Urn'? He can get something, no doubt, just as a bicyclist, as he free-wheels down a slope, can get a blur of green and grey. But it is the pedestrian of those poems who knows best where he has been. I propose, on this occasion, to walk very slowly, and sometimes even to stand still. If Wordsworth could pore over a poised butterfly for thirty minutes[1] surely we can pore over a line of verse for a few. Over lines of verse and over whole short poems. If, for once, the critic is poring over minutiae, instead of sweeping his eyes over great novels and epics, this does not mean that his object engages him any less powerfully. For a poet, to build a work on the grand scale is a rarer performance than to build one on the small, but the small poem has usually certain aesthetic advantages: it tends to be completely finished, more certainly recognizable as right, a thing we can pin our faith to, knowing what we are doing. A jewel five words long, a sentence, a paragraph, unlike the vast total of such minutiae in epic or novel, may achieve a form that cannot be improved on. If a big work is imperfect the imperfection must, of course, be traceable in the sentences that compose it. But only in those few during which the fatal turns are made. Apart from those few the sentences of a careful writer will be good—good in themselves even though running, all told, in a wrong direction. Certainly most poets have paid a close attention, either happy or harassed, to the details of their writing, since in those details they have been surest of themselves. If they do not spend a long time by the clock that is because they work at great intensity. Most of them spend a long time by the clock. Writing slowly, with great attention to detail, all these poets produced millions of written words, and so invite criticism of a Saintsburian amplitude. But since the details of their writing cost them so much care, these details demand as much time and more from critics with the gimlet eye. I am seeking, for the most part, to examine certain details in certain poems, details I think of wide importance because typical. I am seeking throughout this essay to perceive the quality of the sense of order shown by a certain few poets. How do these poets get from one word to the next, and from one larger or smaller group of words to the next? Since they are things written, my phrases, lines, and poems cannot avoid having a fixed order. What can we learn from seeing what it is?

[1] 'To a Butterfly', l. 1.

2

Take first of all Pope, with whom I shall join, at a distance, Johnson.

Pope wrote verse and prose. When he wrote prose he normally placed his words as words are normally placed when we write everyday statements. When he left prose for verse he retained as fully as his purposes would allow the word-order of prose. He honoured that order, as all our great poets have done, [1] with the part exception of Milton (who, having an unusual subject, had, as Pope saw, an unusual excuse). [2] Pope followed close on Dryden, both in time and in aims. And, for Dryden, as for Cowley and most other poets of the time and later, the honouring of the word-order of prose had been a major tenet.

In his first piece of criticism Dryden, happy in his couplets, had shown his stubborn human love of the prose-order of words. He spoke there first of blank verse, which 'the French, more properly, call *prose mesurée*':

[into blank verse] the English tongue so naturally slides, that, in writing prose, it is hardly to be avoided. And therefore, I admire some men should perpetually stumble in a way so easy, and inverting the order of their words, constantly close their lines with verbs, which though commended sometimes in writing Latin, yet we were whipt at Westminster if we used it twice together. I know some, who, if they were to write in blank verse, *Sir, I ask your pardon*, would think it sounded more heroically to write, *Sir, I your pardon ask*.

And this prose-order, Dryden says, should be retained, as far as possible, in the couplet; if only because of the poet's assumed reverence for the genius of the language:

I should judge him to have little command of English, whom the necessity of a rhyme should force often upon this rock [of inversion]; though sometimes it cannot easily be avoided; and indeed this is the only inconvenience with which rhyme can be charged. This is that

[1] See below, pp. 142 ff, for an appendix on the ordering of words in poetry.
[2] Spence, *Anecdotes*, p. 174.

which makes them say, rhyme is not natural, it being only so, when the poet either makes a vicious choice of words, or places them, for rhyme sake, so unnaturally as no man would in ordinary speaking; but when 'tis so judiciously ordered, that the first word in the verse seems to beget the second, and that the next, till that becomes the last word in the line, which, in the negligence of prose, would be so; it must then be granted, rhyme has all the advantages of prose, besides its own.[1]

In the prose he wrote concurrently with his verse, Dryden had helped to improve English word-order, helping to make it more straightforward, uniform, and elegant, more like ordinary colloquial speech, especially the colloquial speech of the time. And in verse he wrote thousands of vibrant couplets in which the word-order of prose was strictly retained, as in the latter two lines of this triplet:

> He was too warm on Picking-work to dwell,　⎫
> He faggotted his Notions as they fell,　　　⎬
> And if they Rhim'd and Rattl'd all was well.[2]　⎭

Gerard Manley Hopkins believed that Dryden's 'style and . . . rhythms lay the strongest stress of all our literature on the naked thew and sinew of the English language . . . [he is] the greatest master of bare [English]'.[3] (Hopkins's voice is raised a little, his worthy purpose being to move Robert Bridges to an estimate of Dryden that is more just.) Certainly Dryden revered the English language as it had always been used in prose—in ordinary prose, if not in prose of all kinds. What Hopkins says of his 'style' and 'rhythms' is true to some degree also of his word-order. There is a strong gust blowing along Dryden's lines, and any inversion of their word-order is begrudged

---

[1] 'Epistle Dedicatory of the Rival Ladies', *Essays*, i.6 f. Cf. Bridges: '[Keats] does not refuse to invert the grammatical order for the sake of rhyme or metre, which, though it may occasionally be a beauty, is generally a licence or abuse, a resource of bad writers, and almost as much to be condemned as those needless or false inversions which are sometimes used by bad writers to give the effect of a heightened style' (*Collected Essays, Papers, &c.*, iv. ('A Critical Introduction to Keats'), 1933, p. 110).

[2] *Absalom and Achitophel*, ii. 418 ff.

[3] *The Letters of Gerard Manley Hopkins to Robert Bridges*, 1935, pp. 267 f.

because a gust when obstructed is weakened—as in the first line of the triplet just quoted.[1]

When, in his turn, Pope wrote verse he had reasons even more urgent than Dryden's for honouring the word-order of prose. Dryden had been a man speaking to men, often about the stuff offered by their own time—politics, religion and the sects, contemporary literature. Pope does touch these contemporary, and partly ephemeral, subjects, but his subjects are usually less strictly contemporary. We may put it this way: that throughout his earlier career Pope was aspiring towards *An Essay on Man*, and some of his last words play with the notion that the period of satire may close with further chapters of that universal work:

> Alas! alas! pray end what you began,
> And write next winter more *Essays on Man*.[2]

Dryden wrote for his fellow men, but particularly for those of his own times. Pope, too, wrote for his fellow men, but for those of later times equally with his own: his subjects were more likely than Dryden's to interest posterity. In the time of Dryden the fashion was for a straightforward use of words in prose and verse: in Pope's time that straightforwardness satisfied not only the standards inherited from Dryden's time, but also those grander ones of 'Nature' that Pope was born to improve. Pope sought to express best what had been thought often, and what would continue to be thought often in the future. And so he needed not only a 'language, such as men do use',[3] but one they were likely to go on using. More consciously, therefore, than most poets he spoke as a poet the language he learned as an ordinary human being. That English, both in its words and in their order, was the staple of his expression, as it had been of Dryden's. At his need he deviated from it farther than Dryden had needed to; in diction at least, he deviated from it nearly as far as Milton had, as far as Keats was to: he had a good share of the strong wild fire of those poets. But he was more conscious

---

[1] Cf. M. L. Barstow, *Wordsworth's Theory of Poetic Diction*, New Haven, 1917, p. 30: 'Dryden did not often succeed in preserving the order of prose in rhymed couplets, [but] was careful to do so in his blank verse.'

[2] 'Epilogue to the Satires', Dialogue ii, 254 f. Note the prose-order of the words.

[3] Ben Jonson, prologue to *Every Man in his Humour*, l. 21.

than Milton and Keats were of what he was deviating from, of how far his deviation had taken him, and of the need for an early return to the common reader.

Pope wanted to express his meaning accurately. All great poets want to, since they have a meaning worthy of accurate expression. But Pope's meaning was unusually dependent on accurate expression. It differed in its nature from the meaning of some other great poets, since it ran two particular sorts together: there was the intellectual meaning that came home to men's 'business', and also and at the same time the emotional meaning that came home to men's 'bosoms'.[1] If he sometimes seemed merely to be saying 'two and two make four' he was saying it to men who were spending their lives in a painful, vain attempt to make the sum work out more conveniently. Pope's truisms, as Tennyson said of Gray's, are 'divine truisms [that] make me weep'.[2] He is often engaged on pulling us back to face the terrors of the obvious. Johnson noted that the pleasure-seekers at Ranelagh dared not go home and think. Pope's poems take us home, and sit with us in the dark:

> Oh! if to dance all Night, and dress all Day,
> Charm'd the Small-pox, or chas'd old Age away; ·
> Who would not scorn what Huswife's Cares produce,
> Or who would learn one earthly Thing of Use? . . .
> But since, alas! frail Beauty must decay. . . .[3]

In so far as Pope's meaning was intellectual, he had to express it with great scrupulousness. An expression that is blurred may suffice for expressing emotion, but not for expressing thought. If Pope's meaning, however, had been merely intellectual he might have stuck to the prose he wrote so well. Wanting also the more-than-intellectual meaning that would 'tear the heart' (I am using words of his own),[4] he wrote verse. The history of the writing of *An Essay on Criticism* and *An Essay on Man* shows him working on them first in prose—so hard did he try to

---

[1] Pope quoted Bacon's expression 'come home to men's business and bosoms' in 'The Design' before *An Essay on Man*.
[2] Allingham MSS., Johnson, *Lives of the Poets*, iii. 445.
[3] *Rape of the Lock*, v. 19 ff.
[4] *Imitations of Horace*, Ep. ii. i ('To Augustus'), l. 345.

master their sense.[1] But the prose versions were merely the conscientious preliminaries to the poems as we have them, poems that are as much lyrics as essays.

3

When a writer forsakes prose for verse he does so at his peril. In ordinary life we cannot get on without prose and, expecting it from everybody, we take what we get without closely criticizing it. When, instead of merely talking prose, we write it we mark ourselves off from many of our fellows: but not decisively. The decisive marking-off comes when we leave written prose for written verse. Turning to verse advertises something special, that the temperature has risen, that there are matters more important to the writer's present purposes than the irregular beat of prose and than the prose-order of words. The abandonment of these is a great loss, and should only be undertaken by those who are sure of an ampler gain. If prose is forsaken for blank verse, or for free verse, not much of the word-order of prose need be lost.[2] But if prose is forsaken for verse with rime, few poets have been equal to avoiding those inversions of the prose word-order that they do not wholly need. Some of their inversions they will need fully. As Bridges saw, 'In ordinary

---

[1] Pope told Spence: 'I had digested all the matter [of *An Essay on Criticism*], in prose, before I began upon it in verse' (*Anecdotes*, p. 142). Similarly 'some of the most material speeches [on ecclesiastical and civil government, which were to have gone into the epic *Brutus* were] written in prose' (ibid., p. 315). Cf. Warton, *Essay on the Genius and Writings of Pope*, i, 1756, pp. 110 f.: 'THE ESSAY ON CRITICISM . . . was first . . . written in prose, according to the precept of Vida [*The Art of Poetry*, ed. A. S. Cook, Boston, Mass., 1892, p. 44: Latin text, i. 75 ff.], and the practice of Racine.

> Quinetiam, prius effigiem formare, SOLUTIS,
> Totiusque operis simulacrum fingere, verbis,
> Proderit; atque omnes ex ordine nectere partes,
> Et seriem rerum, et certos sibi ponere fines,
> Per quos tuta regens vestigia tendere pergas.

[Poetic. lib. i. ver. 75] When Racine had fixed on a subject for a play, he wrote down in plain prose, not only the subject of each of the five acts, but of every scene and every speech; so that he could take a view of the whole at once, and see whether every part cohered, and co-operated to produce the intended event: when his matter was thus regularly disposed, he was used to say, "My Tragedy is finished".' According to Suetonius (*Vita Virgili*, 23), Virgil drafted the *Æneid* in prose. For the composition of *An Essay on Man* see R. W. Rogers, *The Major Satires of Alexander Pope*, 1955, Urbana, pp. 32 ff.

[2] Cf. Dryden, p. 113 above.

speech the words follow a common order prescribed by use, and if that does not suit the sense, correction is made by vocal intonation.'[1] Such correction is impossible in writing (though an intelligent reader might supply it with more or less confidence), but something like it can be secured by using italics or inversions. Italics are crude, especially in verse. Inversions are more elegant. They are easily managed in prose, and, as Bridges noted, are 'of the essence of good style'.[2] In verse, however, they prove more difficult. There are two sorts, as I have already said: (1) those that are required in the interests of the sense; (2) those that are convenient for the metre. And the second kind has a way of tainting the first kind: it takes a great craftsman to persuade us that his inversion is of the first kind when, probably, it looks as if it were merely of the second. So often does metre make inversion an easy way out of a difficulty that most poets use more inversions than their sense needs. They do not wholly need all their unavoided inversions, even when they plead for them on the score of their sonority. The difficulty of writing verse, especially of writing verse that rimes, is the difficulty of keeping the expression unhurt on the spikes of the metre, some of which spikes are concealed. In other words, though rimed verse may prevent your retaining the prose-order of words intact you are a good versifier if you can lose as little of it as possible, except when your loss is in exchange for an order of words that strikes the reader as easy and inevitable: and if easy and inevitable, then better, because such expression is twice as powerful when in metre.

With the minutest exceptions, when Pope wrote verse he wrote rimed verse and, with exceptions only less minute, verse

---

[1] op. cit. p. 109.

[2] op. cit., pp. 108 ff. My next sentence is inverted! Inversion may become a mannerism. Matthew Arnold, for instance, sometimes overdid it, his inversions becoming too noticeable; his article 'The Bishop and the Philosopher' (*Essays, Letters and Reviews*, coll. and ed. F. Neiman, 1960, Cambridge, Mass., pp. 45 ff.) has one paragraph beginning 'The little-instructed Spinoza's work could not unsettle . . .' and another beginning 'Unction Spinoza's work has not . . .'. If he had been more conversant with Dickens's novels he might have been warned by Mrs Micawber's example: ' "We came," repeated Mrs. Micawber, "and saw the Medway. My opinion of the coal trade on that river, is, that it may require talent, but that it certainly requires capital. Talent, Mr. Micawber has; capital, Mr. Micawber has not . . ." ' (*David Copperfield*, chapter xvii).

in the heroic couplet, that is, in that *quasi*-stanza half or wholly closed, having as norm ten beats in all, having pairs of rimes at the rate of one every five beats, those rimes being monosyllabic with a long vowel or diphthong; moreover, 'every rhyme should be a word of emphasis'.[1] This kind of couplet is probably the most exacting of all those metres that are staple metres, jacks-of-all-trades: but only as written by Pope. It was exacting for him because, sharing the human liking for words having the prose-order of ordinary life, he was loath to depart from it except for a better. If we retort that nobody asked Pope to write in a metre so difficult, we should be wrong. Pope was asked to by his age. Contemporary voices implored him to use that metre which, during a hundred years and more, had been cherished by poets of all sorts—dramatic, narrative, lyric, argumentative, and also by the poets of satire, who had kicked and blooded it. One of Pope's strongest claims to be an innovator is that he took a metre which had had grave disabilities for all these poets, whether they knew it or not, and, on most occasions, made the disabilities assets. He converted into opportunities what for Dryden had been 'inconveniences'.[2] Pope, as I have said, was loath to depart from the prose-order of words, except for a better. But he sometimes, even in his later work, found his difficult metre too difficult. He allowed words to take positions demanded only by the rime. For instance, here is a run of three couplets from *The Temple of Fame*, a poem published in his later twenties:

> Here in a Shrine that cast a dazling Light,
> Sate fix'd in Thought the mighty *Stagyrite*;
> His Sacred Head a radiant Zodiack crown'd,
> And various Animals his Sides surround;
> His piercing Eyes, erect, appear to view
> Superior Worlds, and look all Nature thro'.

---

[1] Johnson, *Lives of the Poets*, iii. 258. Early in his career, as we have seen, Dryden deprecated the too frequent closing of the line with a verb (see above, p. 113.). Waller struck the balance: in his 'Preface to the Second Part of Mr. Waller's Poems, Printed 1690', Atterbury wrote of him: 'since the stress of our verse lies commonly upon the last syllable, you will hardly ever find him using a word of no force there. I would say, if I were not afraid the reader would think me too nice, that he commonly closes with verbs, in which we know the life of language consists.' (*Poems of Waller*, ed. G. Thorn Drury, 1901, I. xxi f.) Cf. Johnson at p. 36 above, who found too many 'weak words' in the rime position.

[2] See above, p. 113.

This is Aristotle furnishing out an allegorical group. Look at that line

> And various Animals his Sides surround.

Its sense is not wholly vapid since it tells us in its allegorical way that Aristotle wrote something about natural history; moreover, 'various' had a more definite meaning in Pope's day, when it meant 'of different kinds'.[1] But as was noted by Gilbert Wakefield, that sensitive small critic of the later eighteenth century (and noted in a phrase that happens to be a five-beat line superior to Pope's), it tells us this in 'a very tame and lifeless verse indeed!'[2] If a line is weak in sense it badly needs to have its words left in their prose-order so that at least there is no embarrassing attempt to trim the weakness. How many of Wordsworth's lines have the honesty not to seem less humble than they are! The words of Pope's line depart from their prose-order. In due prose-order they would have run:

> And various animals surround his sides.

The reason for Pope's departure from that order is only too plain: he needed 'surround' at the end for its rime-sound. No reason, therefore, could be more miserable. But if Pope had given the words their due prose-order the line would merely have been weak, instead of being weak and pompous. It would have needed a stronger sense to it before it could have been a good line; and for this reason: only a strong sense can bear the emphasis that falls at certain points of a 'five'-beat line—points that vary with the sense between not less than three and a number not far short of ten.[3] Neither the word 'sides' nor the word 'surround' can, in Pope's line, bear any emphasis. And yet both receive it because they are strong parts of speech—noun

---

[1] I owe this point to Professor James Sutherland.

[2] *Observations on Pope*, 1796, p. 140.

[3] There are three beats in such a line as Pope's:
> The Pindars, and the Miltons of a Curll

(*Dunciad*, iii. 164), and eight in Milton's line:
> Rocks, caves, lakes, fens, bogs, dens, and shades of death

(*Paradise Lost*, ii. 621), and in Pope's:
> And ten low words oft creep in one dull line

(*Essay on Criticism*, l. 347).

and verb—and come, where they do in a 'five'-beat line.[1]

In Pope's mature work, however—and he did mature work from the start, even if not continuously—he was usually a good versifier: that is, he used the patent and latent emphases of the couplet, the patent ones falling on the rimes, and the latent ones becoming patent at the command of the sense. I take it that in the process of compositon he played with the nascent thought and with the norm of the couplet together till he felt sure, at first provisionally, of the confirming of the thought and of the metrical shape of the expression—its two rimes and its full- or half-close (Spence records that he turned his couplets over and over 'with surprising facility').[2] At one point during the process it was the sense that called the tune and, at another, the tune the sense, though neither of them would allow too complete a surrender of their rights. In the end, after many returns, a compromise was arrived at. Sense and tune had been led a dance till they struck together an expressive attitude only foreseen in general, but seen at last in particular and seen as happy. Granted a sense firm enough to stand the kneading, the couplet can mould the meaning till the beats stand like fingers closed up or variously pointed. Coleridge, who said harsh things against Pope's diction in the *Homer*, gave the highest praise to his diction elsewhere, and to the placing of the words chosen:

the almost faultless position and choice of words, in . . . Pope's *original* compositions, particularly in his Satires and moral Essays.[3]

[1] In my book *Pope and Human Nature*, 1958, p. 171 I instanced the phrase, 'the Scaffold, or the Cell' as one in which Pope inverted his words for convenience, to the detriment of the sense, but my friend Dr Harold Brooks has defended it: 'Is Pope not thinking of what Oxford may be *sentenced* to (so that no question arises of the scaffold's coming *after* the cell in time). He may not be counting Oxford's incarceration before sentence; his order of thought may be: the Muse attends you whether you are sentenced to present execution, or to life-long, or at any rate a long, term of imprisonment. I admit that from "prison" to "death" seems the natural crescendo—and the opposite may seem an anticlimax: yet as the incarceration would stretch on into the future, I'm not sure that to pass from imminent execution to long imprisonment is not a natural order of ideas. Milton has something like it, on the fates of divinely elected leaders, in *Samson* (693 ff):
their carcases
To dogs and fowls a prey, or else captiv'd . . .'
[2] *Anecdotes*, p. 280. Cf. Pope's own statement: 'one must tune each line over in one's head, to try whether they go right or not' (id., p. 312).
[3] *Biographia Literaria*, i. 26 n.

4

The configuration that Pope achieved in the couplets vanishes as soon as we revert his lines to prose. This was demonstrated, unfortunately for his argument, in the preface to Joseph Warton's *Essay on the Genius and Writings of Pope*. In the manner counselled by Horace,[1] Warton made what he calls a 'little experiment' on the opening lines of Pope's first Moral Essay:

> Yes, you despise the man to Books confin'd,
> Who from his study rails at human kind;
> Tho' what he learns, he speaks and may advance
> Some gen'ral maxims, or be right by chance.
> The coxcomb bird, so talkative and grave,
> That from his cage cries Cuckold, Whore, and Knave,
> Tho' many a passenger he rightly call,
> You hold him no Philosopher at all.

In Warton's prose these couplets become:

Yes, you despise the man that is confined to books, who rails at human kind from his study; tho' what he learns, he speaks; and may perhaps advance some general maxims, or may be right by chance. The coxcomb bird, so grave and so talkative, that cries whore, knave, and cuckold, from his cage, tho' he rightly call many a passenger, you hold him no philosopher.[2]

Obviously no one is going to claim that the couplets Warton chose for his experiment are the most poetical in Pope. But whatever it is that vanishes in Warton's version, something vanishes indeed. We may call it the designing of the sense, and its shading. On the whole Warton flattens the sense. Pope's 'to books confin'd' is sharper than Warton's 'that is confined to books'. And whereas Pope had designed two of his lines to click into a relationship

> Who from his study . . .
> That from his cage . . .

the relationship vanishes in Warton's prose, and to lose it is to lose a satiric relationship. Pope's couplets have more liveliness than Warton's prose. More than the prose they invite an

---

[1] *Sat.*, I. iv. 39 ff.
[2] *Essay on the Genius and Writings of Pope*, i, 1756, p. viii.

actor to bring their life to the test of speech. If we did a version in prose more faithful than Warton's we should need even more words than Warton used. Although Pope's words are almost in prose-order they acquire a force merely from their contrived coincidence with the configurated emphases of the metre. Take this smaller instance: the opening line of the second epistle of *An Essay on Man*:

Know then Thy-self, presume not God to scan.

Words in their prose-order would have given us 'do not presume to scan God', or, with more decorum, because with more dignity, 'presume not to scan God'. But 'Know then Thy-self, presume not to scan God' weakens the sense of 'God to scan' by weakening the sense of 'scan'. Pope's departure from prose-order produces two emphases instead of one. The emphasis on 'God' is triply strong; the word is emphatic in its own right, its meaning being what it is; it is emphatic because in sense-contrast to 'Thy-self' (which is slowed down by means of the hyphen and, like 'God', given a capital letter); it is emphatic by position. It is so emphatic altogether that it robs the rime word of some of the emphasis that normally falls to the share of a rime word. Even so, 'scan' gets more emphasis in Pope's line than it gets when it falls into its place in prose. The upshot is that the eight words of Pope's partly inverted line give him a sense something like the following: 'Know then thyself: do not presume to get knowledge beyond that, especially not knowledge of God, since the only means even for attempting to get it is the exercise of an insolent curiosity.'

In lines like these Pope departs from the prose-order of words for something better. But he does not depart very far. On occasions he departs farther. For instance:

> Not with such Majesty, such bold relief,
> The Forms august of King, or conqu'ring Chief,
> E'er swell'd on Marble; as in Verse have shin'd
> (In polish'd Verse) the Manners and the Mind.[1]

What the ready prose of Joseph Warton would have made of this superb half-comic sentence, I dare not think. And although its

---

[1] *Imitations of Horace*, Ep. II. i ('To Augustus'), ll. 390 ff.

being superb owes something to its being contorted, it is contorted scrupulously: in whatever order the clauses and phrases are placed, they retain in themselves the prose-order of their words, except that we get 'forms august' instead of 'august forms'—I shall revert to this. And when, as not infrequently in Pope, we find a couplet designed like a fairly complicated figure in Euclid, the design as it exists on paper is often executed not so much on the order of the words as on the letters of the words. In illustration of this I turn at last to Johnson. Writing his couplets in haste, as Dryden did, Johnson, like Dryden, wasted and bedevilled many chances. The latent configuration of the emphases often found him with a sense too grossly simple to need their proferred elaborations. Lines like

> For gold his sword the hireling ruffian draws[1]

are as frequent in poems of his as they are frequent in those of the minor poets: inversions creaking with excuses instead of inversions carving the sense into fuller expressiveness. But on one occasion at least Johnson, alone of the other eighteenth-century poets, could take his stand as a designer of couplets beside Pope:

> How small of all that human hearts endure,
> That part which laws or kings can cause or cure.[2]

Within the couplet design could not well be more superb. But it is not a design that greatly disturbs the word-order of prose: it works mainly with sounds. And all this in the interests of the sense. Johnson can design a couplet occasionally, Pope often. But the brilliant conciseness of the result must not blind us to the Dryden-like glory of lines which wield as from the shoulder words in their strictest prose-order:

> The proper study of Mankind is Man.[3]

> The glory, jest, and riddle of the World![4]

> But wonder how the Devil they got there![5]

> Nor think the doom of man revers'd for thee.[6]

---

[1] *The Vanity of Human Wishes*, l. 25. There is nothing wrong with the placing of 'For gold': it links the line to the argument of the paragraph. This sort of initial inversion is common in prose. It is the rest of Johnson's line that creaks.

[2] The opening couplet of Johnson's conclusion to Goldsmith's *Traveller*.

[3] *Essay on Man*, ii. 2.   [4] ibid., l. 18.

[5] 'Epistle to Dr. Arbuthnot', l. 172.   [6] *The Vanity of Human Wishes*, l. 156.

The couplets that are elaborately designed engage our fascinated attention, but lines like these knock us down.[1]

Johnson stuck to prose as a general thing, and he was wise to. He is a great poet: as Anna Seward divined, 'excepting his orthographick works, every thing which Dr Johnson wrote was Poetry'[2]—and some of the sensitive, creative definitions of the Dictionary make even that exception unnecessary. But though a great poet Johnson was not a great metrist. His poetry exists mainly in his prose, where it takes its ease, that state which the eighteenth century preferred even to joy, as being more commonly and surely within man's reach. His poetry is at ease mainly because it does not suffer the taunts of a metre it cannot master. But even Johnson's prose approaches near to a free sort of metre. Most of his sentences have a rhythm that is strongly marked. They are unusually musical, especially at the close of a paragraph where they follow the patterns of the classical orators; he deprecated 'periods negligently closed'.[3]

5

So much for the great poets of the eighteenth century.

When we turn to the great poets of the early nineteenth we find them in two minds about the claims of prose-order. They are zealous for it up to a point, and since, of course, they are writing in metres less exacting than the couplets of Pope, they find it easier to come by. Even so, though Wordsworth is almost another Dryden when it comes to love of the prose-order of words, he sometimes fails to achieve it, and gets nothing in lieu; and when, as often, he does achieve it, sometimes finds it barren or, worse, finds it silly. Wordsworth took a pure-minded delight in humdrum thought which, when not brushed aside by an equally pure-minded delight in majestic,

---

[1] Gray, who was proud of his debt to Dryden, was a master of prose-order when he needed to be. It was especially necessary in comic verse. A remarkable instance is the following:

> Old, and abandon'd by each venal friend,
> Here H[olland] form'd the pious resolution
> To smuggle some few years, and strive to mend
> A broken character and constitution.

(*On L[ord] H[ollan]d's Seat Near M[argat]e, K[en]t*, ll. 1 ff.)

[2] Boswell's *Life*, i. 40 n.   [3] *Rambler*, 193.

makes him feed his metre with appropriately humdrum words. These words, retaining an appropriate prose-order, receive an enforcement they cannot bear from the stress of the metre. There is at least one instance of this in Shakespeare. The norm of thought and expression in *Julius Caesar* is a bare simplicity. Usually that simplicity is a Roman simplicity, but when the thought is too near that of trivial occasions it is made silly by the metre:

> To-morrow, if you please to speak with me,
> I will come home to you, or, if you will,
> Come home to me and I will wait for you.[1]

This is sometimes Wordsworth's failing, as it had been the failing of most eighteenth-century writers of tragedy. There was nothing wrong, at bottom, with Wordsworth's liking for the humdrum thought and humdrum words; what was wrong was that it was often accompanied by a liking for dignified metre.[2]

As for Keats, it was partly because of its Miltonic inversions that he abandoned 'Hyperion'. His growing dislike of Milton's style was accompanied with a growing liking for Chatterton's:

He is the purest writer in the English Language. He has no French idiom, or particles like Chaucer—'tis genuine English idiom in English Words. I have given up Hyperion—there were too many Miltonic inversions in it. Miltonic verse can not be written but in an artful or rather artist's humour.[3]

Keats exaggerated the Englishness of Chatterton; but though, like Spenser, Chatterton inverted the position of noun and adjective as often as he found it metrically convenient, he had a strong liking for words in their prose-order.

6

Where prose-order is concerned one small matter of large importance is the placing of noun and adjective. To disturb their prose position is to disturb the prose-order profoundly. In

---

[1] I. ii. 309 ff.

[2] Cf. Coleridge, *Biographia Literaria*, ii. 54: 'If disproportioning the emphasis we read [the last three stanzas of 'The Sailor's Mother'] so as to make the rhymes perceptible, even *tri-syllable* rhymes could scarcely produce an equal sense of oddity and strangeness, as we feel here in finding *rhymes at all* in sentences so exclusively colloquial.' As Coleridge saw, the same is equally true of the metre, without which the rime would be lost.

[3] *Letters*, p. 384; cf. p. 425.

English prose the adjective precedes its noun, but not always in English verse.[1] In medieval English verse the influence of the French had led to transposition. But in the later seventeenth century poets were trying to undo what they had come to see, in general, as mischief. Modern critics who persist in the belief that French influence played strongly on those poets should admit that it did not play strongly enough to make them continue to invert noun and adjective. In the latter half of the following century, however, poets increasingly showed an archaic readiness to invert them. Johnson mocked at Thomas Warton for affectations of this kind. The first two lines of his parody sport two instances of 'words in disarray' (i.e. two instances of inversion) flanking, for no reason except convenience and archaicism, one instance of prose-order:

> Hermit hoar, in solemn cell,
> Wearing out life's evening gray,

'*Gray evening* is common enough', commented Johnson, 'but *evening gray* he'd think fine.'[2] This kind of inversion is a powerful

---

[1] Cf. Gascoigne, *Certayne Notes of Instruction*, note II: 'You shall do very well to use your verse after thenglishe phrase, and not after the maner of other languages: The Latinists do commonly set the adjective after the Substantive: As for example *Femina pulchra, ædes altæ*, etc. but if we should say in English a woman fayre, a house high, etc. It would have but small grace: for we say a good man, and not a man good, etc. And yet I will not altogether forbidde it you, for in some places, it may be borne, but not so hardly as some use it which wryte thus:

> Now let us go to Temple ours,
> I will go visit mother myne etc.

Surely I smile at the simplicitie of such devisers which might aswell have sayde it in playne Englishe phrase, and yet have better pleased all eares, than they satisfie their owne fancies by suche *superfinesse*' (*Complete Works*, ed. J. W. Cunliffe, Cambridge, 1907–10, i. 470). In the notes to *Davideis* (II. *n.* 6) Cowley speaks wisely: 'There is great caution to be used in English in the placing of *Adjectives* (as here) after their *Substantives*;' and he continues: 'I think when they constitute specifical *differences* of the *Substantives*, they *follow* best; for then they are to it like *Cognomina*, or *Surnames* to *Names*, and we must not say, the *Great Pompey*, or the *Happy Sylla*, but *Pompey the Great*, and *Sylla the Happy*; sometimes even in other cases the *Epithete* is put last very gracefully, of which a good *ear* must be the *judge* for ought I know, without any *Rule*. I chuse rather to say *Light Divine*, and *Command Divine*, than *Divine Light*, and *Divine Command*.'

[2] Boswell's *Life*, iii. 159. Cf. the Life of Cowley: 'The artifice of inversion, by which the established order of words is changed . . . is practised, not by those who talk to be understood, but by those who write to be admired' (*Lives of the Poets*, i. 40); and the Life of Collins: 'he puts his words out of the common order, seeming to think, with some later candidates for fame [e.g., Thomas Warton], that not to write prose is certainly to write poetry' (id., iii. 341).

disturbance of prose-order, and it struck Johnson with the force of a hysteron-proteron:[1] inversions he found 'harsh', that is, un-pleasing.[2] Most of the poets of the early and later nineteenth century are so many Thomas Wartons where this sort of inversion is concerned.

We found one instance of this particular disturbance of prose-order in Pope's 'Forms august'. There are a few others, as, for example, this instance in *The Temple of Fame*:

> Four Swans sustain a Carr of Silver bright.[3]

This instance, however, does not represent Pope's normal practice in those few: it is too merely convenient for the rime: there is no need to add to the brightness of 'bright' when 'silver' is the important word. In four consecutive lines of the 'Epistle to Robert Earl of Oxford' we get two instances:

> And sure if ought below the Seats Divine
> Can touch Immortals, 'tis a Soul like thine:
> A Soul supreme, in each hard Instance try'd,
> Above all Pain, all Passion, and all Pride.[4]

It will be noted that 'august', 'Divine', and 'supreme' are all two-syllable adjectives having the accent on the second syllable. They are, therefore, to that extent still French. For this reason Pope is more willing to place them after the noun.[5] When so placed, they do not seem placed out of their prose-order so oddly as does 'bright'. Moreover, there are further justifications for Pope's way of placing these particular adjectives. First, there was good precedent for the use of 'Seats Divine'. Wye Saltonstall had given

> Aspire not thou unto those seates divine

in translation of Ovid's *alta palatia* of Caesar,[6] and Milton has

---

[1] Cf. Hawkesworth, reviewing Goldsmith's *Deserted Village* in *The Monthly Review*, 1770, p. 442: 'In this [poem] there is a strain of poetry very different from the quaint phrase, and forced construction, into which our fashionable bards are distorting prose.'

[2] *Lives of the Poets*, iii. 418.   [3] l. 210.   [4] ll. 21 ff.

[5] Cf. also 'Who never mentions Hell to ears polite' (*Mor. Ess.*, iv. 150).

[6] *Tristia*, I. i. 69; Saltonstall, *Ovids Tristia*, 1633, B 2 r. The translation had been reprinted in 1637 and 1681. (Ovid on several occasions has *sedes ætheræ*, and Virgil once has *cælicolæ sedes*, but their seventeenth- and early eighteenth-century translators, who translate these phrases variously, do not use 'seats divine'.)

'seat divine' in his versification of Psalm lxxx; it also exists in a cancelled passage of Pope's *Iliad*.[1] As we have seen, Cowley saw fit to argue the rightness of inversions where 'divine' was concerned. The additional justification of 'Forms august' is obvious: that phrase needs all the size and bloated sublimity it can get. As for 'Soul supreme', in Pope's line it is predicative: 'a soul that was supreme when each hard instance put it to the trial'.[2] There are no such means for justifying 'Silver bright' or 'Hermit hoar'.

There is an interesting criticism by Conington of a passage from *An Essay on Man* (i. 43 ff):

> Of Systems possible, if 'tis confest
> That Wisdom infinite must form the best,
> Where all must fall or not coherent be,
> And all that rises, rise in due degree;
> Then, in the scale of reas'ning life, 'tis plain
> There must be, somewhere, such a rank as Man. . . .

Conington remarks:

Pope did not generally condescend to the artificial inversion which places the adjective after the substantive. Here, in a passage where simplicity was an object, we have 'systems possible' followed by 'wisdom infinite',—combinations, too, which have the effect of producing a disagreeable monotony, occurring in the same part of the lines to which they respectively belong.[3]

When we read Pope's lines, I do not think we are aware of any inversion, and the reason is obvious: both 'possible' and 'infinite' are key-words in the argument, and can take the stress we wish to give them because they follow their respective nouns.

7

So much for the order of words in short runs. There remains the order of words in sentence and paragraph.

In the eighteenth century the isolated sentence flourished in

---

[1] See Johnson, *Lives of the Poets*, iii. 123 n.

[2] Cf. *Imitation of Horace*, Ep. II. ii. 119: 'He walks, an Object new beneath the Sun'.

[3] See *The Works of Alexander Pope*, ed. Elwin and Courthope, 1871–89, ii. 351, n. 4.

prose as the maxim. But though Pope did write maxims in prose (and separate couplets), he and Johnson preferred to combine sentences in sizeable writings. The combining of two or three sentences presented merely the difficulty experienced by any writer. The combining of paragraphs presented more. The means of combination was the 'transition', and a great deal of Ovidian ingenuity was expended on making each transition strong and pleasurable. If the transitions were not strong the design fell back into its parts; if not pleasurable the reader complained, as Gray did, of 'a string of transitions [in a poem of Tickell's] that hardly become a schoolboy'.[1] The paragraphs with their transitions made up the design. Pope noted that even the shorter pieces of the ancients were 'written by a plan'.[2] His own, whether short or long, he designed beautifully. With their collocation of a certain number of balanced or contrasted units the poems of Pope resemble architecture—houses built by Kent or palaces built by Wren. They also resemble painting. For some time Pope worked hard at learning to draw and paint and, turning back to his writing, he took as much of drawing and painting with him as he could. His poems are designed. No writer can help concerning himself with sequence, since all you can do with words is to arrange them to follow one another. But it seems that Pope, with all the materials for a poem to hand, would sometimes have liked to present them at a clap, as a painter can his, an architect, and even a landscape gardener. I detect some ambition this way when Pope uses the exclamation 'Lo!': it represents for him the suddenness with which one comes on a picture:

> Lo! where Mæotis sleeps, and hardly flows
> The freezing Tanais thro' a waste of snows.[3]

Pope's poems, then, are poems designed.

8

I spoke of Pope's having all the materials for a poem to hand. In his day it was thought that the materials for a poem lay ready

[1] Gray, *Correspondence*, 1935, i. 295.
[2] Spence, *Anecdotes*, p. 1.
[3] *Dunciad*, iii. 87 f.

to any hand, not only to that of a poet. Every thought worth thinking (those were the only thoughts man needed to concern himself with) had already been thought. The universe had been complete ever since God rested on the first sabbath. Clearly, then, there is some connexion between the way Pope designed a poem and the philosophy and 'natural philosophy' of the time. At that time things were seen as separate but related: Pope spoke of

> . . . this frame, the bearings, and the ties,
> The strong connexions, nice dependencies,
> Gradations just. . . .[1]

The philosophers were mathematicians manipulating units, however small—with Leibnitz they were infinitesimal. The psychologists saw experience as happening bit by bit, as a rapid sequence of pinpricks: Hartley's account of man is of 'nothing but a bundle of "vibratiuncles"—a kind of barrel-organ set in motion by the external forces of the world',[2] and of all noises those of a barrel-organ are the most disjointed, however rapid their sequence. The historians saw time in pools. Swift 'treats time bi-dimensionally, as if it were laid out flat upon the table of history like a sheet of paper'.[3] When Dryden, Pope, and Gray looked back over what for us is the history of poetry they saw a number of 'clans' or 'schools'; and though Gray wrote a poem called 'The Progress of Poesy', its progress, like one of Queen Elizabeth's, was merely a string of visits.[1] And until late in the day the eighteenth-century critics were content to

---

[1] *Essay on Man*, i. 29 ff. The subtle sense of these lines is so well expressed that it seems pedantic to note the obvious justification of the placing of the last two words —it avoids a second repetition of a striking pattern, a monosyllabic adjective followed by a polysyllabic noun. In this *Essay* Pope made excellent use of inversions of this kind.

[2] Leslie Stephen, *History of English Thought in the Eighteenth Century*, ch. ix. 66.

[3] M. K. Starkman, *Swift's Satire on Learning in 'A Tale of a Tub'*, Princeton, 1950, p. 9.

[4] This is true of the 'progress' represented in the poem. But in one of his notes Gray shows himself aware of a continuity between two of the schools: 'Chaucer was not unacquainted with the writings of Dante or of Petrarch. The Earl of Surrey and Sir Tho. Wyatt had travelled in Italy, and formed their taste there; Spenser imitated the Italian writers; Milton improved on them. . . .' Dryden had shown some of the history of English poetry (see D. Nichol Smith, *Warton's History of English Poetry*, 1929, pp. 13 f.). It was Thomas Warton who achieved the sense of an evenly chronological sequence (ibid., p. 18).

accept the first play in the Folio, *The Tempest*, as the first written. This 'philosophy', then, has some connexion with the way Pope designed his poems.

Not too much, however. We of the twentieth century, admiring the American 'historians of ideas', must beware of exaggerating the strength of any 'strong connexions' that exist at any time between philosophy and poetry. 'Philosophy and poetry', as Johnson noted, 'have not often the same readers',[1] and were not intended to have. Poetry is for the 'common reader', and, therefore, only for the philosopher and scientist as he sheds his special interests and becomes as a common reader. A poet, being, so to speak, a common writer, makes too amateurish and fickle a philosopher and scientist. Turning away from the newest account of a system, the newest 'argument from design', Pope, like any common man, saw not design but gliding movement. For him, as for any poet of the nineteenth century, moons rose, seasons passed, 'colours [stole] into the Peare or Plum',[2] the Thames heaved 'floating tides'; in reaches higher up, it had once made Denham exclaim

> O could I flow like thee, and make thy stream
> My great example. . . .[3]

and though the Tanais is freezing, its flow is not yet quite solid.

Permanently, then, and in innumerable instances, the notion of design coexisted with the notion of continuity. If the eighteenth-century poet wanted help from poetry he had only to think of his beloved Ovid. The designing of the *Metamorphoses* was a classic of concatenation, and yet the course of each metamorphosis was a concise miracle of smooth continuity. Pope had translated one of the smoothest:

> . . . the creeping rind invades
> My closing lips, and hides my head in shades . . .
> And all the nymph was lost within the tree.[4]

And though, Johnson, to take him as an instance, spoke of the historian as 'arranging and displaying' his given materials,[5] he

[1] *Lives of the Poets*, iii. 164.
[2] Herrick, 'Lovers how they come and part', l. 6.
[3] 'Cooper's Hill', ll. 189 f.
[4] 'The Fable of Dryope', ll. 96 ff.   [5] *Rambler*, no. 122.

was himself acutely conscious of continuity as it existed in certain examples. He was conscious of the automatic continuity of human lives: in *Rasselas* we are told that men 'glide along the stream of time', and the story leaves Imlac 'contented to be driven along the stream of life'. Again in *Rasselas* there are the words 'The Progress of Sorrow' which, in the second edition, Johnson added to one of his chapter headings (the chapter, however, was one of the shortest). He was perhaps especially conscious of the continuity of slow decay: his verbs are never more powerful than when expressing the wearing-away of time.

The poems of the eighteenth century, therefore, are designed with care and yet have a necessarily strong continuity within the sentence, sometimes a strong continuity within the paragraph, sometimes—when the transitions are drops of molten metal— a strong continuity within the poem.

9

This limited sense of continuity, this preference for design, led Pope and Johnson to prefer certain sorts of literature to others.

They had no sincere interest in narrative, that manner of writing in which continuity is broken as seldom as possible. Pope and Johnson read narratives and enjoyed them. Pope saw that *Robinson Crusoe* was the best of the many good stories of Defoe.[1] Johnson even enjoyed reading romances, though uneasily: he tried to justify a taste he feared to be unfitting.[2] We hear that he devoured *Amelia* 'without stopping'.[3] Why? He liked it: he read it with 'inclination'. But he read it doubly fast because that was all any novel could be worth. If he had thought better of it he would have stopped. As for the ballads, Johnson mocked at them especially when they were offered by modern poets as would-be serious poems. His extemporized stanza of a ballad[4] demonstrates why he disliked them: there was nothing to them except a hollow continuousness; they had not enough

---

[1] Spence, *Anecdotes*, pp. 258 f.
[2] See, for example, Boswell's *Life*, iv. 16 f.
[3] ibid., iii. 43.
[4] 'I put my hat upon my head . . .' *Poems*, ed. D. Nichol Smith and E. L. McAdam, 1941, p. 158.

stuff in them; they were too much like 'that kind of conversation which consists in telling stories', and which he did not 'much delight in'. [1] Pope wrote some comic ballads, but published them anonymously. They are, of course, very good: when Pope did tell a story, he told it well. If readers cannot follow the story in *The Dunciad* that is because they read its concentrated epic pieces too fast: the way to read *The Dunciad* is to see what happens in one couplet before proceeding to the next. The story of *The Rape of the Lock* is well told, especially in its first form; in its second it is much longer but scarcely as story. The events of this poem are presented in chronological order, except that the Baron's sacrifice in Canto ii precedes the action of Canto i. But elsewhere Pope breaks up the chronology and rearranges the bits, which as bits are more like pictures than actions, in an order he prefers. There is some of this breaking up and re-arranging in 'Eloisa to Abelard'. The 'Elegy on the Death of an Unfortunate Lady' gives us a story, but only as it exists in the implications of picture, invocation, rhetorical questions, imprecation, exclamation, epitaph, conclusion. In arranging such a sequence there is no one overmastering reason why any one arrangement cannot be made as effective as at least one or two others. In a story, remembered or invented and then told chronologically, there is no such choice. And to surrender their power of choice was not a thing Pope and Johnson liked to do. In that age, when the young novel was striding on from masterpiece to masterpiece, the poets were still using 'narrative' as the homeric epithet for old age. [2]

Like Pope, Johnson wrote a few narratives. Fortunately for us, the poignant need for ready money drove him to write *Rasselas*. Needing to get the best price, he had to write a story. But it was rather a tale than a novel, and its many well-placed short essays show it to be by the author of *The Rambler*. If he preferred 'The Vision of Theodore' to his other works it was on account of its power of seducing the mind to recognize truth, and to think about it.

Sometimes in Pope a narrative is merely an illustration and

---

[1] *Johnsonian Miscellanies*, ed. G. B. Hill, 1897, i. 265.
[2] The epithet appears to have originated in Longinus: see *On the Sublime*, ch. ix.

the process is, therefore, of less account than the result. Look, for instance, at these lines from 'An Epistle to Dr. Arbuthnot':

> 'Tis sung, when *Midas'* Ears began to spring,
> (*Midas*, a sacred Person and a King)
> His very Minister who spy'd them first,
> (Some say his Queen) was forc'd to speak, or burst.
> And is not mine, my Friend, a sorer case,
> When ev'ry Coxcomb perks them in my face?[1]

Short as the anecdote is, Pope is as much in it as Midas or any of the others. ''Tis sung' is Pope making an introduction, an introduction serving as a transition. '(Some say his Queen)' diverts the interest towards the accidents of transmission, and towards satire—on women: if it was a woman who spied them first of course she would have to speak, and if it was not in this case a woman then the king and queen were not on good terms. After four lines of pointed narrative Pope is back at his argument.

10

After narrative we may consider argument. Obviously argument, like narrative, is dependent on sequence. Pope constructed several arguments in essays and epistles. But, even when borrowed, they only satisfy us in short bursts. Johnson, you will say, is famous as an arguer: his 'supreme enjoyment', said Boswell, 'was the exercise of his reason'.[2] But how do you exercise reason? If directly as an intuition, then the ideal form for Johnson's reason is the sentence; if, on the other hand, reason is reason-ing, then its ideal form, for Johnson at least, is the steps of a few sentences, and not more than a few; 'the labour of excogitation is too violent to last long'.[3] Johnson is most characteristically himself when writing a sentence of intuitive reason beginning with 'Every man . . .' or 'He . . .' or 'A man . . .'; or when writing a short reason-ing paragraph. There are arguments which Johnson kept up for longer, but not many of them. The arguments of the two great prefaces, those to the Dictionary and the edition of Shakespeare, have as little continuity (though they have as much) as the tombstones ranged in a village churchyard. We see the difference as soon as we

[1] ll. 69 ff.   [2] *Life*, i. 66.   [3] *Rasselas*, ch. xliv.

135

turn to Burke, who as a prose writer seems to belong to the following century. Johnson praised his 'stream of mind',[1] which 'winds into a subject like a serpent'.[2]

Pope and Johnson, then, are often in the position of writers who make descriptions, writers whom they do not esteem highly. This is Johnson on Thomson's *Seasons*:

The great defect of *The Seasons* is want of method; but for this I know not that there was any remedy. Of many appearances subsisting all at once, no rule can be given why one should be mentioned before another.[3]

And Johnson agreed with Dennis's similar criticisms of *Windsor Forest*:

The objection made by Dennis is the want of plan, of a regular subordination of parts terminating in the principal and original design. There is this want in most descriptive poems, because as the scenes, which they must exhibit successively, are all subsisting at the same time, the order in which they are shewn must by necessity be arbitrary, and more is not to be expected from the last part than from the first.[4]

But Johnson did not see much difference between the designs of these mainly descriptive poems and the designs of *The Vanity of Human Wishes* and the *Imitations of Horace*.

II

I have said that the eighteenth-century poets, though they spoke much of design, must have been also aware of unbroken movement, or at least of recurrent lengths of it. In the same way the poets of the nineteenth century, though they spoke most of continuity, must have been also aware of design. But less aware: surely design came nearer to fading out of the nineteenth-century mind than continuity did out of the eighteenth? Instead of seeing the elegance of the transitions, the nineteenth century saw everything as one long transition. Change, they discovered, was happening all the time, and therefore, since it had taken so long to discover this, happening imperceptibly. The philosophers turned from mathematics to the natural sciences, which observe and account for growth, movement, 'becoming', evolu-

---

[1] Boswell's *Life*, ii. 450.   [2] id., ii. 260.
[3] *Lives of the Poets*, iii. 299 f.   [4] id., iii. 225.

tion. As for the psychologists, what his once-admired Hartley had seen as association working mechanically became for Coleridge association having a 'streamy nature'.[1]

We can see what was happening if we compare the reasons, or some of them, why poets of the eighteenth and early nineteenth centuries keep returning to *The Faërie Queene*. Pope's 'Imitation' of Spenser shows that he chose to see *The Faërie Queene* as composed of pictures,[2] of pictures fiercely coarse. The old lady to whom he read Spenser also saw pictures—the poem, she said, was a gallery of them (pictures perhaps by Claude or by Hogarth).[3] But for Wordsworth *The Faërie Queene* was movement:

> Sweet Spenser, moving through his clouded heaven
> With the moon's beauty and the moon's soft pace.[4]

As we should expect, Keats, like Pope, saw pictures rather than movement, though not the Hogarthian ones. By that time, however, even pictures had become something else. When Pope saw the picture presented by Windsor Forest, he saw design: but for Coleridge 'Landscape is music . . . the rhythm of the soul's movements,'[5] and Ruskin remarks 'an expression about all the hill lines of nature . . . a music of the eyes, a melody of the heart'.[6]

---

[1] *Anima Poetae*, 1895, p. 65.

[2] Pope's 'Imitation' may be designed to mock at Ambrose Philips who, on the score of his 'Pastorals', had been hailed as 'Spenser's eldest born'. 'On the contrary', Pope may be saying in his 'Imitation', 'there is no relationship: Spenser is fierce where Philips is tame'.

[3] Spence, *Anecdotes*, p. 296.

[4] *The Prelude*, iii. 283 f.

[5] I have not succeeded in checking this quotation.

[6] *Works*, iii. 468. One might compare an eighteenth-century composer and a nineteenth, and say that Mozart's pieces are, in the main, designed, and that the later ones of Beethoven progress with something more like a biological development. It was only possible for Beethoven to achieve this at the expense of melody: Mr Benjamin Britten has noted that with him sets in the rot of melody. Instead of melodies Beethoven has melodious snatches. Fragments are combined in a single whole more readily than melodies, which cannot but be complete things in themselves. This discovery was made by Mozart in the great concerted numbers of his operas where you get not melody but a snatch of melody repeatedly varied. Mozart's melodies come to an end even though what immediately follows seems phoenix-like to spring out of the very being of what has just ended. Beethoven in his later work breaks up the design-cum-continuity of Mozart in the interests of a more biological continuity lasting over wide sweeps without marked stages. Mozart is usually more like Pope, and Beethoven more like narrative.

I have quoted powerful words of Coleridge, but perhaps it was Wordsworth and Shelley who were most sensitive to gliding succession. Has anything seen by man glided with more mysterious smoothness than the white doe of Rylstone? By the time of the *Lyrical Ballads* Wordsworth was thoroughly aware of continuity. The avowed object of 'The Thorn' was to 'follow the turns of passion'; of 'The Idiot Boy' and 'The Mad Mother' that 'of tracing the maternal passion through many of its more subtle windings': another poem in the *Lyrical Ballads* had a present participle in its title: 'Old Man Travelling'. And Wordsworth provides an instance of the word *continuousness* anterior to that cited as first in the *OED*: he invented it as he discussed a passage in an early draft of 'Resolution and Independence'.[1] It was from this passage in the poem, as finally printed, that Coleridge wanted to excise a stanza. Unfortunately Wordsworth complied. We therefore have to read the poem in its earlier form if we want its tremulous continuity to remain unbroken.[2] It goes without saying that Wordsworth's sense of continuity is sometimes the sort that Johnson rightly mocked at. Some of the poems have too much of the dogged continuity of the pedlar or the tired beast:

> My horse moved on; hoof after hoof
> He raised, and never stopped.[3]

12

The great poets of the early nineteenth century prefer continuity to design. And the change from the design of Pope and Johnson to the continuity of Wordsworth is effected mainly by Gray.

Gray was one of those poets who write little, but whose little told powerfully. One of his greatest achievements was the writing of the little odes. His big odes were charged by Johnson with having too much 'pomp of machinery',[4] but the little odes—

[1] *The Early Letters of William and Dorothy Wordsworth*, ed. E. de Selincourt, 1935, p. 304.

[2] Coleridge, noted that one of the marks of a poetic genius was that he could reduce 'succession to an instant' (*Biographia Literaria*, ii. 16 f.) He did not see that in the early nineteenth century it required genius to express unbroken succession.

[3] 'Strange fits of passion . . .', ll. 21 f.

[4] *Lives of the Poets*, iii. 437.

those on the spring, the cat, and Eton College—have a small amount of the mechanical and a large amount of life, of rapid development. There is, to begin with, the metre. Partly—of all humble but useful things—it is ballad metre. It should be read as such: the opening of the 'Ode on the Spring' should be read as quickly as we read any rattle like

> He had not sailed a league, a league,
> A league but barely three. . . .

It is too near to Dryden's versification to be dawdled over, as we dawdle over Pope's. In that opening quatrain Gray does rig up the expected classical tableau, but perfunctorily: his first stanza is, as it were, a flinging down of his singing robes as he runs forward. This first stanza opens with the 'Lo!' for which I suggested an explanation when speaking of Pope. Altogether, it should be read fast, especially its first quatrain:

> Lo! where the rosy-bosom'd Hours,
> Fair VENUS' train appear,
> Disclose the long-expecting flowers,
> And wake the purple year!

Gray's metre in these little odes means business. It moves quickly forward. When directing how the *Elegy* should be printed, he stipulated that even these slow stanzas should have no interval between them, 'because the Sense is in some Places continued beyond them'.[1] The business of his metre is mainly narrative. Though Gray was writing odes, he cared very much for narrative. Unlike Pope and Johnson, he greatly admired the ballads: after his complaint of Tickell's schoolboy transitions, he added: 'I forgive him for the sake of his ballad ["Colin and Lucy"], which I always thought the prettiest in the world.'[2] Like Pope and Johnson, Gray thinks, but, unlike them, he thinks as he runs. Though he begins with a description and continues with a narration he snatches thoughts as he goes, and it is with a thought that he touches the tape. Pope and Johnson saw

---

[1] *Correspondence*, i. 341. Matthew Arnold, in his essay on Gray, commended the 'evolution' of thought in the two big odes. De Quincey had already noted such evolution in Dryden's poems, whereas Pope thought 'in jets' (*Collected Writings*, 1897, xi. 119).

[2] *Correspondence*, i. 295.

that their readers were greeted with thought straight off, or early. All that led up to their discovery of what that thought should be is well over before the poem begins. But Gray is as much interested in the occasion and process of arriving at the thought, as in the thought itself. And it is this interest that he passes over to Wordsworth[1] and Keats. From the 'Ode on the Spring' come 'Resolution and Independence' and 'The Small Celandine' and 'Ode on a Grecian Urn'.

Gray's thoughts are among his best things. He is as good at them as Pope had been. It was Gray's truisms that Tennyson called divine, and that made him weep. Now, no one has ever wept over Wordsworth's truisms, except perhaps himself and Dorothy. Over other things in Wordsworth, perhaps, but not over his truisms. He has not the gift of piercing us through with an observation. When his poems are memorable, and they often are, they are usually memorable as wholes, as big impressions almost independent of words. The maxim that closes 'The Small Celandine' satisfies the double standard demanded by Johnson: it is both 'Natural' and 'new'. But it only satisfies that double standard by virtue of its matter: the expression of the 'what oft was thought' is far from being 'ne'er so well'. We divine that the thought is good rather than perceive its goodness with ocular delight. The words, clumsy as they are, are just not too clumsy:

> To be a Prodigal's Favourite—then, worse truth,
> A miser's Pensioner—behold our lot!
> O Man, that from thy fair and shining youth
> Age might but take the things Youth needed not!

When it came to Keats he learnt from Gray's continuously speeding poem not to stop the continuity with the last word of his poem but to continue the sense beyond it. That is, he saw process in the way the scientists were coming to see it, as unbreakable. In the 'Ode on the Spring' the retort the insects make to the poet ends with

> We frolick, while 'tis May.

[1] Jeffrey noted that 'Love, and the fantasies of lovers, have afforded an ample theme to poets of all ages. Mr. Wordsworth, however, has thought fit to compose a piece ['Strange fits of passion . . .'], illustrating this copious subject, by one single thought.' (Elsie Smith, *An Estimate of William Wordsworth by his Contemporaries 1793–1822*, 1932, p. 103). That one thought is reserved to close the poem.

That taunt ends the poem as far as words go. But not as far as thought goes.[1] For the taunt carries the implication that the poet has wasted the May that fell to him, and that accordingly he is foolish—less wise, indeed, than creatures much lower down the Scale of Being. A similar implication persists beyond the last word of the 'Ode on a Grecian Urn'. The urn, says Keats, will remain a friend to man, saying to him

> Beauty is truth, truth beauty

—a hard saying to men in their misery, but the only saying possible for an urn whose pictured forms have been so carefully selected that life as pictured by them is unexceptionally beautiful. 'Yes,' sighs the poet, 'that "Beauty is truth, truth beauty" is all you marble men and maidens know on earth and all you need to know—but', his thinking continues silently, 'with men it is far otherwise: for them the actual is often ugly.'[2]

13

I have spoken of Pope's love of conciseness. In the nineteenth century certain poets sought it, Meredith with eagerness. But on the whole, conciseness scarcely interested the nineteenth century: they had little leisure for concentration. Pope valued

[1] Occasionally, in an epitaph, Pope leaves the reader with the need to go on thinking; the best instance is the couplet designed for Dryden's monument, quoted below, p. 152.

[2] Keats seems to be remembering two famous couplets from the last Epistle of *An Essay on Man*: iv. 309 f.:
> Know then this truth (enough for Man to know)
> 'Virtue alone is happiness below;'

and the concluding couplet:
> . . . VIRTUE only makes our Bliss below,
> And all our Knowledge is, OURSELVES TO KNOW.

That virtue and happiness are connected as cause and effect is, says Pope, 'enough for Man to know'. It is pleasantly otherwise for the figures on the urn, 'all *they* need to know' being that 'whatever is, is' beautiful. For men,
> What right, what true, what fit, we justly call,
> Let this be all my care—for this is All.
> (*Imit. of Horace*, Ep. i. i. 19 f.)

For men 'All our knowledge is, OURSELVES TO KNOW'. But 'all [the figures on the Urn] know' is again pleasantly otherwise. The implication that persists beyond the close of Keats's poem, the implication that for men matters are sadly different, leaves the field open for a philosophic poet to comment on those different matters, Keats himself attempting to be such a philosophic poet in certain passages in other poems.

it as a means for avoiding tediousness and glibness, an avoidance necessary for anyone expressing what had been thought often. The designing of his couplets was an undertaking possible only for a poet not in a hurry. He was unhurried because there was nothing new under the sun, nothing new even in the latest people he satirized.[1] Though he wrote his first drafts quickly, he brooded over them at leisure. His material being known already, the expression of it had to strike the recipient as justified by its finality. In the nineteenth century matter often seemed, and sometimes was, new. In that age, instead of refining the old, making it clearer and brighter, words often kept pace with discoveries. The poet often pressed on to more and more discoveries, and his words with him. Where such advances are in progress words cannot form themselves into the final expressiveness. Or not usually: when they do, it is by some lucky accident. They are the excited words of a reporter, not words carved on a monument: they are words on the stretch.

APPENDIX

THE ORDERING OF WORDS IN POETRY

That the words of poetry should retain their prose-order as much as possible has been the constant admonition of critics, most of whom have been practising poets. Commentary on the subject constitutes a firm body of doctrine. That sensible counsellor, George Gascoigne, whom I quote elsewhere on the ordering of noun and adjective, is for prose-order in general:

Therefore even as I have advised you to place all wordes in their naturall or most common and usuall pronunciation, so would I wishe you to frame all sentences in their mother phrase and proper *Idióma*. . . .

He goes on to allow that departures from prose-order may have to be countenanced 'where rime enforceth' ('Certayne Notes

[1] Cf. T. Burnet's letter of 1 June 1716: 'I am now at my leisure hours reading Horace with some diligence and find the world was just the same then, that it continues to be now. . . .' (*The Letters of Thomas Burnet to George Duckett 1712–1722*, ed. D. Nichol Smith, 1914, p. 99). Pope began to 'imitate' Horace because, on one occasion, Bolingbroke noted 'how well [one of the satires] would hit my case' (*The Poems of Alexander Pope*, Twickenham edn., iv (ed. John Butt), p. xiii).

of Instruction', note II; *Complete Works*, ed. J. W. Cunliffe, Cambridge, 1907–10, i. 470) which frankly admits that metrical perfection cannot be expected of an English poet when he writes rimed verse—he lived before the advent of Milton, and also of Herrick. He counts departure from prose-order as a loss and does not also see that poets can sometimes gain by making those departures. In the seventeenth century there are Dryden's persuasive remarks on the subject, which I quote in the text at p. 113 above; and the couplet of the Earl of Mulgrave in his *Essay upon Poetry*, deprecating those departures that are merely for convenience:

> No words transpos'd, but in such just cadence,
> As, though hard wrought, may seem the effect of chance.

(Spingarn, ii. 288). For Goldsmith's view see his 'Life of Parnell', *Works*, ed. Gibbs, 1885, iv. 173. Wordsworth touched on the matter in his Preface to the *Lyrical Ballads*, and again powerfully in a passage in the Alfoxden MS notebook, quoted in *The Prelude*, ed. E. de Selincourt, rev. H. Darbishire, 1959, p. xlii, *n.* 2:

Dr. Johnson observed, that in blank verse, the language suffered more distortion to keep it out of prose than any inconvenience to be apprehended from the shackles and circumspection of rhyme. This kind of distortion is the worst fault that poetry can have; for if once the natural order and connection of the words is broken, and the idiom of the language violated, the lines appear manufactured, and lose all that character of enthusiasm and inspiration, without which they become cold and vapid, how sublime soever the ideas and the images may be which they express.

(How amply Wordsworth might have illustrated these distortions from his own poetry!) There are also the remarks by G. M. Hopkins, *Letters to Robert Bridges*, ed. C. C. Abbott, Oxford, 1935, p. 89; and a characteristic passage in a letter of Ruskin. Ruskin takes some lines from Shakespeare's *Richard II*,

> Even so, or with much more contempt, men's eyes
> Did scowl on gentle Richard; no man cried 'God save him!'
> No joyful tongue gave him his welcome home:
> But dust was thrown upon his sacred head;

in which, as he says, there is 'not *one* transposition from beginning to end', and invites his correspondent 'to try the effects of
a few', as follows:

> So—or with more contemning did men's eyes
> On Richard scowl. No man God save him cried,
> No joyful tongue him home his welcome gave;
> But dust upon his sacred head was thrown, etc.

He continues:

You see in a passage like this where there is deep feeling, Shakespeare prefers writing a line which will not scan (Did scowl on
Richard, etc.) to using the least transposition. Neither is it any
excuse for transposition to say that such in a *perfect* language would
be the natural order of the words. The imperfection of our language
compels us to express the government by the order of the words,
and in an English poem that order of words is natural which is
suited to the genius of the language, and which a person not thinking
about his words would use, and that is *un*natural which a person
thinking about the philosophy of language instead of its meaning
would use. If it is my habit to say 'I want an apple' it is vain to tell
me that apple is the principal idea in my mind and that it would be
natural to say 'Apple I want'. It is natural in every language to use
the customary forms, and philosophical language never could be the
language of passion, unless it became fragmentary. The unruly
child at the dessert does indeed roar Apple, but the *want* is wanting
altogether. (*Works*, iv. 390 f.)

I have reserved the remarks of two poet-critics for special
consideration. The ordering of words in poetry was discussed by
Coleridge during his criticism of Wordwsorth's ill-considered
phrase 'the real language of men' (*Biographia Literaria*, ii. 41 ff.).
Coleridge was mistaken, I think, in the way he interpreted such
divergence as exists in a poem from the order words take in
written prose. He goes so far as to say, on one occasion, that
'the sense [of a "poem"] shall be good and weighty, the language
correct and dignified, the subject interesting and treated with
feeling; and yet the style shall, notwithstanding all these merits,
be justly blamable as *prosaic*, and solely because the words and
the order of the words would find their appropriate place in
prose, but are not suitable to *metrical* composition' (p. 60). And
yet his instances, whatever they prove about 'the words', i.e. the
diction, of prose and poetry, prove several things about the order

of the words: (1) that in a poem prose-order is the norm; (2) that deviations from it are of two sorts: (*a*) deviations for the sake of technical convenience, deviations, therefore, that we wish away; and (*b*) deviations that improve the quality of the sense. The first few lines of his instance from Spenser show deviations that are plainly justifiable:

> By this the northern waggoner had set
> His sevenfold teme behind the steadfast starre,
> That was in ocean waves yet never wet,
> But firme is fixt, and sendeth light from farre
> To all that in the wide deep wandering are.

Here prose-order is the norm. It is retained except (i) towards the end of l. 3, (ii) at the beginning of l. 4, and (iii) at the end of l. 5. At (i) the inversion makes acceptable what would be an intolerable jingle if prose-order were retained: 'never yet wet'. At (ii) 'But firm is fixt' is a variation of 'But is fixt firme'; here the words are so strong in themselves that order makes little difference—in any event the reader would give them due emphasis. At (iii) the inversion is completely justified, being an improvement in the interests of the poetical. It gives us 'wide deep wand-', a group of strong accents, and tails off into quietness and tremulousness that suggest a fearful vastness. On the whole, however, the inversions of the *Faërie Queene* are dearly bought. They could not be avoided, Spenser having chosen to write in a stanza-form that calls for more rimes on a single word-ending than English can readily supply. If it were not for them Spenser would write continuously a firm, clear and forthright English.

Coleridge's instance from Daniel of what may be 'justly blamable as *prosaic*' shows a retention of prose-order not more complete than Spenser's.

Robert Bridges has some interesting remarks on inversion in his *Collected Essays, Papers, &c.*, IV, 'A Critical Introduction to Keats', 1933, pp. 108–10. They are vitiated, of course, by his way of looking at language: he sought to impose a usage he considered abstractedly as logical on material inimical to logic: e.g. he here assumes an absolute standard, and calls the French position of the noun and adjective 'in most cases' the 'proper' position, forgetting that in English, as in French, the only criterion of what is proper is the criterion of what is in general use; Gascoigne and Ruskin, as we have seen, knew better. I quote one remark of Bridges above, p. 114 n. Another that is relevant here is:

The best simple writers have the art of making the common grammatical forms obey their ideas, and Keats has usually a right order of ideas in a simple grammatical form, and a preference for this style over more elaborate constructions [such as those Miltonic ones he came to dislike in 'Hyperion'] is no doubt what he intended to advocate. . . . (p. 109).

This is true; but 'simple' writers are more numerous, I think, than Bridges believed.

The principle reiterated in these passages was strengthened for these writers by the example of Virgil: in Porson's words, 'Virgil has everywhere arranged his words naturally and properly as in prose. No violent transposition, or inversions; every word is precisely where it ought to be!' (S. Rogers, *Recollections*, 1859, p. 123).

For an overwhelming justification of the inversions that metre encourages, though fearfully, see Shakespeare's Sonnet 90:

> If thou wilt leaue me, do not leaue me last,
> When other pettie griefes haue done their spight,
> But in the onset come . . .

The right of a poet, even more than of a prose-writer, to invert the prose-order of words ranks with his right to use metre itself; but it is a right he exercises at his peril.

THE 'MINOR POEMS' IN THE 'TWICKENHAM' POPE

THE FIRST sight of this stout and handsome volume cannot but prompt the regret that its chief architect saw it only prospectively. Norman Ault made the preparing of it his main occupation for some twenty years before his death in 1950. His first public move towards it was made in 1935 when he edited the *Poems on Several Occasions* of 1717 under the title of *Pope's Own Miscellany*. As that title was meant to suggest, Pope not only edited its contents but composed many of them himself. Without knowing it from the start Ault was repeating a discovery of A. E. Case, but he went further than Case in his claims for Pope as author. Then followed several articles mainly on the canon of Pope's writings—articles which were collected in 1949 as *New Light on Pope with Some Additions to his Poetry Hitherto Unknown*. In view of these two books our regret that Ault did not see the present one is not regret at its sharpest: some monument to his 'long labours' was already visible. And if, during his last years, he doubted whether his edition of the minor poems would appear before his death, he may well have felt assured that it would be completed for him by his friend, the general editor of that slowly swelling series in which this volume now takes a distinguished place. Not all frustrated labours promise and achieve the speedy and conscientious fulfilment that Professor John Butt has accorded these.

Norman Ault could always be relied on to add to our knowledge of any biographical or textual matter he set his hand to. Concerned here first of all with the shorter poems that Pope acknowledged and admitted—and it is the first glory of this volume that such poems preponderate in it—he managed to assemble a surprising number of manuscript and printed versions from which to confirm or establish the text. The further task which, from the point of view of great literature, was the less rewarding was, from the point of view of scholarship, the more difficult: the finding of poems which Pope wrote but did not acknowledge, or admitted though not in so many words. Ault's success this way lies in the thirty or so poems—short or occasionally longer than short—that he claimed for Pope, and to the credentials of which Professor Butt has had, like mitred Rochester, to nod the head.

For his task on text and canon Ault was well equipped in another field than the scholarly and bibliographical. He had a talent for recognizing evidence of a stylistic sort. He brought to his work a memory retentive of that vast concourse of sense and sound which for him was the rest—including the *Iliad* and *Odyssey*—of Pope's poetry. Pope is eminently a memorable poet, but few have held more of his lines in their memory than did Ault. He also had an ear for recognizing the recurrence of smaller units, of diction and phrases and 'tricks' of expression. This gift of his can be illustrated by his discovery of what he neatly called Pope's device of the 'pathetic parenthesis', a device which is perhaps most familiar to us from Gray's use of it in the 'Elegy':

> He gave to Mis'ry all he had, a tear,
> He gain'd from Heav'n ('twas all he wish'd) a friend.

If Ault lacked enough external evidence of Pope's authorship of a tempting poem, the presence of stylistic points such as these was brought forward as evidence worth considering, even as evidence conclusive. Not all of his admirers agreed as to the worth of this evidence. And in any event Ault cannot be said to have discerned and handled it with enough nicety. Nor did he see clearly enough that style is a subtler matter than shreds and patches: he was no Swinburne gifted as a critic to touch and demonstrate the intangible. But at least he was trying to assert the principle that for the purposes of an editor of poetry stylistic evidence is evidence that must weigh. After his fashion he was acting on the belief we all confess outwardly, that the style is the man. And it is possible that he had more judgment of this sort than he managed to give adequate account of.

Perhaps Professor Butt has been a little too cautious in neglecting the stylistic side of Ault's work where it did not enforce an attribution already sufficiently ensured from other quarters. In

his introduction, after a most clear and convincing account of
evidence that may be called solid, he adds that 'stylistic evidence
alone has not been used in this edition to attribute a poem to
Pope'. This policy may well be sound enough though we cannot
but honour the editor whose convictions about style sometimes
get the better of him. In the case of several rejected poems, however, there is stylistic evidence that is not wholly unsupported by
evidence of the solid sort. Several poems here relegated to the
section 'Poems of Doubtful Authorship' and only listed by
name, call for re-consideration. The evidence of the solid sort is
set out by Ault in *Pope's Own Miscellany*. It does not amount to
much. On the other hand, the stylistic evidence is strong. Taken
altogether, the evidence is enough to admit them—so the
present reviewer holds—into the canon. Chief among these
poems is 'Upon Cleora's Marriage and Retirement':

I

Happy, *Cleora*, was the time,
E're courts and musick were a crime,
When maidens cou'd uncensur'd go,
With a she-friend from show to show.

II

When bright *Cleora* cou'd appear
Drest to the season of the year;
And gayly ramble up and down,
The Toast and envy of the town.

III

When in a scarf (our sins forgiven,
No matter how we dress for heaven)
She drove to church, display'd her fan,
Took orange chips, and thought on man.

IV

Such was the life *Cleora* led,
Who then like blest *Cleora* sped?
Yet for the thing that pleases best,
Cleora gave up all the rest.

V

And now confin'd to homely cares,
Domestick drudgery and prayers,
Coop't in a lonely fenny house,
One dog, the parson, and her spouse!

VI

No basset now, no midnight chat,
Of who said this, or who did that:
For scandal too (the joy of life)
No creature but the doctor's wife.

VII

All this for sins of flesh and blood?
Tis hard: but yet 'tis for her good.
For now there's time, and some pretence
Why she may think on providence.

VIII

Beside, whate'er her future fate,
The matter is not now so great;
Half of her hell she suffers here,
And has but t'other half to fear.

These verses do not disgrace the principles and standards of correctness that Professor Butt rightly guards on Pope's behalf. And in addition they share Pope's known vision of the 'human situation'—or of a feminine facet of it—and his Tennysonian sensuousness, the wit and playful poignancy, the intimacy of knowledge and sympathy, and the indulgence we expect of him when his theme is young women.

A detail of entitlement calls for comment, if only because it concerns one of the most moving of the poems Pope did not collect, the two 'elegiac' stanzas sent to the Misses Blount in a letter of September 13, 1717:

All hail! once pleasing, once inspiring Shade,
  Scene of my youthful Loves, and happier hours!
Where the kind Muses met me as I stray'd,
  And gently pressd my hand, and said, Be Ours!—
Take all thou e're shalt have, a constant Muse:
  At Court thou may'st be lik'd, but nothing gain;
Stocks thou may'st buy and sell, but always lose;
  And love the brightest eyes, but love in vain!

This poem was first printed, it seems, by Bowles in a footnote to the letters, and first placed among the poems by Dyce, who called it 'Lines'. Under that title and 'Lines Written in Windsor Forest' we have always known it. Pope's letter offers it as 'a Hymn [made] as I past thro' these Groves', and this has been the ground for giving it here the new title 'A Hymn Written in *Windsor* Forest'. It seems probable that Pope called his poem a hymn merely because it suited him on one intimate occasion to represent its practical object as success in love. The term does not cover more than a part of the content of the poem. 'Lines Written in Windsor Forest' seems preferable.

And so to the poetry of this volume as a whole—for of course we are here given not only an exhibition of scholarly principles at work on fascinating materials but also some of the greatest poetry Pope wrote. And if we speak of 'poetry' we must also speak of poems. Indeed in a collection of minor pieces, the higher test is whether or not the collection falls into separate things. What do we most hope to find in a collection of small things—things small by any standards, and things small by comparison—written by a poet we know on other accounts to be great? Is it not evidence of a recurrence of acts of mental intensity that have the effect of dividing off one thing from the next? Here there is plenty of division—more than in the 'major' poems—of the mechanical sort. There is plenty of variety of metre and 'colours' of diction. Moreover, in the moods conveyed there is that familiar Popean range—tenderness; fierceness; a cathedral solemnity; fastidious, ribald and smirking amusement; and so on. The division, however, between poem and poem does not depend on the separateness of technical method or of expressed emotions: Pope's poems, even his minor ones, are divided, as it were, biologically. When we are in the midst of the minor poems we do not feel that we are reading a single poem of epical length accidentally broken up by typography. Moving from one to the next, we alight at the centre of a succession of individual items. Sometimes, it is true, Pope has used couplets, and even runs of them, twice over, and where we are conscious of a repetition perhaps—for it is by no means certain—a feeling of things individually organized breaks down. It may also break down in the less good poems—after all,

Pope may not have acknowledged some of the poems here collected because he considered them inferior as literature. Usually, however, the feeling exists strongly. 'On lying in the Earl of Rochester's Bed at Atterbury' is a poem wholly and compactly itself:

> With no poetick ardors fir'd,
>   I press the bed where *Wilmot* lay:
> That here he lov'd, or here expir'd,
>   Begets no numbers grave or gay.
>
> But 'neath thy roof, *Argyle*, are bred
>   Such thoughts, as prompt the brave to lie,
> Stretch'd forth in honour's nobler bed,
>   Beneath a nobler roof, the sky.
>
> Such flames, as high in patriots burn,
>   Yet stoop to bless a child or wife;
> And such as wicked kings may mourn,
>   When freedom is more dear than life.

And not less this sublime 'Epitaph designed for Mr. Dryden's Monument':

> This *SHEFFIELD* rais'd. The sacred Dust below
> Was *DRYDEN* once: The rest who does not know?

Perhaps another way of making the same point is to say that we cannot read this couplet without being prompted to commit it to memory on the spot, just as we cannot fail to pick up a ring or brooch we find lying on the pavement. Or take the 'Epilogue to Jane Shore. Design'd for Mrs Oldfield'. Not all of its fifty lines can be quoted here, but does not the following excerpt help to prove that its like exists nowhere else, not even in Pope's poems?

> Prodigious this! the Frail one of our Play
> From her own sex should mercy find to day!
> You might have held the pretty head aside,
> Peep'd in your fans, been serious, thus, and cry'd,
> The Play may pass—but that strange creature, *Shore*,
> I can't—indeed now—I so hate a whore—
> Just as a blockhead rubs his thoughtless skull,
> And thanks his stars he was not born a fool;

So from a sister sinner you shall hear,
'How strangely you expose your self my dear!'
But let me die, all raillery apart,
Our sex are still forgiving at their heart;
And did not wicked custom so contrive,
We'd be the best, good-natur'd things alive.
    There are, 'tis true, who tell another tale,
That virtuous ladies envy while they rail;
Such rage without betrays the fire within;
In some close corner of the soul, they sin:
Still hoarding up, most scandalously nice,
Amidst their virtues, a reserve of vice. . . .

Two of the three poems here singled out are couplet poems. There used to be the notion that the couplet as written in the eighteenth century, in contradistinction to the couplet as written in the early seventeenth, was so closed a metre as to make cohesion into anything we call could a poem impossible. In answer to this view we can only say that to remove a couplet from Pope's poems is to engage in a surgical operation.

A word finally on Pope's comic poems—comic and usually indecent, and forming a fair proportion of the new poems. In his *New Light on Pope* Ault considered that he had distinguished a new Pope which he called 'Pope the Clown'. The designation cannot, surely, be considered a happy one. Pope cannot be equated with a clown since his poems never lack a Miltonic exquisiteness. His ideal for a comic poem always has wit as an ingredient. It draws its subsidiary matter from odd and learned quarters. It unites an economy of syllables with brilliancy of rhymes, and it is not considered ready for view until its native ease has been polished into grace. Even when he writes a ballad in the popular style, that style is not without its sophistication. In the ballad 'Duke upon Duke' the responsibility for which is likely, as Ault argues, to be Pope's, we come on stanzas such as this:

The Duke in Wrath call'd for his Steeds,
    And fiercely drove them on;
Lord! Lord! how rattl'd then thy Stones,
    Oh Kingly *Kensington*!

And again in 'The Discovery,' another poem likely to be Pope's in the main:

> Most true it is, I dare to say,
>   E'er since the Days of *Eve*,
> The weakest Woman sometimes may
>   The wisest Man deceive.
>
> For *D[avena]nt* circumspect, sedate,
>   A *Machiavel* by Trade,
> Arriv'd Express, with News of Weight,
>   And thus, at Court, he said.
>
> At *Godliman*, hard by the *Bull*,
>   A Woman, long thought barren,
> Bears *Rabbits*,—Gad! so plentiful,
>   You'd take her for a Warren. . . .
>
> A vow to God He then did make
>   He would himself go down,
> *St. A[ndré]* too, the Scale to take
>   Of that *Phœnomenon*. . . .

There is something in the comic poetry, which includes certain portions of the satirical, that corresponds with the biographical fact that its author himself refrained from vigorous laughter: 'I never saw him laugh very heartily in all my life,' said his sister, and we can see that this was so when we look at the noble, drawn, melancholy, intellectual face of the Roubillac bust here reproduced as frontispiece. The laugh we accord his comic strokes does not lack heartiness, but that heartiness coexists with a delight in the fineness of the art that rules the occasion.

POPE'S LETTERS IN PROFESSOR SHERBURN'S EDITION

THE EDITOR of a bulky correspondence has a hard task. Letters are dispersed, exist unsuspected, alight for a moment in a saleroom, and have to be assembled, discovered, kept trace of; they are hand-written, perhaps tattered, perhaps undated, and have to be represented in print and given some sort of a date; they are puzzling, and have to be explained. It follows from all this, that their editor needs many gifts, some alert as a journalist's, some of the slow and burrowing sort—a letter of our own has rubbish in it that would puzzle even ourselves in a few years' time, and more than two centuries have passed over the ephemeralities of Pope's. One gift, clearly, must be that of a noble stoicism: the editor of George Eliot's letters, we recall, was denied permission to consult one series of them, and a note by Professor Sherburn reads: 'The excerpts come from [a] catalogue. Unfortunately the entire letter has not been available for publication. It is one of Pope's best.' Much is at stake here, and we take the opportunity to quote the following considered remarks from Professor Sherburn's preface:

To owners and especially dealers in autographs acknowledgements are made at the beginning of each letter, as a help to students and as an act of gratitude on my part. Almost without exception dealers have been ready to allow . . . transcripts to be made—and this in spite of the current tradition that such procedure cuts the money value of a letter. Having watched the prices of Pope letters now for twenty-five years, I should like to register the opinion that publication or other reproduction has far less bearing on the price of a letter than some imagine. If dealers or owners have suffered financial loss through helping me, I am very sorry. They have been generous, and my hope is that interest in Pope, increased through this edition, may eventually reward them.

Pope wrote many letters, and many have survived. Among his reasons for writing them were reasons that have made for their survival. Letters in the vernacular were coming to be thought of as literature, and valued as permanent possessions. They were beginning to constitute literary property, as Addison saw when he took pieces from his own and gave them a place in the *Tatler*. For the same literary end Pope, who improvidently had not kept a copy, recalled some of his, though, on the available evidence, he did not use them. Later in his life he carried through a brilliant scheme for the publication of the best of the letters—brilliant because he did it without seeming implicated. About a tenth of the letters that survive were printed in his lifetime. Since then many of his 'good letters'—to use his own term for one of Gay's—have been printed, and many of the plainer kind, notably in the edition that Elwin and Courthope completed some seventy years ago.

To their number Professor Sherburn has been able to add a third more. Many of these new letters are 'good letters', but he has printed everything he could lay his hands on. The alternative, a system of omission and cutting, is deplorable where a great writer is concerned—nobody can trust a selection made by anybody else, and the stone one builder rejected may be found useful by another. The frequent printing of Pope's letters particularly in his own lifetime, entails 'long labours' on their editor. Nevertheless, Professor Sherburn has collated completely: he has even collated the text of Elwin and Courthope where their originals exist, with results that lead us to infer that where originals are lost—conspicuously in the long correspondence of Pope, Broome and Fenton—we cannot wholly trust their unique transcript.

It would require many quotations to represent the worth of the new letters—their variety, vivacity and the interestingness of their opinions of this and that. Space forbids; but it can be said that the new letters include a delightful collection of sixty or so addressed either to the Earl or the Countess of Burlington, which often treat, as we should expect, of architecture, and treat of it, again as we should expect, in playful earnest. On all the letters together let us quote the sober, amusing estimate with which Professor Sherburn concludes his preface:

Some readers, viewing the extensiveness of Pope's epistolary achievements, will be inclined to sigh with a former colleague of mine who does not love Pope, and exclaim, 'Who would have thought the little man had so much ink in him.' To less prejudiced readers the letters here presented will give a portrait of Pope and his mind such as has not been seen before.

It will be noticed that we have already begun our praise of the present edition. These five volumes are the magnificent result of some forty or so years of devotion and scholarship. The distinction of Professor Sherburn is that he is equipped at all the many points. He is the best all-round Popean there has ever been—the author of *The Early Career of Alexander Pope*, a biography vivid because of its generous temper and fascinating depth of knowledge, and of *The Best of Pope*, which he furnished with first-rate critical introductions to the poems selected. Moreover, he can write excellent English, believing, as some younger American scholars seem to forget, that excellent English is not less excellent American. His notes to the letters are a pleasure to read, not least for their spirit. Their tone would have pleased Pope. Indeed, we wish that Pope himself could have thanked his editor in princely compliment. It goes without saying that future scholars, specializing on pieces of the whole, will challenge an interpretation, argue a dating, expose a half-buried reference or quotation, correct a fact here and there, but it will always be with a sense of gathering samphire on Dover Cliff.

Professor Sherburn's index occupies some 200 pages of double columns, and its amplitude is itself an index to the amount of thumbing it will receive. The new letters are recommended as helping 'to fill out our picture of Pope': all the letters together help fill out our picture of the age to which Pope gave his name. Any scholar working on that age will need to know all that there is to his purpose in Pope's letters, as in Pope's poems— whether it is the working of the postal systems, social manners, pin-money, the state of certain roads, politicians and the changing 'climate' of politics, writers great and small, gardening and the cultivation of pineapples (in which Pope was a pioneer), the life of a courtier, the relation of author, publisher and book-buyer (during the years when, largely owing to Pope, the patron, both individual and party, was on the way out), fire insurance, theatre practices, painting, funeral monuments, the 'Edder-down Quilt'—and so on endlessly.

Much of the particular evidence has been available before, but this edition is where it will now have to be read, and though we had some of the facts already, there will now be the chance that we shall have one of Professor Sherburn's trenchant comments on them. The reader's debt to the commentary is particularly obvious where Pope himself, and particularly his character and personality, is concerned. There has been much written about all this, but Professor Sherburn is in a position to have the last word, which he wisely makes cordial in admiration and, at intervals, regretful.

The most important reason, however, why we need the best possible edition of these letters is that they contain literature—the sort of thing we find, to limit ourselves to scraps, in the phrase for his dead aged mother, 'this Winter-flower . . . faded', in his suggestion on a manuscript of Aaron Hill's 'in Black Lead, half afraid to be legible', in his being 'so sick of [the piracy of his letters] as to be almost afraid of the Shadow of my Pen'. They contain literature: unlike the poems, they are not composed of it. How could they be, being letters? What spoils the early ones is their ceremony and the occasional laboriousness of their wit. Some ceremony and wit were inevitable constituents of letters written in or soon after the age of Anne, and much of both when their author was addressing his social superiors— 'I endeavour (like all awkward Fellows) to be agreeable by Imitation'—who were sometimes also much senior to him.

Even in the early letters, however, Pope is critical of the expected style, calling ceremony 'the Smoak of Friendship', speaking of 'long letters about nothing', and of the recipient 'paus[ing] at each Period, to look back over how much Wit you have pass'd'. Fortunately, too, the wit often conveys a Congrevian fineness of matter, as when he writes that country folk 'all say 'tis pitty I am so sickly, & I think 'tis pitty they are so healthy'. Fortunately, again, the matter is often that of literary criticism, in writing which Pope is always the gloriously sound and pointed author of *An Essay on Criticism*.

While some of the early letters are too literary in the bad sense, many of the later belong to that plainest of plain forms, the letter conveying what nowadays would go on a postcard or down a telephone. The style of these later letters, even when at their plainest, is as interesting as the elaborate earlier style at its best. It is neatly brisk—one of the most telling phrases ever applied to Pope is Fenton's 'brisk as a wren'—and 'laconic', a term which recurs with odd frequency in the opening sentences of Pope's letters to Warburton. Pope, however, was not always in a hurry, and it is from what we feel to be his stillnesses that the finest things enter the letters, as the poems. For one thing, he had much capacity for the deepest feeling. It exists quite apart from the unpleasant things in his nature.

The reason we feel convinced of its genuineness is not so much its recurrence as its access to a peculiar sort of evidence. Only a sincerely loving person could have come by the matter he expresses. We know, of course, that the person concerned, being a poet, was less dependent than other men on direct experience: a poet could no doubt have made up the evidence, as Shakespeare did the evidence that there was deep feeling in his *dramatis personæ*. But leaving aside the question whether or not Pope was this sort of poet, we do not need to invoke his poetship, for we have the ample evidence of his friends.

Swift, Gay, Arbuthnot, Burlington and the rest did not think his feeling was a literary fiction. Their letters give us clear evidence that they knew he meant the wonderful things his letters often said. Here are instances:

And you [Gay], whose Absence is in a manner perpetual to me, ought rather to be remembered as a good man gone, than breathed after as one living;

or:

I find my other Tyes dropping from me; some worn off, some torn off, others relaxing daily: My greatest, both by duty, gratitude, and humanity, Time is shaking every moment, and it now hangs by a thread! I am many years the older, for living so much with one so old [his mother]; much the more helpless, for having been so long help'd and tended by her; much the more considerate and tender, for a daily commerce with one who requir'd me justly to be both to her; and consequently the more melancholy and thoughtful; and the less fit for others, who want only in a companion or a friend, to be amused or entertained;

or:

So will the death of my Mother be! which now I tremble at, now resign to, now bring close to me, now set farther off: Every day alters, turns me about, and confuses my whole frame of mind;

or, finally, on her death:

It is indeed a Grief to mee which I cannot express, and which I should hate my own Heart if it did not feel, & yet wish no Friend I have ever should feel.

Johnson, who had less evidence before him than we have, had enough to conclude his paragraph on Pope's filial piety with: 'Life has, among its soothing and quiet comforts, few things better to give than such a son.'

Feelings such as these of Pope's are so deep as to seem free of time, but they are one thing at twenty, another at forty and a different again at sixty. And it is because of this, among other matters, that we so much welcome Professor Sherburn's decision to give us the letters in a single chronological sequence—a decision which has meant much work, sometimes thankless work, on undated scraps. In the edition of Elwin and Courthope the letters are arranged in about a hundred sequences, some long, some very short—some consist of a single item— according to correspondent. Supporting this arrangement was presumably the argument that any batch of letters from any one person to another has its own homogeneity. It was the arrangement that Pope favoured when he himself printed his letters. But to honour this particular homogeneity is to damage interests even more clamant. Consider the nature of letters. One letter is followed by others to the same person, each separate and yet each linked. The separateness, however, is as important as the linkedness, and it is destroyed if we present each of the many correspondences as if it were a novel in so many short chapters. For this arrangement destroys the space that originally existed between the letters, intervals that were filled for writer and recipient with 'slices of life.' On the other hand, those intervals are faithfully suggested if the letters to any one person are interspersed with the letters the writer happened to send to others.

Nor does the one chronological sequence really harm our sense of the homogeneity of each correspondence within itself. For the reader readily forms a picture of each recurring correspondent, which the recurrence of others does not efface. When he meets another letter to Caryll after letters to Oxford, Fortescue, Swift and the rest, he effortlessly recalls Caryll and his interests, and indeed Pope's last letter to him. He has indeed been waiting for the further letter, as Caryll did.

If the one chronological sequence is right for the letters themselves, it is even more patently so for their author. He is the one constant, being always himself, but a changing thing, being a man existing through time. The one sequence of his letters represents the steps he took along the road of the seven ages, a road which seems of the proper human solidity and proportions now that we can pace it with him. The quasi-biography latent in his forty years of letter-writing has never been properly discernible till now. And our sense of continuity—of deepening tone, and also of untiring zest of contrivance—is so strong that we end by seeing Pope, the maker and recorder of it all, as a greater man than before.

Our sense of the one continuity is strengthened, as it were from below, by another innovation of Professor Sherburn's: he has prefixed to the letters of each year a concentrated account of Pope's life during that year. Perhaps the idea for this he owed to Professor Griffith, whose brilliant bibliography of Pope is humanized by a similar method. To read their accounts side by side and step by step is to read the best whole biography of Pope available. But their joint biography exists, as we have said, on a different plane from the mental biography the letters give us. So powerful is the tone of this that we cannot say we have had Pope complete till Professor Sherburn has allowed us to hear it. In saying that we do not forget the poems. Their tone is deep, and their autobiographical matter almost ubiquitous. Sometimes the letters and the poems sound the same tone. But here is more of it, and we hear it in a new way because it comes to us, as experience came to Pope, under what he might have called a felt subjection to time.

VII

POPE'S 'EPISTLE TO HARLEY': AN INTRODUCTION AND ANALYSIS

To be a poet is, to begin with, a matter of being; from time to time being becomes doing, and the poet writes down a poem. There is the antecedent cause, the poet's general readiness to write poetry—as when Henry Taylor remarked that Tennyson was 'full of poetry, with nothing to put it in' or when Keats foresaw that in writing *Endymion* he would have to 'make 4000 Lines of one bare circumstance and fill them with "Poetry".'[1] And there is the efficient cause, the occasion, as when, at last, Tennyson found his theme. Occasions vary in their importance for the writer and the reader. On the one hand, it is clear that there must have been an occasion for Keats's 'Ode to Melancholy', a decisive moment striking into the general poeticalness of Keats's life. But we may suppose that he was scarcely aware of it. If he was sharply so, he did not require any awareness of it from his reader. On the other hand, the occasion of 'On first looking into Chapman's Homer' dictated the very title of the poem. In that title Keats dated the poem ('On *first* looking') and localized it ('looking into' a particular copy of 'Chapman's Homer'). Some poems are better left undated and unlocalized. The poetry they contain is of the kind that seems more impressive from being left floating in a general poeticalness. Not being tied to any one place, it seems more widespreading, not to any one time, more lasting. We are more impressed by Keats's melancholy when we are left to think of it vaguely as chronic: if its opening cry suggests an occasion, we accept it as prepared by many turns before this last turn of the screw. Other poems, it is equally true, need to be seen as being occasional. If Keats had agreed that poetry takes its origin from emotion recollected in tranquillity, he might have left the experience on first looking into Chapman's Homer to

---

[1] *Autobiography*, 1885, ii. 192 (letter of 3 June 1862); and *Letters* p. 52.

mature unexpressed until the time came, if it ever came, when he wrote generally of the realms of gold. But we know that he could not have borne postponement any more than Wordsworth could: we know that the poem was commanded into being by the voice of Chapman, speaking out loud and bold. The occasion was sacred, as sacred as the emotion it aroused.

If a poet does mark the occasion of a poem, this means that for some reason he wants the poem kept close to the practical world. With the result that we lack his permission to treat it as the sort of poem made out of or aspiring towards what is called 'pure poetry'. 'On first looking into Chapman's Homer', though it may tempt the purists, cannot be so treated. It must be kept in its place in the career of Keats. Even if that poem were not one of Keats's best, it would still be greatly valued for being a poem greatly placed in a great career. In saying this I am, of course, speaking of an organism as if it were a machine, and, worse, as if the machine had its parts loose: ultimately we cannot divide the man either from his poems or from his career. Some part of our minds is aware of Keats the man even when we are reading the 'Ode to Melancholy'. We should read it differently it if were by Browning. And if somebody were to retort that Browning could not have written it, that is another way of saying that Keats did. It seems to be according to human nature that people prefer to tie down the poems they like to time and place, or certainly to place—time is more difficult to handle: place, even if its particulars change, remains generally extant, whereas any one time becomes increasingly buried. Even though the evidence is much against Gray's having 'wrote' the 'Elegy', or any part of it, in the 'country churchyard' of Stoke Poges, people, who possess no sense of time but who do possess a sense of place, insist that he did. We cannot rule out this evidence on the ground that Stoke Poges is only honoured by readers who do not greatly care for poetry even when it is so obviously rich as that of the 'Elegy'. In *Rasselas* Imlac notes that piety may be improved on a pilgrimage; and it is possible that at Canterbury, if not on the way there, the Wife of Bath improved hers as well as did the Parson. A reading of the 'Elegy'—if the pilgrim quali-fies for consideration by reading it at all—will probably be more vivid for a visit to a haunt of the poet. However poetical readers of poetry cannot but remain human beings, and human beings (in the 'civilized' world, at least) have always been interested in careers, and especially in the great careers of great men. And when it comes to a poem that is declared occasional, the reader has his practical instinct already provided for. He does not need either to seek or to invent the particulars. He has his time and place fixed for him. If we are vaguely aware of Keats the man when reading the 'Ode to Melancholy', we are more particularly aware of him when reading 'On first looking into Chapman's Homer'. When a poem is declared to be occasional, we can call ourselves readers of it only if we recover as much of its occasion as we can.

2

During the eighteenth century, as everybody knows, there was too much writing-up of occasions. Innumerable 'copies of verses' 'on' this or that event printed in innumerable volumes called *Poems on Several Occasions* were firmly linked to the practical life. Human beings are so constituted that they respect the evidence of practical life whenever they meet it, but there is little to respect in most of the poems which were linked with it in the eighteenth century. We rarely condemn even trivial occasions as having been too trivial; nor do we condemn their celebration by means of verses; what we condemn is the pride that seeks the printer. When we do not condemn the printing this means that the poems to some extent remain what Pope called 'living Lays'. And when we choose to turn back to such living occasional poems, it follows that we must attend not only to their words but to their occasion, their practical historical context. To take an instance. Dr Delany wrote 'Verses left with a Silver Standish, on the Dean of St Patrick's Desk, on his Birth-day', and Swift a poem in reply. Surveying Swift's achievement as a poet, Delany complimented him on his 'living Lines', and though Delany had no comparable power of vivification, his own poem was vivified a little. In 1949 it still has enough to it to interest, say, twenty readers (was not Swift always avid for statistics?). One of those twenty, a research student burrowing towards his doctorate, may read the poem because he is interested in Delany. A few others of those twenty read it because they are interested in Swift, and so in Delany, and so in every scrap of them that survives. The rest of the score read it because of an interest in English poetry of the eighteenth century, or in English poetry, or in poetry of all times and places. But if they look at the poem at all, their interest must be dubbed—of all avoided terms—'academic', unless they learn what sort of a thing a standish was, and what was its status as a gift in the mid-eighteenth century. It will not prove possible for them to achieve ocular possession of the bright particular standish that Swift found on his desk, though that for most of them would be a further help: 'the Shape you see', the poem had said, pointing at the actual thing. But Delany was practical enough, when he, or another,[1] published the poem, to be aware of this inevitable deficiency, and to see that he had made allowances for it. The twenty readers must, at any rate, have 'some' acquaintance with a standish. And I do not see that this requirement can be disputed as necessary for anyone setting up as a critic of the poem. And if this be granted, it follows that the usefulness of the historical knowledge increases in proportion as the poetry it illuminates increases in quality. After we have learned what a 1732 standish amounted to, we see more clearly what lay in these poems of Delany and Swift; but the knowledge stands us in still better stead when we read a better poem on a similar occasion, when we read Pope's 'On receiving from the Right Honourable the Lady Frances Shirley, a Standish and two Pens'.

The poem that is the subject of the present discussion is another of Pope's occasional poems. His occasion is august, and he exhibits it with a proper pride. It is fixed firmly in a context of history: of political history—Harley had been a great politician; in a context of literary history—manuals of it find a place for Parnell as well as for Pope and Swift; in a context of polite society—the poem is an epistle. If Parnell did not speak out loud and bold, the occasion and Pope did.

[1] We do not know who was responsible for the publication of both poems in the *Gentleman's Magazine* two months after presentation. Perhaps the agent was Lord Orrery, who joined Delany with a poem and gift of his own, and who, as other evidence suggests, 'took pride in [his poem]' (see *Poems of . . . Swift*, ed. H. Williams, 1937, p. 609).

3

When concluding his notes to the *Iliad*, Pope thanked his assistants, one of whom had been Thomas Parnell:

I must end these Notes by discharging my Duty to two of my Friends, which is the more an indispensable piece of Justice, as the one of them is since dead: The Merit of their Kindness to me will appear infinitely the greater, as the Task they undertook was in its own nature of much more Labour, than either Pleasure or Reputation. The larger part of the Extracts from *Eustathius*, together with several excellent Observations were sent me by Mr. *Broome:* And the whole Essay upon *Homer* was written upon such Memoirs as I had collected, by the late Dr. *Parnell*, Archdeacon of *Clogher* in *Ireland:* How very much that Gentleman's Friendship prevail'd over his Genius, in detaining a Writer of his Spirit in the Drudgery of removing the Rubbish of past Pedants, will soon appear to the World, when they shall see those beautiful Pieces of Poetry the Publication[1] of which he left to my Charge, almost with his dying Breath.

This note was dated 25 March 1720, and the publication of the volume of the *Iliad* containing it followed on 12 May. Parnell had died some eighteen months earlier, in October 1718. The two poets had been close friends, and at some date in 1720, it seems, Pope told a friend that Parnell's death 'was . . . much in my mind', and that

to [his] Memory I am erecting the best Monument I can. What he gave me to publish, was but a small part of what he left behind him, but it was the best, and I will not make it worse by enlarging it.[2]

While preparing the monument Pope must have taken seriously the commission which, early in 1719, Swift conveyed to him through Charles Ford:

I think Pope should bestow a few Verses on his friend Parnels

[1] Pope, as Professor Griffith has said, was the best business man among the English poets. Here he is giving his projected volume a puff of 'advance publicity'. But if he is encouraging readers, he is not deceiving them: the poems were indeed 'beautiful', and are so still.
[2] Pope, *Correspondence*, ii. 24.

memory, especially if it is intended (as I think I have heard,) that some of Parnels scattered Things are to be published together.[1]

By 25 September 1721 the poem was written, though not finally. It took the form of a dedication to Robert Harley,[2] to whom on 21 October Pope sent a unique fair copy along with the body of his book.[3] The packet contained this letter:

> From my Ld Harley's in Dover Street
> Octob. 21. 1721.

My Lord,

Your Lordship may be surpriz'd at the liberty I take in writing to you; tho.you will allow me always to remember, that you once permitted me that honour, in conjunction with some others who better deserv'd it.[4] Yet I hope, you will not wonder I am still desirous to have you think me your gratefull & faithful Servant; but I own I have an Ambition yet farther, to have Others think me so; which is the Occasion I give your Lordship the trouble of this. Poor Parnell, before he dyed, left me the charge of publishing these few Remains of his: I have a strong Desire to make Them, their Author and their Publisher, more considerable, by addressing & dedicating 'em All, to You. There is a pleasure in bearing Testimony to Truth; and a Vanity perhaps, which at least is as excusable as any Vanity can be. I beg you, My Lord, to allow me to gratify it, in prefixing this paper of honest Verses to the Book. I send the Book itself, which I dare say you'l receive more Satisfaction in perusing, than you can from any thing written upon the Subject of yourself. Therfore I am

---

[1] *Letters of Jonathan Swift to Charles Ford*, ed. D. Nichol Smith, 1935, p. 74.

[2] For the sake of uniformity I call him throughout by his family name.

[3] Pope sent Harley the text of the volume. It was quite convenient to do this since the text was contained in a series of complete gatherings, namely, B–P⁸. I assume that after receiving Harley's permission to print the dedication, that is, soon after 6 Nov., the date of his reply, Pope revised it, designed the preliminaries, and had them printed on Sheet A. The book was published on 7 Dec., though it bears the date 1722. The contents of the preliminaries are as follows: A1ʳ, title-page in black and red:

POEMS|ON|Several Occasions.|—|Written by|Dr. *THOMAS PARNELL*,| Late Arch-Deacon of *Clogher:*|AND|*Published by Mr.* POPE.|—|*Dignum laude Virum Musa vetat mori.* Hor.|=|*LONDON:*|Printed for B. Lintot, at the *Cross-Keys*, between|the *Temple Gates* in *Fleet-street*, 1722.

A1ᵛ, blank, A2ʳ–A3ᵛ, Pope's dedicatory poem, signed '*Sept.* 25. 1721. *A. POPE.*', catchword 'HESIOD'; A4ʳ, title for the first poem of Parnell's, 'Hesiod: or, the Rise of Women.'; A4ᵛ, blank.

[4] Pope refers to joint communications from members of the Scriblerus Club.

a good deal in doubt, whether you will care for such an addition to it? I'll only say for it, that 'tis the only Dedication I ever writ, & shall be whether you permit it or not: For I will not bow the knee to a less Man than my Lord Oxford, & I expect to see no Greater in my Time.

After all, if your Lordship will tell my Lord Harley that I must not do this, you may depend upon a total Suppression of these Verses (the only Copy whereof I send you). But you never shall suppress that Great, sincere, & entire, Admiration & Respect, with which I am always | My Lord, | Your most faithful, most o- | bedient, & most humble Servant, | A. Pope.

To which Harley replied:

Brampton-Castle, Nov. 6. 1721.

S^r

I received you Packet by the Carrier, which could not but give me great Pleasure, to see you preserve an Old Friend in Memory: for it must needs be very agreeable to be Remembred by those we highly Value. But then, how much Shame did it cause me! When I read your fine Verses inclos'd, my Mind reproach'd me how far short I came of what your great Friendship & delicate Pen would partially describe me. You ask my Consent to Publish it; to what Streights doth This reduce me! I look back, indeed, to those Evenings I have usefully & pleasantly spent with Mr Pope, Mr Parnel, Dean Swift, the Doctor,[1] &c. I should be glad the World knew you admitted me to your Friendship: and, since your Affection is too hard for your Judgement, I am contented to let the World see, how well Mr Pope can write upon a barren Subject. I return you an exact Copy of the Verses, that I may keep the Original, as a Testimony of the Only Error you have been guilty of. I hope very speedily to Embrace you in London, and to assure you of the particular Esteem & Friendship wherewith I am | S^r | Your most faithful | & most humble Servant | Oxford.

I keep the Printed Paper, because I think | you have more of them.[2]

Here is the text of the dedication as Pope printed it:[3]

[1] Dr Arbuthnot.

[2] I print the text of these two letters by kind permission of the Marquess of Bath. I owe my text of them to the kindness of Professor Sherburn, who has since printed them at ii. 90 f. of his edition.

[3] The text of the poem as Harley received it in manuscript is printed in smaller type.

TO THE

Right Honourable,

R O B E R T,

Earl of *OXFORD*

AND

Earl MORTIMER.

S UCH were the Notes, thy once-lov'd Poet
   sung,
'Till Death untimely stop'd his tuneful Tongue.
Oh just beheld, and lost! admir'd, and mourn'd!
With softest Manners, gentlest Arts, adorn'd!
Blest in each Science, blest in ev'ry Strain!   [5]
Dear to the Muse, to HARLEY dear—in vain!
  For him, thou oft hast bid the World attend,
Fond to forget the Statesman in the Friend;
For *Swift* and him, despis'd the Farce of State,
The sober Follies of the Wise and Great;   [10]
Dextrous, the craving, fawning Crowd to quit,
And pleas'd to 'scape from Flattery to Wit.

To the Right Honourable,
Robert Earl of Oxford & Earl Mortimer

Such were the Notes thy once lov'd Poet sung,
When Death untimely stop'd his tuneful tongue.
Oh just beheld, and lost! admired, and mourn'd!
With softest manners, gentlest arts adorn'd!
Blest in each Science, blest in evry Strain!   [5]
Dear to the Muse, to Harley dear—in vain!
  For him, thou oft hast bid the World attend,
Fond to forget the Statesman in the Friend;
For Swift and him, despis'd the Farce of State,
The sober Follies of the Wise and Great;   [10]
Dextrous, the craving, fawning Crowd to quit,
And pleas'd escape from Flattery to Wit.

Absent or dead, still let a Friend be dear,
(A Sigh the Absent claims, the Dead a Tear)
Recall those Nights that clos'd thy toilsom Days,   [15]
Still hear thy *Parnell* in his living Lays:
Who careless, now, of Int'rest, Fame, or Fate,
Perhaps forgets that OXFORD e'er was Great;
Or deeming meanest what we greatest call,
Beholds thee glorious only in thy Fall.   [20]
And sure if ought below the Seats Divine
Can touch Immortals, 'tis a Soul like thine:
A Soul supreme, in each hard Instance try'd,
Above all Pain, all Anger, and all Pride,
The Rage of Pow'r, the Blast of publick Breath,   [25]
The Lust of Lucre, and the Dread of Death.
In vain to Desarts thy Retreat is made;
The Muse attends thee to the silent Shade:
'Tis hers, the brave Man's latest Steps to trace,
Re-judge his Acts, and dignify Disgrace.   [30]
When Int'rest calls off all her sneaking Train,
When all th' Oblig'd desert, and all the Vain;

Absent, or dead, let either Friend be dear,
(A Sigh the Absent claims, the Dead a Tear)
Still think on those gay Nights of toilsome Days,   [15]
Still hear thy Parnell in his living Lays;
Who careless now of Int'rest, Fame, or Fate,
Perhaps forgets that Oxford e'er was Great;
Or deeming meanest what we greatest call,
Beholds thee glorious only in thy Fall.   [20]
Yet sure, if ought below the Seats divine
Can touch Immortals, 'tis a Soul like thine:
A Soul supream, in each hard Instance try'd,
Above all Pain, all Anger, and all Pride,
The Rage of Pow'r, the Blast of publick Breath,   [25]
The Lust of Lucre, and the Dread of Death.
In vain to Desarts thy Retreat is made;
Fame, and the Muse, pursue thee to the Shade.
'Tis theirs, the Brave man's latest steps to trace,
Re-judge his Acts, and dignify Disgrace,   [30]
Wait, to the Scaffold, or the silent Cell,
When the last lingring Friend has bid farewell,
Tho' In'trest calls off all her sneaking Train,
Tho' next the Servile drop thee, next the Vain,

She waits, or to the Scaffold, or the Cell,
When the last ling'ring Friend has bid farewel.
Ev'n now she shades thy Evening Walk with Bays,   [35]
(No Hireling she, no Prostitute to Praise)
Ev'n now, observant of the parting Ray,
Eyes the calm Sun-set of thy Various Day,
Thro' Fortune's Cloud One truly Great can see,
Nor fears to tell, that MORTIMER is He.   [40]

A. POPE.

Sept. 25.
1721.

Tho' distanc't one by one th' Oblig'd desert,   [35]
And ev'n the Grateful are but last to part;
My Muse attending strews thy path with Bays,
(A Virgin Muse, not prostitute to praise),
She still with pleasure eyes thy Evening Ray,
The calmer Sunsett of thy Various Day;   [40]
One truly Great thro' Fortune's Cloud can see,
And dares to tell, that Mortimer is He.

A. Pope.[1]

We know from his letter what Harley thought of the poem,
even in its inferior penultimate form. We can only infer what
Swift thought. But we may infer with confidence his deep grati-
fication. He had suggested something perhaps like Dryden's
'To the Memory of Mr. Oldham', but here was a poem swelling
beyond Parnell to his circle the Scriblerus Club, and to one of
its greatest literary figures, Swift, and to its great public figure,
Swift's hero, to whom it was dedicated. The original suggestion
was overwhelmed, and with Pope's finest poetry, the only poetry
not translation which, during 1721 and longer, he seems to have
allowed himself to write.

4

It was Pope's practice to crowd even shorter poems with as
much matter as possible, and that of different sorts. He there-

---

[1] This manuscript is the property of the Marquess of Bath, with whose permission its text is here printed. Norman Ault printed the last ten lines in his *New
Light on Pope*, 1949, p. 23.

fore planned these shorter pieces with an Ovidian care. Such care was particularly necessary when the poem was short: a short poem of bits and pieces must offer those bits and pieces neatly packed. A poet, Horace had counselled, must use art, but art that hides itself. But from whom? The art that is beyond the discovery of the attentive reader is the art that is part and parcel of the 'inspired' thought, and which is the result of a poet's mind habituated to want to produce certain effects. There was art in the making of

> eyes thy Evening Ray,
> The calmer Sunsett of thy Various Day

and in the re-making of it into:

> Eyes the calm Sun-set of thy Various Day.

There was art here, or, to begin with, the needs of the metre would not have been met; and better art in the revision. But we cannot explain it. The finger can touch it a little more certainly when we find that

> Above all Pain, all Anger, and all Pride

becomes, when reprinted in the *Works* of 1735 (where the Epistle is given pride of place)

> Above all Pain, all Passion, and all Pride.

But though surer, our explanation is not more than superficial. When, however, we turn from the clauses and phrases of the poem to its structure, we meet an art which is more readily tangible. An argument has a course: we may be able to discuss sequence and relationship when we cannot discuss the nature of what it is that is sequential or related. How much, then, can we say of the sequence and relationships of Pope's poem?

I have suggested that when Swift proposed that Pope should write the 'few Verses', he had in mind those few of Dryden's on the death of Oldham; and there can be no doubt that at some point, or points, Pope had. The occasion was similar: the great poet mourning the untimely loss of the smaller poet who had become his friend. Certainly Pope echoed Dryden's poem, both echoing Virgil.[1] But, as we might expect, Pope compresses Dryden's poem into 'few Verses' indeed:

> Such were the Notes,[2] thy once-lov'd Poet sung,
> 'Till Death untimely stop'd his tuneful Tongue.[3]
> Oh just beheld, and lost! admir'd, and mourn'd!
> With softest Manners, gentlest Arts, adorn'd!
> Blest in each Science,[4] blest in ev'ry Strain![5]
> Dear to the Muse . . .
> . . . the Dead [claim] a Tear . . .
> . . . *Parnell* in his living Lays.

Parnell has to rest content with these few lines and snatches. But even of these he is not the sole tenant. Pope's poem is not an elegy (in the sense of 'a few Verses on his friend Parnels memory'): it is an epistle. Unlike an epitaph, an elegy is a poem expressing a relationship, that between the dead and the surviving friend; and usually the surviving friend is the author. But to include an elegy in an epistle is to introduce a further relationship, that between the author and the recipient.

---

[1] Cf. with Pope's
  Oh just beheld, and lost! admir'd, and mourn'd!
Dryden's
  Farewell, too little and too lately known.
Both recall Virgil's lines on Marcellus, *Æneid*, vi. 869 f.:
  Ostendent terris hunc tantum fata nec ultra
  Esse sinent. . . .
which Dryden had translated with
  This Youth (the blissful Vision of a day)
  Shall just be shown on Earth, and snatch'd away.
Dryden had also referred to Oldham as Marcellus:
  Once more, hail, and farewell! farewell, thou young,
  But ah! too short, *Marcellus* of our Tongue.

[2] 'Such . . .': Pope was publishing only a selection from the pieces Parnell left him, that made in the first place by Parnell (see p. 166 above). The rest that were in his possession Pope kept by him till his death, when Spence pleaded in vain against their destruction. Some, or all, of these poems existed in one or more other copies, and were printed later in the century (see the bibliography in G. A. Aitken's edition, 1894, p. lxviii f.). These posthumous poems did not add to Parnell's fame, which was high until well into the nineteenth century. Some of them had been printed during his lifetime.

[3] Cf. the 'Elegy [on] Waller's *Poem of Divine Love*', in Dryden's third miscellany, *Examen Poeticum*, 2nd edn. 1706, p. 116:
  Such were the last, the sweetest notes that hung
  Upon our dying Swan's melodious Tongue.

[4] That is, 'subject' of knowledge.

[5] Pope is complimenting Parnell on the variety of metres used in his poems.

The presence of the recipient removes Pope's poem farther from Dryden's. Moreover, Pope removes himself from his poem as much as he can. Dryden had used the 'I' boldly: Pope hides himself behind 'the Muse'. Though we *feel* that it is he who is speaking, we *see* him speaking of others. It is a nice point to his credit as a man. Of course Pope signs the poem. But that is not to be inside it. Johnson deprecated those personal poems that did not introduce the person(s) by name in the body of the poem.[1] To be named in a poem was a chance of immortality highly esteemed. Pope withdraws in favour of his three friends. And also in favour of poetry, since 'the Muse' suggests that poetry is the work of an impersonal agent, impersonal and therefore impartial, an agent acting from the days of Homer downwards—rather than the work of this or that man. Pope's withdrawal is also in favour of friendship, since it suggests that, unlike poetry, friendship is dependent on men, a thing men are proud to have achieved of themselves. The withdrawal of the author from his poem—he exists suggested as a person only in his extraneous signature—united the dead and the recipient without his agency, as it were over his head.

The relationship between Parnell and Harley is stated at once. Harley, whose name and title had been emblazoned at the head of the poem in large capitals, intrudes even into the few lines that are all that Parnell is allowed. Parnell is 'thy' poet;[2] he has been 'beheld' and 'admir'd' by Harley, and is now 'lost' and 'mourn'd' by him. But so far, at least, the relationship has been fairly level: if Harley has his capitals and his pervasiveness, Parnell has his concise, warm, bright praise. The first paragraph ends, however, with the balance tilted in favour of Harley:

> . . . to HARLEY dear—in vain!

(At the moment I am not concerned with the significance of the typography.)

---

[1] *Lives of the Poets*, i. 35 f. and iii. 257.

[2] The affixing of the possessive pronoun to the proper name indicates, especially since the name is that of a poet, that a precious thing is being treasured against the possible attacks of barbarians. Milton had showed the power of the possessive in 'What needs my Shakespeare for his honour'd bones'.

The bright Parnell is already diminished, but he persists farther into the poem, even as far as into its third paragraph. In the second, however, he suffers an almost total eclipse. His relationship with Harley, which is given its concisest expression in 'him, thou', dims beside a new relationship, that between Harley and another survivor, Swift, whom Pope signalizes as greater than Parnell simply by the place he gives his name in the line and the place of the line in the paragraph:

> For him, . . .
> For *Swift* and him, . . .

(Again, I am not yet concerned with the significance of the typography.) The Parnell-Harley relationship persists into the third paragraph in 'Absent or dead', Swift being the absent friend, Parnell the dead—Swift had last seen Harley just before his fall in 1714. (The transition between these paragraphs is as firm as any in Pope: 'Absent or dead' quietly carried Swift and Parnell over the second chasm, just as the 'For him' had quietly carried over the first all that had been so far said of Parnell.) In those three words, however, the Parnell-Swift and the Swift-Harley relationships cease, survived by that between Harley and Parnell, which suddenly blazes to its height. Even Parnell, now on his last appearance, has a flash of splendour, as the author of 'Lays' which are 'living' (Pope had put on his title-page the words from Horace, 'Dignum laude virum Musa vetat mori'). But he never gets clear of Harley: even his immortal soul is still related to him; 'careless now' he 'Perhaps forgets'— what? Matters of concern to the practical world, and some matters perhaps still of concern to a spirit, 'Int'rest, Fame, or Fate', but also something particular about Harley, 'that OXFORD e'er was Great'. What he 'beholds' is again something particular about Harley, Harley 'glorious in thy Fall'. If Parnell persists vividly, still it is as the weaker end of a relationship. And at this point even that uneven relationship, as a thing receiving expression, ceases. The final dismissal of Parnell is done gradually in 'if ought below the Seats Divine Can touch Immortals': Parnell fades into the general shining crowd of the dead. And now Harley is free to occupy the rest of the poem, a great person followed, observed, and proclaimed by 'The

Muse', who speaks with more authority than Pope of himself
could, and who speaks with a startling honesty:

(No Hireling she, no Prostitute to Praise)

'Nor fears to tell' what it is she sees: 'A Soul supreme', 'One
truly Great'.

Harley's greatness is even attested by means of a change in
the quality of the transitions between the paragraphs of the
poem. The first two were presented as coming within the poet's
control, so to speak, as a discernible part of his plan, of the logic
of his procedure. Their force lay in their deliberate rightness.
The third is a transition that is more like a boiling-over than an
arrangement. Even the transitions of arrangement had been
lovingly done: 'For him . . . Absent or dead' were transitions
charged with feeling. But the feeling rises when the third transition, instead of controlling feeling, is overborne by it. The
emotion of the poem by now is rising sharply. 'Such *were* the
Notes, thy *once*-lov'd Poet sung': the beautiful poems were first
seen as things belonging to the past. Now they are alive again,
are 'hear[d]'[1] and 'living Lays', just as their dead author is still
alive, though 'careless now' of worldly matters, unless—and
here is the passionate transition—he still, a soul himself, remem-
bers Harley's soul, a soul so supreme that, if anything is recalled
by the careless, living dead, ''tis a Soul', anybody's if 'like thine'.

Between the last two paragraphs the force of the transition is
quiet. It is still a transition affecting the emotions: the urgency
of the 'And sure' is past, and quiet emotion simmers in its 'In
vain,' words heavy for Pope's first readers with the *nequiquam*s
of the Roman poets. But though 'made of' emotion, the transition is one of arrangement. The first two words of the last
paragraph repeat the last two of the first:

. . . in vain! . . .
In vain . . .[2]

They are beautifully in place. Their quietness is also necessary
to separate the preceding climax from that with which the poem
closes.

[1] Pope may be recalling a practice of reading verses aloud favoured by Harley
(see *Journal to Stella*, ed. H. Williams, 1948, p. 145 f.).

[2] Gray owed something to this patterning. He began and ended his sonnet on
the death of West with these words.

5

The plan of the poem is also observable in its words taken as units, even in its typography.

Look first at its use of the word 'great'. Pope introduces this word when, not content with dubbing public affairs a 'Farce', he also dubs them

The sober Follies of the Wise and Great.

In such a context 'Great' means no more than 'highly placed'. At meetings of the Scriblerus Club, so potent was the charm of Swift's irony that statesmanship appeared temporarily as no fit work for the wise: when you did get an odd case, such as Harley's, of a man not only 'great' but wise, then his political duties seemed one of his comical weaknesses, perhaps disguised from himself, as from the public, by its soberness.[1] On its second and third appearances in the poem, the word 'great' has the same meaning: Parnell, now among the immortals,

Perhaps forgets that OXFORD e'er was Great;
Or deeming meanest what we greatest call,
Beholds thee glorious only in thy Fall.

The remainder of the poem shows Harley to be wise as well as great, shows him escaping the dangers of office, namely 'Pride', 'The Rage of Pow'r',[2] and 'The Lust of Lucre'. And the escape is possible because, for once, great place is occupied by 'One *truly* Great'. Pope's stride across the boundary between two meanings of a common word, between 'great of place' and 'great of soul', helps the poem to achieve its last climax.

[1] Pope's meaning was missed by Gilbert Wakefield: 'There seems to my judgement an incongruity in this association of characters. Should [Pope] not have written,
The sober follies of the *proud* and great?
no otherwise distinguishable from the *freaks* of Bedlamites, than as acted by men not literally frantic' (*The Works of Alexander Pope*, 1794, p. 285). Pope is adapting to new ends a common phrase of the time: Joseph Trapp in his poem 'To the Right Honourable Mr. Harley, On His appearing in Publick after the Wound given Him by *Guiscard*', had compared Harley to Julius Caesar as being 'like him Wise and Great'. In *The Drapier's Letters* Swift was to refer to Harley as 'the greatest, the wisest, and the most uncorrupt Minister, I ever conversed with' (ed. H. Davis, 1935, p. 127).
[2] Johnson borrowed this Johnsonian phrase for *The Vanity of Human Wishes*, l. 33.

There is a similar progression in the use of the word 'friend', and again with the advantage of pulling the sections of the poem more closely together. For Parnell's sake Harley is

> Fond to forget the Statesman in the Friend.

And later there is the gnomic line:

> Absent or dead, still let a Friend be dear.[1]

This straightforward use of the word implies that friendship of this quality is friendship as Harley and Pope understand and practise it. But alas, not all friends are staunch, and, at a crisis, though the fair-weather ones may survive such hangers-on as are interested, obliged, and vain, they depart at last: the Muse

> . . . waits, or to the Scaffold, or the Cell,
> When the last ling'ring Friend has bid farewel.

We should not be so sure of the irony in this last use of the word, its almost visible inverted commas, if its use earlier in the poem had not made it clear that for Pope friendship was of first importance.

Further, Pope marks the progress of the poem by means of proper names, and his manner of printing them. It was the practice of contemporary printers to distinguish proper names by a special type, by using italic (*Pope*), large caps. (POPE), small caps. (POPE), a mixture of large and small (POPE), or in the italic versions of these last three. In the printing of Pope's poem, as many as three of these methods are used, and therefore used designedly. Parnell and Swift are given italics. This leaves the ground clear for typography that matters. Harley is distinguished by ordinary initial caps. and small caps. ('HARLEY' and 'OXFORD') until his final appearance in large caps. as 'MORTIMER'. The typography, however, is only a second string to Pope's bow. By good fortune Pope's dedicatee had four names clustered in an 'extraordinarily worded Earldom':[2] Baron Harley of Wigmore (the ancient seat of the Mortimers,

---

[1] Cf. Pope to Swift, 22 March 1740–1: 'Death has not used me worse in separating from me for ever, poor Gay, Arbuthnot, &c, than Disease & Distance in separating You so many years' (Pope, *Correspondence*, ii. 337).

[2] G. E. C., *The Complete Peerage*, 1945, x. 264.

in Herefordshire, the 'Desarts' of the poem), Earl of Oxford, and Earl Mortimer. Pope makes use of three of them (to have used the fourth, Wigmore, would have been pedantic—no one used it). When he is speaking of Harley as the friend of Parnell and Swift, he uses his family name, the name representing him as a human being on a level with other human beings born with the names Parnell and Swift. When he is speaking of Harley as holding high office, he gives him the name which, after his elevation to the peerage in 1711, was in general use, the name 'Oxford'. But Harley had also the title Mortimer. He had been given it for fear that claimants to the Oxford title still survived—it had become extinct as recently as 1702. The further title had been extinct much longer. At the time Harley acquired the title Oxford, lawyers had called that name 'the noblest in the land'.[1] But the associations of 'Mortimer' were nobler still: it sounded nobler, and had nobler literary connotations. Who could forget that line of Mortimer's soliloquy in 1 *Henry VI*:

> Here dies the dusky torch of Mortimer,

or the two epistles passing between an earlier Mortimer and Queen Isabel in Drayton's still-popular *England's Heroical Epistles?* Moreover, the latter Mortimer was the hero of Drayton's *Barons' Wars*, entitled in its first form *Mortimeriados*. So in the last line of the poem 'OXFORD' gives place to 'MORTIMER'. This climax of Pope's must be brief, if it is to fit a poem in which so much has found a place. To attain brevity Pope uses every device he has. If we had been given 'OXFORD' we should have missed both the almost brandishable sonority of 'Mortimer' and its connotations of heroic greatness.

And, finally, among the agents binding together the remarkably varied matter of the poem, there is the diction, which works through alternations, beginning in the second paragraph, of softness and harshness. The poem opens almost as might a pastoral: its pipe is the oaten reed. And this innocency is, so to

---

[1] op. cit., p. 262. Scott in the Introductory chapter to *Waverley* was to speak of 'the most sounding and euphonic surname that English history . . . affords, and . . . the chivalrous epithets of Howard, Mordaunt, Mortimer, or Stanley'.

speak, the woof of the poem, the weft being harsh as hemp. A constant interchange is kept up between phrases like 'tuneful Tongue', 'softest Manners', 'silent Shade', 'calm Sun-set' and words like 'Farce', 'Blast', 'Lust', 'sneaking',[1] 'Hireling', the harshest Saxon beloved of satirists rasping through the Sicilian. The harsh words keep the poem from languishing. Pope gives no particulars, and so cannot rely on the means of vividness that details provide readily. But the general is not necessarily feeble. Pope does not fall into the error remarked by Johnson, who complained that Sprat's life of Cowley gives 'so little detail that scarcely anything is distinctly known'.[2] Pope can give no details without writing a different sort of poem, one much longer and one necessarily less dignified. He chooses his focus and sticks to it. But though he cannot give details, he can be sharp.

6

If Pope's poem is an occasional one, and one with an occasion of this status—a rough parallel in our own time would be to suppose that Mr T. S. Eliot were presenting the poems of Sidney Keyes to Sir Anthony Eden—it follows that we cannot forget the man, Pope. If he excludes himself from his Epistle as much as he can, we grab him when he affixes his signature to it. His poem is as much a political article in a newspaper as a poem: if it is an epistle, it is also an 'open letter'. We judge it as we judge any poem, we also judge it as we judge any prose testimonial: we ask whether or not Pope's verses can meet the claim he made for them in the covering letter to Harley, the claim that they are 'honest verses'. (I do not concern myself with the further question asked by Pope's contemporaries: 'Is Pope attacking the Hanoverians and the Whigs in praising a fallen Tory statesman of the last Stuart?' Grattan was to note that to write Pope's Epistle required courage.[3])

They can seem incompletely honest only to those who are

---

[1] In Pope's day pronounced as we should pronounce *snaking*.

[2] *Lives of the Poets*, i. 1.

[3] 'Repeated Pope's lines to Lord Oxford with great enthusiasm. They required courage in Pope.' Grattan, in Rogers' *Recollections*, 1859, p. 94.

blinded by the blaze of the climax praising the 'Soul like thine'.[1] But, of course, to make that praise blind us was Pope's aim. Praise of that degree is implied as a hoped-for possibility in any dedicatory poem, as a probability in any dedicatory poem by a major poet. In trying to rise to a great occasion, a poet has to see the occasion as even greater than it is. Being a poem, it must go all out, at least at its climax. At this point in his poem Pope is deep in panegyric, and that sort of writing is notoriously liable to bathos: two years earlier the author of *A letter of Advice to a Young Poet* had noted that 'All panegyrics are mingled with an infusion of poppy'.[2] If in a passage of panegyric the poet vacillates, his very metre rots. But there may be a simpler explanation of the effect produced by those four lines: it may be due to Pope's describing sublime virtue in terms of its opposite. He does not tell us what Harley's soul was, but what it was 'beyond', and he therefore turns to the things in a politician that men hate, things that prompt in all but some of the saintly a vivider emotion. Pope knew that his panegyric was better poetry—better because more fiercely sensuous—for turning round from virtue and facing instead

---

[1] The first tribute to Pope's praise of Harley is that recorded by Aaron Hill in his letter of 13 October 1746 (*Correspondence of Samuel Richardson*, 1804, i. 112 ff.). Hill relates how, in conversation with Pope, he forced him into a trap from which he could escape only by affecting to belittle either his poem or a great man—for how could he square the sense of the line, 391, in *An Essay on Criticism*—

For fools *admire*; but men of sense *approve*

—with the evidence that Arthur Onslow, the Speaker of the House of Commons, was greatly moved by Pope's praise of Harley: 'at reading a new play at Lord Tyrconnel's there was present a gentleman, distinguished both for rank and genius, who, on a discourse about the difficulty of a delicate and manly praise, repeated those fine lines, in compliment to the earl of Oxford, printed before D. Parnell's poems.—I added, that this gentleman had been so generously warmed, in his repeating them, that he was the most undeniable example I had ever seen of all Longinus's effect of the sublime, in its most amiable force of energy! for, (breaking off into a humanised excess of rapture, that expressed philanthropy with such a natural beauty, that, had he been my greatest enemy, I must have, from that moment, been compelled to love him for it) he told us, "He could never read those verses without rapture; for, that sentiments such as those were, appeared to carry more of the god in them than the man, and he was never weary of admiring them!"' (If Pope had remembered his *Essay* closely he could have evaded Hill's trap. What the 'fools' are gaping at ('admiring') is not sublime poetry but the succession of striking phrases, 'each gay turn'.)

[2] Swift, *Works*, ed. Scott, 1814, ix. 448.

The strong Antipathy of Good [, the] Bad.[1]

Pope, then, does blind us with his climax of praise. But though the soul of Harley as a politician is seen as perfect, Pope's vision of it is arrived at by selection rather than by fabrication. To see that this is so, we have only to consult the writings of Swift. For all his disappointment at Harley's failure to get him the post of historiographer and no nearer or greater glory than the deanery of St Patrick's, Swift saw to it that nothing prevented his reporting the cause of Harley aright to his own age and to posterity. The hard work he put in as historian and critic of that administration has the purposiveness of a campaign. And though Swift's praise of Harley lacks the sensuous glow of Pope's, it is not less superlative. For Swift Harley was, to choose only four of his judgements, 'the most fearless man alive',[2] 'an utter despiser of money for himself',[3] 'the humblest of men in the height of his power',[4] and 'Fear, cruelty, avarice, and pride, are wholly strangers to his nature'.[5] Swift's bequest to Pope of his miniature of Harley marks the closeness of their views on the subject.

Swift, however, wrote of Harley with the judiciousness of the responsible historian, and therefore with due sense of his failings. If, for him, the good in Harley heavily outweighed the bad, he paid due attention to what existed in the other scale. In a dedication, Pope cannot actually demonstrate that he is being judicious as, in his prose accounts, Swift could and did. He is judicious, nevertheless. He sees in his hero some of the failings Swift sees, and at least hints them. Pope does not, and cannot, say outright that Harley was a procrastinator, that his admired calm was sometimes that of the hopeful drifter; that, as Johnson came to put it, he was caught with

pow'r too great to keep, or to resign.[6]

But reading his poem carefully, we see that Pope was not blind to these faults. To 'bid the World attend' is a finer compliment

---

[1] 'The Epilogue to the Satires', Dialogue II, 198.
[2] *The Journal to Stella*, p. 206.
[3] *Correspondence*, ed. F. E. Ball, 1910, i. 280.
[4] Quoted by E. S. Roscoe, *Robert Harley*, 1902, p. 198.
[5] *Prose Works*, ed. Temple Scott, 1902, x. 93 f.
[6] *The Vanity of Human Wishes*, l. 134.

to Parnell's wit than to a statesman's sense of responsibility; there is some ground for political uneasiness in the word 'Fond'; no statesman should despise 'the Farce of State' lest he should come too near despising the state itself; nor can we admire the statesman who likes his private pleasures to the point of having acquired a 'dexterity' in 'escaping' to them, even if it is only from the 'craving, fawning Crowd'.[1] Harley, Pope says outright, did suffer a 'Fall'; during two years of unduly prolonged imprisonment (owing to alleged Jacobite sympathies) he faced 'the Scaffold or the Cell'. Nor does Pope blink what is least pleasant in Harley's rustication; he has made a 'Retreat' after his 'Fall', and that to the 'Desarts' on the Welsh border, where instead of buzzing with curiosity the 'Shade' is 'silent';[2] he is under a 'Cloud', and a 'Disgrace' that stands in need of being given its 'digni[ty]'. The climax of Pope's poem is a blaze, but the recovering eye is aware that Harley is human after all. Pope does not suffer any repercussion from that fierce line

No Hireling she, no Prostitute to Praise.

[1] Swift has several descriptions of the crowds at Harley's levees, e.g. 'I cald at Ld Treasr's it was his Levee day but I went up to his Bedchamber; & sd what I had to say; I came down & peept in at the Chamber where a hundred Fools were waiting, and 2 Streets were full of Coaches' (*Journal to Stella*, p. 499).

[2] From 1650, according to the *OED*, *shade* came to be used metaphorically of the 'comparative obscurity' of 'retirement'. Pope had already written in *Windsor Forest*, ll. 431 f:

Ev'n I more sweetly pass my careless days,
Pleas'd in the silent shade with empty praise.

The usage seems to have been prompted by Ovid, *Amores*, ii. xviii. 3: 'ignava Veneris cessamus in umbra'.

'GRONGAR HILL'
AN INTRODUCTION AND TEXTS

IN THE last ten[1] years or so readers of poetry have been presented with the Four Quartets of Mr Eliot, each 'quartet' a poem about two hundred lines long, named after a place that most readers had not known to exist. And here is a poem from two centuries ago, a poem of similar length, named after a hill in Carmarthenshire almost as obscure as any Burnt Norton.[2] On this basis of length and stated subject, one might well compare a 'quartet' of Mr Eliot's with Dyer's 'Grongar Hill'. Among all their many differences, we should find one obvious point of agreement: both poems would disappoint the readers who expected from them a literary equivalent for the picture postcard, or, since they are longish poems, for those paper concertinas of local views that one used to buy at the seaside. In other words, neither a 'quartet' of Mr Eliot's nor 'Grongar Hill' is a poem made up of description, of description of what the later eighteenth century began to call scenery. There were poets in the nineteenth century who tried to make even longish poems that had nothing to them save scenery, but a poem that is all description is a poem relying on the five senses, and normally they cannot operate for long without provoking the jealous participation of the intellect. At some point, not usually long delayed, thinking breaks in. We do not like our sense experience raw, or not for long, and it is thinking that cooks it. If we go on a walking tour, the peaks and the meadows, the lakes and the torrents, are one sort of ingredient and only one, in a complicated activity to which thinking and affection contribute other sorts. A longish poem made out of 'pure description' —that is Pope's phrase of about the time of 'Grongar Hill'—

---

[1] This was written in 1948; I note the date because of certain things said later.

[2] A group of farm people I spoke to in 1959 a few miles from Grongar Hill had no idea where it was.

does not correspond to anything we experience in the normal course of living. But that has not prevented some poets from trying their hand at such poems.

Our hope that Dyer would not be among them may shrink when we discover that in 1720, six years before the poem was first published, he had taken up painting. Four years later, in 1724, he went off to Italy to study pictures. We do not know enough about his life to know how his study proceeded. Some evidence exists that it prospered. At any rate, Dyer did not forget his painting in his poem. He saw his poem as needing all the help it could get from his professional knowledge, especially of painting in the Italian style, of what the painters of his time, their eye trained by Claude Lorrain and Salvator Rosa, were finding to admire most in the visible world. Dyer tried to define his twin allegiance to poetry and to painting in the first paragraph of his poem. 'Silent nymph': that 'stands for' painting: painting is silent because, unlike poetry which uses words, it uses colours. But Dyer, with the hill spread out before him, sees that he wants words as near paint as words can get. He therefore imagines himself as calling on the presiding genius of painting, who, though silent, keeps a store of colours, to help the presiding genius of poetry who, though using nothing but words, on this occasion needs words that describe what a painter would paint:

> Come with all thy various hues
> Come, and aid thy sister Muse.

Writers of the later seventeenth and early eighteenth centuries had frequently discussed the neighbouring provinces of poetry and painting, and soon Lessing's *Laokoon* was to draw all the discussion into fine shape. Dyer is setting out, then, to paint a picture with words.

I have said that our hope that the poem would not prove to be all description might shrink when we found its author to be a painter. But even at the outset we are reassured. For even in the way he begins his poem, calling on the help of painting, there is evidence of an intellectuality. Dyer does not merely colour his poem with words like 'purple' and 'lustre', as if he were a child colouring paper: he understands what he is

doing; he introduces us to problems in aesthetics, problems
that were engaging the critics of his time. And something else
might have reassured us. If Dyer was a painter, he was a
painter painting in the eighteenth century. In that century, of
all others, 'pure description', sustained for any length that we
should count tedious, was unthinkable. For the eighteenth
century was the time when everybody made it their business to
assert the primacy of man, his superiority over the rest of the
creation. Even Thomson, who painted pictures furiously in
words, saw that

> . . . Man superior walks
> Amid the glad creation.[1]

and, seeing that, he saw to it that man walked superior in
his poem as long and pictorial as a roll of wallpaper. It was
agreed on all hands that 'The proper study of mankind is man'
—that the study proper to the individuals composing the
human race was the human race. Mankind was the proper
subject for every man, however much he liked cultivating his
own individual gifts and idiosyncrasies. Even the musicians
and painters of the time, the sculptors and the architects,
undertook the study. The painters, for instance, seldom painted
a picture without allowing a place for man in it, or if not a place,
a trace. It was the age of magnificent portraits, cartoons, and
social scenes, and if it was also the age of landscape pictures,
almost all of them have their shepherds or girls or house or
bridge or spire. And if they lack these, they do not lack a trace
of man in animals that he has tamed.

Moreover, in the history of English poetry Dyer's poem is
not the first poem with a place name for title. In particular,
right back in the 1640's, there had been Denham's 'Cooper's
Hill', a poem which after being venerated for half a century,
started a fashion, a craze even, so that, by the end of the
eighteenth century, every English hill, boasted a poet on its
summit. The craze for the hill poem was part of the craze for
the local poem: we have above all Pope's *Windsor Forest* and
Gray's 'Ode on a Distant Prospect of Eton College'. But the
craze for the local poem was not a craze merely for topography;

---

[1] See above, p. 31.

it was a craze for thinking amid topography—by 'thinking' I mean contemplating, mental perception. When Pope used the phrase 'pure description', he applied it to his early poems— *The Pastorals* and *Windsor Forest* primarily. But even in those poems the result of the proper study was vividly present. And so it was in all descriptive poems written before the nineteenth century. Only later did poets seek to escape from their fellows. 'Grongar Hill', a poem by a writer who made the proper study, is as much concerned with man as with a hill, as much concerned with man as were *Windsor Forest*, 'Cooper's Hill' or (to name another early and thoroughly human descriptive poem) Marvell's 'Upon Appleton House'.

I have called in Marvell's poem because 'Grongar Hill', in the form it finally assumed, forsook the heroic couplets of Denham and Pope for the four-beat couplets of Marvell and the author of 'L'Allegro' and 'Il Penseroso'. And perhaps, for this reason, the thinking of 'Grongar Hill' reminds one more strongly of seventeenth-century thinking than of eighteenth. I do not mean seventeenth century thinking at its best, as in the gouge-like thinking of Shakespeare, Donne and Herbert, or at its strenuous worst in the thinking, say, of Cleveland, which has violence rather than power; I mean the reflective thinking done by poets who were writing to be set to music, and so writing thoughts to please rather than impress. Early in his poem Dyer speaks of 'modest' Muses. He can claim to have only the sort of thoughts that occur of themselves to one whose quiet and pleasant mind is not averse to being struck with a reflection. Such minds may be common. What is not common is the capacity to put the quiet and pleasant thought in a form that shares those qualities. An instance comes at lines 116–21. The most famous, however, is more than pleasant—it has the quality which in the eighteenth century was called 'shining'. It is a reflection, but has the luminousness and melodiousness, the purity and simplicity, of the equally famous lines that close the poem. I am referring, of course, to lines 89–92. In the form they take in a version of the poem probably earlier than the version I shall transcribe, they resemble even more closely those of seventeenth-century poets, having their string of images some familiar, others surprising:

Yet Time has seen, that lifts the low,
And level lays the lofty Brow,
Has seen this broken Pile compleat,
Big with the Vanity of State;
But transient is the Smile of Fate!
A little Rule, a little Sway,
A Sun-Beam in a Winter's Day:
So long the Monarch grasps his hold,
So long the Miser sees his Gold,
So long we bloom, so soon we pine,
So long we taste, so soon resign,
Life glides away from you to me;
The World's a Caravansary.

I have said that even a poem written nearer to our own time could not well be without its thinking, but in a poem of the nineteenth or twentieth century the poet is usually thinking about himself, seeing himself as crowned with all the idiosyncracies that mark him off from his fellows. In an eighteenth-century poem the thinking turns on man in general. Which do we find the more interesting? The answer, surely, depends on the quality of the thinking. Thomas Hardy thinking of himself ('He was a man who used to notice such things', 'Said my own voice talking to me') is more interesting than some minor eighteenth-century versifier thinking about man in general; just as obviously, Pope thinking about man in general ('The glory, jest and riddle of the world') is more interesting than a later versifier thinking about himself. But we have seen a time when it was assumed that thought about people as individuals was the only sort of thought worth having. That time has, I think, passed. Eighteenth-century readers expected a writer, even if he were a poet, to think about mankind; we do not expect it, but I believe we are getting to welcome it more warmly than some of us did once upon a time: nowadays an interest in mankind is being forced upon us by the way the world has gone and is going.

The thinking about man done by the poets of the eighteenth century remains pertinent to readers in the twentieth. How could it not? It is pertinent by definition. Sometimes it comes very near us as men in societies. There is, for instance, this

snatch of dialogue from one of Pope's epistles, a couplet painfully on the spot in this decade of shortages:

> What riches give us, let us then enquire [;]
> Meat, Fire, and Cloaths. What more? Meat, Cloaths,
> and Fire.[1]

Otherwise it comes very near us as individuals sharing a common
lot of love and hate. There are frequent instances up and down
Dyer's poem, and we may call them 'silver' commonplaces.
Dyer cannot equal Gray in the making of memorable lines—
those 'divine truisms' that Tennyson said made him weep.[2]
Gray could manage them in lines of five beats and less. Dyer's
are in lines of four beats, and they have none of the forcefulness
Gray put into lines of whatever length. They earn no higher
epithet than 'silver'. Of course they are commonplaces by
design. And perhaps of necessity. Few of us can hope to say
anything about humanity that is not commonplace in the inferior sense. Few can hope to achieve a generalization so startling
as Johnson's in *Rasselas*: 'Perhaps, if we speak with rigorous
exactness, no human mind is in its right state',[3] and in any
case prose not poetry is the proper medium for epoch-making
pronouncements like this. Imlac's remark is now in process of
becoming a commonplace, because it has passed into the hands
of the psychologists—Freud believed that we are all neurotic.
The commonplaces found in poetry are usually as old as poetry
itself. They 'strike the heart' (I am using terms beloved in the
eighteenth century) as well as lay a dusty finger on 'the head'.
And Dyer is lucky in that the commonplaces of 'Grongar Hill'
have a freshness simply because they have not been too much
handled. Unless we have the power and knowledge and skill to
make an effort of the historical imagination, it is impossible to
feel the due power of Gray's truisms simply because they are as
much a part of the language as 'a merry Christmas' is. 'Grongar
Hill' was fairly well known, judging by the number of reprints, until well into the nineteenth century, but few have
read it since the days of their grand-fathers, and so we are the
more ready to be fair to it.

---

[1] *Moral Essays*, iii ('Of the Use of Riches', To Bathurst), 81 f.
[2] See above, p. 116.   [3] See below, p. 244.

Where it is reflective poetry, it is poetry according to Johnson's definition: it exemplifies 'the art of uniting pleasure with truth by calling the imagination to the help of reason'.[1] When it is giving us an equivalent of what a painting gives us, there is an even balance in the poem between thought and imagery. It shows in little what the local poem showed at large, picture plus thinking, the loved physical substance and the happy thought. It is obvious that Dyer liked the earth as much and as well as he liked to think quietly about the problems of its human tenants. And when that joint liking is strong enough, and can put itself into musical words, the result is poetry. Dyer, it is abundantly clear, liked the earth. Particularly its light and shade, and the objects light and shade transfigured. Along with his quietness there is a vigorous delight in power and movement: the eye is active. A recurrent image is that of the embrace. He chose as the theme of his poem the hour before sunset; the evening, he said, was purple, and the epithet for him retains much of its colour. It was the hour before sunset, the hour when gilt lies thickest. Liking his light so, he liked his shade to match. He is even drawn to shade deep and permanent enough for toads to breed in. The dank shades of decayed medieval masonry were already producing their delightful 'gothick' shudder—see lines 71–83. He can also deal with size and complexity: he gives you the feeling that Grongar Hill is vast, solid, intricately various to a man climbing it with his eyes open.

I say climbing 'it', Grongar Hill. But we are dealing with a poet writing in the eighteenth century, and therefore with one who did not feel the same sort of humility before the fact that would be felt by a nineteenth-century poet. By the later date photography was having its effect on descriptive method, bullying poets into observing the distinction between what is visible from a named point and what is not—though it may be known to be round the corner or over the horizon. In the eighteenth and earlier centuries painters verbal and otherwise introduced into a scene what they would have liked it to have included—what they knew they could have seen if they could

---

[1] See below, p. 232.

have been in two places at once. Dyer does not behave quite in this way. It is rather that at some points he is given an inch and takes an ell. And the reason for this is sound at bottom. He is really writing a poem in praise of the Vale of Towy, the loveliest and most evocative[1] of all the valleys of South Wales, and so draws on his knowledge of the whole of it. Grongar Hill indeed is not the best hill to choose. A better would have been Bryn Castell-gwrychion, a mile or two away, rising fifty feet higher than Grongar, and commanding a view grander and more extensive. Indeed at some points he seems to have described the views from that hill rather than Grongar. A local historian, Mr J. F. Jones, tells me that

From Grongar (as also from Bryn Castell-gwrychion) can be seen in the extreme west: the town of Carmarthen ringed by hills (except on the viewing side); beyond, and a little to the left, Green Castle, embowered by trees (this was a seventeenth century castellated residence); between Carmarthen and Grongar, the tall spire of Abergwili Church pushes up above the trees, while near it is the Bishop of St David's Palace; on the right of this stands Merlin's Hill; nearer to the observer are Llanegwad Church and Village, and Llanarthney Church and village; nearer still is Dryslwyn Castle. Looking south-eastwards was the old mansion of Golden Grove (associated with Jeremy Taylor) surrounded with trees. Eastwards of Grongar would be Aberglasney [Dyer's home], Berllar-dywyll (a mansion of somewhat lesser pretensions than Dyer's home), Llangathen Church (containing the tomb of Bishop Rudd, from whose descendants Dyer's father bought Aberglasney), with Bryn Castell-gwrychion as a background. Slightly east south east from Grongar can be seen both the ancient fortress (ruins) of Dynevor, and the later family mansion of the same name set amidst its parkland; while Carreg Cennen Castle is only just discernible over the top of a distant intervening hill.

Now from Bryn Castell-gwrychion can be seen: Carreg Cennen

---

[1] Cf. the Ward Lock *Guide to Tenby, &c.*, 7th ed. 1947, p. 126. 'The Vale of Towy has been called "the heart of South Wales". "It is famous in Welsh life, Welsh history, and Welsh song. In the days of the Welsh Princes it was the political centre of the southern kingdom, and, save Glamorgan, was the most distinguished strip of South Wales. As arms and men abounded here in the days of the Plantagenets . . . so for the same reason do country houses, prosperous or ancient families, and fine farms distinguish the Vale of Towy at this time above most parts of South Wales." '

Castle set on its rocky base, visible in all its glory,[1] with the rocky slopes of the Black Mountains behind; the smoke of the town of Llandeilo rising above the hill on whose further side it stands; a few miles beyond are the houses of Llangadog village, while dimly in the background can be seen the hills and mountains of north Carmarthenshire.

From this hill of Bryn Castell-gwrychion can be got one of the most extensive views of the vale of Towy: from Green Castle (only a few miles upstream from the estuary), up past Carmarthen, along the main reaches of the valley where its course would be winding and slow, past Grongar, curving behind the Dynevor hill and past Llandeilo, where its upper reaches would be hidden between hills at first, and further away, between mountains clad with fern.[2]

If the higher hill were in fact his point of vantage it is easy to see why he named his poem as he did. It was a poem in English intended not only for Welsh readers, and probably for English readers in the first place. Of necessity, therefore, he avoided the use of all thorough-going Welsh names, and the more readily because, by supreme good fortune, the inferior hill standing next to Bryn Castell-gwrychion had a name to charm any ear, whether Welsh or English. Having called his poem as he did, we must assume that he tried to remain true to the facts of Grongar Hill where they suited his purpose, though feeling free to heighten fact in accordance with his memory of the better things round the corner.

The textual history of the poem, even without taking account of the 'pindarique' version, is unusually interesting. It has been examined by Professor R. C. Boys in his edition of the poem.[3] I print below the version that appeared in David Lewis's *Miscellaneous Poems, by Several Hands*. This book was published in 1726, and in the same year, Professor Boys believes, another

[1] The Ward Lock *Guide* describes this castle as 'a ruined fortress south-east of Llandilo [, which] forms one of the most striking sights of this part of Wales': approached on one side it appears as ' "a castle like a rock upon a rock", so perfectly do the walls blend with the crags upon which they stand. They themselves stand up [300 ft.] like cliffs upon a sea-coast' (pp. 135 f.).

[2] In a letter to me, Mr Jones continues: 'On reading his poems on the spot, I seemed to feel a greater linkage between the Grongar countryside and his "Country Walk" than between that countryside and his "Grongar Hill".'

[3] Baltimore, 1941.

version of the poem appeared in a *New Miscellany*, a version I have not seen in the original, but which is reprinted by Professor Boys. There is some doubt about priority as far as this text and that of Lewis is concerned. Professor Boys conjectures 1726 as the date of the *New Miscellany*, but Professor Case in his *English Poetical Miscellanies* 1521–1750[1] firmly dates it 1725. The date must be left in doubt until further evidence is available—a search in the periodicals has not disclosed any advertisement of publication. The text of the *New Miscellany* has some variants from the Lewis text, the most interesting of which I have already quoted. Here is David Lewis's text:

GRONGAR *HILL*.

Silent Nymph, with curious Eye!
Who, the purple Ev'ning, lye
On the Mountain's lonely Van,
Beyond the Noise of busy Man,
Painting fair the form of Things,   [5]
While the yellow Linnet sings;
Or the tuneful Nightingale
Charms the Forest with her Tale;
Come with all thy various Hues,
Come, and aid thy Sister Muse;   [10]
Now while *Phœbus* riding high
Gives Lustre to the Land and Sky!

2. 'the purple Evening', like 'the Even still' (l. 18), is a temporal phrase: cf. Collins's '*Ode to Evening*': 'Elves|Who slept in Buds the Day'; 'Lie', strictly speaking, should be 'lyest' unless, as seems likely, Dyer was aiming at conveying the sense 'art wont to lie'.

3. In this opening of the poem Dyer is speaking generally: the hill called Grongar does not enter the poem till l. 13. There was much confusion in the eighteenth century between the terms *hill* and *mountain*: it is embodied in this poem, the title of which is Grongar *Hill*, but which refers to that hill as a mountain at l. 41. Nowadays a mountain does not officially exist till it is 2,000 ft. above sea level, but as the *OED* notes there is local variation, and the terms are used comparatively. Where an eighteenth-century writer was impressed by the comparative height of a hill he called it by the grander name: the *OED* quotes an English writer of 1766 who describes St Germain, near Paris, as 'situated upon a very high mountain'; it also quotes Gilbert White's description of the Sussex Downs as 'that chain of majestic mountains'. On the other hand, as the *OED* reminds us (s.v. 'hill') *hills*, as used in India often refers to ground 5,000 feet high, because they are so much lower than the heights of the Himalayas.

---

[1] Oxford, 1935, no. 335.

Grongar Hill invites my Song,
Draw the Landskip bright and strong;
Grongar, in whose Mossie Cells   [15]
Sweetly-musing Quiet dwells:
Grongar, in whose silent Shade,
For the modest Muses made,
So oft I have, the Even still,
At the Fountain of a Rill,   [20]
Sate upon a flow'ry Bed,
With my Hand beneath my Head;
And stray'd my Eyes o'er *Towy*'s Flood,
Over Mead, and over Wood,
From House to House, from Hill to Hill,   [25]
'Till Contemplation had her fill.
     About his chequer'd Sides I wind,
And leave his Brooks and Meads behind,
And Groves and Grottoes where I lay,
And Vistoes shooting Beams of Day: [30]
Wider and wider spreads the Vale;
As Circles on a smooth Canal:
The Mountains round, unhappy Fate,
Sooner or later, of all Height!

17 ff. Dyer recalls his visits to the foot of the hill. He does not begin to climb it till l. 27.

20. fountain=source, or spring: cf. l. 105.

21 f. This is an early description of a posture that becomes common later on. The portrait by Wright of Derby of Sir Brooke Boothby in 1781, now in the National Gallery, shows the same posture complete with gloves. The catalogue of the 'Romantic Movement' Exhibition held by the Arts Council, 1959, explained Sir Brooke's attitude as homage to his friend Rousseau, but the pose was well established here before Rousseau gave it impetus. Gray assumes the attitude in 1742; see below, p. 210.

27. Judging from the appearance of the hill today there seems little point in 'chequered' except as homage to Milton (see 'L' Allegro', l. 96). Dyer learns from Milton the art of keeping the syntax going, see e.g. ll. 6 f. above; and also something of the art of writing four-beat verse.

30. *visto,* an alternative form of *vista,* is here used in the sense of 'a long narrow opening', the length of which is reduced by perspective, so that the light seems to shoot through it. Francis Kilvert, the diarist, notes a similar effect, as it happens also in Wales: 'At the Lower House the orchard boughs were so thick and close that the sun could not penetrate them, and the sunlight only got into the orchard at a gap in the west side through which it came streaming in low in a long bright streak along the brilliant green rich velvety-looking grass like sunshine through a painted Cathedral window' (*Kilvert's Diary* 1870–79, ed. William Plomer, 1944, p. 40).

Withdraw their Summits from the Skies,   [35]
And lessen as the others rise:
Still the Prospect wider spreads,
Adds a thousand Woods and Meads;
Still it widens, widens still,
And sinks the newly-risen Hill.   [40]
  Now, I gain the Mountain's Brow,
What a Landskip lies below!
No Clouds, no Vapours intervene,
But the gay, the open Scene
Does the Face of Nature show,   [45]
In all the Hues of Heaven's Bow!
And, swelling to embrace the Light,
Spreads around beyond the Sight.
  Old Castles on the Cliffs arise,
Proudly tow'ring in the Skies!   [50]
Rushing from the Woods, the Spires
Seem from hence ascending Fires!
Half his Beams *Apollo* sheds,
On the yellow Mountain-Heads!
Gilds the Fleeces of the Flocks;   [55]
And glitters on the broken Rocks!
  Below me Trees unnumber'd rise,
Beautiful in various Dies:
The gloomy Pine, the Poplar blue,
The yellow Beech, the sable Yew,   [60]
The slender Firr, that taper grows,
The sturdy Oak with broad-spread Boughs.
And beyond the purple Grove,
Haunt of *Phillis*, Queen of Love!

41. The poet now represents himself as standing at an eastern point of the brow of the hill.

42. Not exaggerated.

45 f. Note the opposition of nature (the earth) and heaven. It is more pointed in the 'pindarique' version, ll. 100 f.

56. No rocks would seem to have been visible from Grongar Hill, or not near enough to be seen to glitter. The sky-line is that of the Black Mountains, which have rocks of carboniferous limestone that may be seen to glitter brightly by those who are near enough to them.

57–62. This passage is best considered as a 'tree-piece', a descriptive indulgence which poets of epic and romance usually allowed themselves. As for pines and firs, such trees are very noticeable in the wood which at present clings to the northern top of the slope of the hill; as for yews they are prominent features of most church yards (Llangathen Church is visible from Grongar Hill); there are a few poplars in the Towy valley.

195

Gawdy as the op'ning Dawn,   [65]
Lies a long and level Lawn,
On which a dark Hill, steep and high,
Holds and charms the wand'ring Eye!
Deep are his Feet in *Towy's* Flood,
His Sides are cloath'd with waving Wood,   [70]
And antient Towers crown his Brow,
That cast an awful Look below;
Whose ragged Walls the Ivy creeps,
And with her Arms from falling keeps;
So both a Safety from the Wind   [75]
In mutual Dependance find.
   'Tis now the Raven's bleak Abode;
'Tis now th' Apartment of the Toad;
And there the Fox securely feeds;
And there the pois'nous Adder breeds,   [80]
Conceal'd in Ruins, Moss and Weeds:
While, ever and anon, there falls,
Huge heaps of hoary moulder'd Walls.
Yet Time has seen, that lifts the low,
And level lays the lofty Brow,   [85]
Has seen this broken Pile compleat,
Big with the Vanity of State;
But transient is the Smile of Fate!

---

66. *Lawn.* There is much flat grazing land, the valley of the Towy being un-usually broad.

ᶜ 67 ff. From Grongar the obvious hill is Dryslwyn, remarkable for its humped cottage-like proportions and the ruined castle on top—huge rough fragments of walls, pierced by arched openings, and a tall corner of one tower. It is perched on top of steep slopes that run down into the bank of the river, so that l. 69 is fairly accurate. The slopes are not now 'clothed in waving wood'; they are dotted with hawthorns. As for the fauna, I may note that within a few miles of the place I saw a dead adder on the road—it had been run over by a car: but adders are not often met with now. Foxes were common in earlier days. Mr Jones thinks Dynevor hill and its castle are meant: in his favour is the *size* of the masonry described at ll. 71–87. Against his view is to be counted the prominence of Drys-lwyn and the oddity of its shape—in the 'pindarique' version of the poem (see below, p. 201, l. 48) the same hill is described as having a 'Form uncommon'.

   Dyer likes to exaggerate the frequency with which ruins shed fragments of themselves: cf. 'The Ruins of Rome', ll. 38 ff:
     . . . The pilgrim oft
   At dead of night, 'mid his oraison hears
   Aghast the voice of time, disparting tow'rs,
   Tumbling all precipitate down-dash'd,
   Rattling around, loud thund'ring to the Moon . . .

A little Rule, a little Sway,
A Sun-Beam in a Winter's Day   [90]
Is all the Proud and Mighty have,
Between the Cradle and the Grave.
   And see the Rivers how they run,
Thro' Woods and Meads, in Shade and Sun,
Sometimes swift, and sometimes slow,   [95]
Wave succeeding Wave they go
A various Journey to the Deep,
Like human Life to endless Sleep!
Thus is Nature's Vesture wrought,
To instruct our wand'ring Thought;   [100]
Thus she dresses green and gay,
To disperse our Cares away.
   Ever charming, ever new,
When will the Landskip tire the View!
The Fountain's Fall, the River's Flow,   [105]
The woody Vallies, warm and low,
The windy Summit, wild and high,
Roughly rushing on the Sky!
The pleasant Seat, the ruin'd Tow'r,
The naked Rock, the shady Bow'r;   [110]
The Town and Village, Dome and Farm, ⎫
Each give each a double Charm,   ⎬
As Pearls upon an *Æthiop's* Arm.   ⎭
   See on the Mountain's southern Side, ⎫
Where the Prospect opens wide,   ⎬   [115]
Where the Ev'ning gilds the Tide; ⎭
How close and small the Hedges lie!
What streaks of Meadows cross the Eye!

93. The 'see', like the 'from hence' at l. 52, is frustrating—there are many streams in this part of the vale other than the Towy itself and some of them perhaps qualify to be called rivers. But only one—the Towy—is visible from Grongar Hill.

105. *fountain* is again used in its tamest possible sense, see l. 20.

109. The most obvious of the pleasant seats is the imposing one of Aberglasney, where Dyer himself lived.

111. The town is Carmarthen. *Dome* is straight from L. *domus*, dwelling.

114. The view southwards is the finest of all, the Towy making a great horse-shoe curve in the middle distance.

117 is accurate.

A Step methinks may pass the Stream,
So little distant Dangers seem;   [120]
So we mistake the Future's face,
Ey'd thro' Hope's deluding Glass;
As yon Summits soft and fair,
Clad in Colours of the Air,
Which, to those who journey near,   [125]
Barren, and brown, and rough appear;
Still we tread tir'd the same coarse Way.
The Present's still a cloudy Day.
    O may I with my self agree,
And never covet what I see: [130]
Content me with an humble Shade,
My Passions tam'd, my Wishes laid;
For while our Wishes wildly roll,
We banish Quiet from the Soul:
'Tis thus the Busy beat the Air;   [135]
And Misers gather Wealth and Care.
    Now, ev'n now, my Joy runs high,
As on the Mountain-turf I lie;
While the wanton *Zephir* sings,
And in the Vale perfumes his Wings;   [140]
While the Waters murmur deep;
While the Shepherd charms his Sheep;
While the Birds unbounded fly,
And with Musick fill the Sky.
Now, ev'n now, my Joy runs high.   [145]
    Be full, ye Courts, be great who will;
Open wide the lofty Door,
Seek her on the marble Floor,
In vain ye search, she is not there;
In vain ye search the Domes of Care!   [150]

119. Dyer is here speaking with his eye on the object, and his poem suffers unless the reader knows the view itself. The Towy is wide, but because of a bank that obstructs the sight of its hither shore, it appears from Grongar Hill to be so narrow at the base of its horse-shoe curve that a step would seem enough to clear it.

146. It may be that there is no omission of a line here, and that l. 146 is intended to rime with ll. 155–7. The text published in the *New Miscellany*, probably about the same time as the text printed here, reads:

> Be still, ye *Courts*, be great who will;
> Open wide the lofty Door,

and so on, where *still* rimes 'internally' with *will*, though it has a sense inferior to *full*. The collected *Poems* of 1761 add after l. 145 the line:

> Search for Peace with all your skill:

Grass and Flowers Quiet treads,
On the Meads, and Mountain-heads,
Along with Pleasure, close ally'd,
Ever by each other's Side:
And often, by the murm'ring Rill,   ⎫   [155]
Hears the Thrush, while all is still, ⎬
Within the Groves of *Grongar Hill*. ⎭

157. *Groves* is still applicable because of the wood mentioned at l. 59 *n.*

So far I have done no more than mention the most interesting version of all the versions of 'Grongar Hill'. The text we usually read is that of 1761, the last of a long series—long, that is, as these things go. Dyer began to write about Grongar Hill when he was a mere boy of sixteen, and went on re-writing and revising for some thirty years. It is odd that the two most interesting versions should have been laid before the world almost simultaneously. In 1725 (or 1726?) appeared the original of the version usually printed, and about the same time came out a version in the form of a pindarique ode:[1] it was printed in *Miscellaneous Poems and Translations. By Several Hands. Publish'd by Richard Savage, Sone of the Late Earl Rivers*, 1726. Of all forms for the 'Grongar Hill' we know, that of a pindarique is, surely, the most unpredictable. After the neat, close tetrameters to come on the irregular and the high flying! And to come on these two versions almost at the same moment! It is as if Gray, when he published the 'Elegy', had published another version of it in the metre of *The Bard*. The small poet, John Dyer, provides us with one of the completest surprises in the history of English poetry.

Here, then, is his pindarique, with its strong individuality, its power and torment as well as its clumsiness, its flashes that

[1] In the Preface to *Miscellaneous Poems* Lewis notes that he has 'admitted nothing which [he] knew to be before publish'd', except for one or two Latin originals and a poem of his own distributed among his acquaintances. He goes on: 'one [poem] of another Author, inserted here from his own genuine Manuscript, is I am inform'd already got abroad; but, as he assures me, surreptitious and disguis'd'. It seems likely that this refers to 'Grongar Hill' in its two forms—certainly the word 'disguis'd' suggests a marked difference such as that between the pindarique and the four-beat version of Dyer's poem.

remind us of splendid things in Milton, Dryden, Pope, and Keats. The word 'tire(d)' occurs in it three times: only the healthy and vigorous are pleased to acknowledge the pleasure of repose.

GRONGAR HILL.

By *Mr.* JOHN DYER, *of* Carmarthenshire.

I

Fancy! Nymph, that loves to lye
On the lonely Eminence;
Darting Notice thro' the Eye,
Forming Thought, and feasting Sense:
  Thou! that must lend Imagination Wings,   [5]
  And stamp Distinction, on all worldy Things!
    Come, and with thy various *Hues,*
    Paint and adorn thy *Sister* Muse.
  Now, while the Sun's hot Coursers, bounding high;
  Shake Lustre on the Earth, and burn, along the Sky.   [10]

II

More than *Olympus* animates my Lays,
Aid me, o'erlabour'd, in its wide surveys;
And crown its Summit with immortal Praise:
Thou, aweful *Grongar!* in whose mossy Cells,
    Sweetly-musing *Quiet* dwells: [15]
  Thou! deep, beneath whose shado'wy Side,
Oft, my sick Mind serene Refreshment took,
Near the cool winding of some bubbling Brook:
There have I, pensive, press'd the grassy Bed,
And, while my bending Arm sustain'd my Head,   [20]
Stray'd my charm'd Eyes o'er *Towy*'s wand'ring Tide,
Swift as a Start of Thought, from Wood to Mead,
Glancing, from dark to bright, from Vale to Hill,
Till tir'd Reflection had no *Void* to fill.

1 ff. *Fancy* must mean man's power of experiencing the external world, and *Imagination* man's power of transforming it into poetry.
24. A line that Goldsmith might have written.

III

Widening, beneath the Mountain's bushy Brow,   [25]
Th' unbounded Landskip softens off below;
   No skreeny Vapours intervene;
   But the gay, the splendid Scene,
Does Nature's smiling Face all *open* show,
In the mix'd Glowings of the tinctur'd *Bow*.   [30]
And, gently changing, into soft and light,
Expands immensely wide, and leads the *journeying* Sight.

IV

White, on the rugged Cliffs, Old *Castles* rise,
   And shelter'd Villages lie warm and low,
   Close by the Streams that at their *Bases* flow.   [35]
Each watry Face bears pictur'd Woods, and Skies,
Where, as the Surface curls, when Breezes rise,
Faint fairy Earthquakes tremble to the Eyes.
Up thro' the Forest's Gloom, distinguish'd, bright,
   Tops of high Buildings catch the Light: [40]
The quick'ning sun a show'ry Radiance sheds,
And lights up all the Mountain's russet Heads.
Gilds the fair Fleeces of the distant Flocks;
And, glittering, plays betwixt the broken Rocks.
Light, as the Lustre of the rising Dawn,   [45]
Spreads the gay Carpet of yon level Lawn:
Till a steep Hill starts horrid, wild, and high,
Whose Form uncommon holds the wond'ring Eye;
Deep is its Base, in *Towy*'s bord'ring Flood,
Its bristly Sides are shagg'd with sullen Wood: [50]
Towers, ancient as the Mountain, crown its Brow,
Aweful in Ruin, to the Plains below.
Thick round the ragged Walls pale Ivy creeps,
Whose circling Arms the nodding Fabrick keeps;
While both combine to check th' insulting Wind,   [55]
As Friends, in Danger, mutual Comfort find.

50. 'shagg'd', a favourite eighteenth-century borrowing from *Comus*, l. 429.
53. 'pale Ivy creeps' is borrowed from Pope's 'Eloisa to Abelard', l. 243.

V

Once a proud Palace, This,—a Seat of Kings!
Alas! th' o'erturning Sweep of Time's broad Wings!
   Now, 'tis the Raven's bleak Abode,
And shells, in marbly Damps, the inbred Toad.   [60]
There the safe Fox, unfearing Huntsmen, feeds;
And climbs o'er Heaps of Stone to pendant Weeds.
The Prince's Tenure in his Roofs of Gold,
   Ends like the Peasant's homelier Hold;
Life's but a Road, and he who travels right,   [65]
Treats Fortune as an Inn, and rests his Night.

VI

   Ever changing, ever new,
Thy Scenes, O *Grongar!* cannot tire the View:
   Lowly Vallies, waving Woods,
   Windy Summits, wildly high,   [70]
   Rough, and rustling in the Sky!
The pleasant¹ Seat, the ruin'd Tower;
The naked Rock, the rosy Bower;
The Village and the Town, the Palace and the Farm,
Each does, on each, reflect a doubled Charm;   [75]
As Pearls look brighter on an *Æthiop*'s Arm.

VII

Southward, along the Mountain's waving Side,
The Vale grows liberal, and the Prospect wide.
Glowing, beneath a kind and purply Sky,
Broad flower-dress'd Meadows and rich Pastures lie.   [80]
Green Hedges, in long Parallels, are seen;
And silv'ry Lawns draw Streaks of Light between:
Distant, those *Thorns* diminish'd scarce appear;
As Dangers scape, unseen, that are not *near*.
Smiling, like this fair Prospect, soft and gay,   [85]
The flatt'ring Glass of Hope our *Future* shows;
But Ills, *at hand*, their Face, unmask'd display,
And Fortune *rougher* still when *nearer*, grows:
Still we tread, tir'd, along the same deep Way;

---

60. 'shells'=encloses as in a shell.

---

¹ Misprinted 'pleasaht'.

And still the *present* proves a *cloudy* Day.   [90]
O, may I ever with my self agree,
Nor hope the unpossess'd Delights I see!
Nobly content, within some silent Shade,
My Passions calm, and my proud Wishes laid:
Ne'er may Desire's rough *Sea* beneath me roll,   [95]
Drown my wish'd Peace, and *tempest* all my Soul!
While, idly busy, I but beat the Air,
And, lab'ring after Bliss, embosom Care!

VIII

Here, while on humble Earth, unmark'd I lie,
I subject *Heav'n* and *Nature* to my Eye;   [100]
Solid, my Joys, and my free Thoughts run high.
For me, this soft'ning Wind in *Zephyrs* sings,
And in yon flow'ry Vale perfumes his Wings.
To sooth my Ear, those Waters murmur deep;
To shade my Eye, these bow'ry Woodbines creep.   [105]
Wanton, to yield me Sport, these Birds fly low;
And a sweet *Chase* of Harmony bestow.
Like me too yon sweet Stream serenely glides;
Just *views* and *quits* the Charms which tempt its Sides:
Calmly regardless, hast'ning to the Sea,   [110]
As I, thro' *Life*, shall reach *Eternity*.

107. A 'Chase of Harmony' suggests counterpoint: cf. *fuga*. Dyer may have invented the expression: Mr A. H. King, the Superintendent of the British Museum Music Room, tells me that it does not occur in contemporary lists of musical terms.

109. A use of verbs with 'just' characteristic of Pope: see above, p. 169; 'Oh just beheld, and lost!'

IX

GRAY'S 'ODE ON THE SPRING'

I HAVE already quoted[1] the opening quatrain of the poem:
here is the whole first stanza:

> Lo! where the rosy-bosom'd Hours,
> Fair VENUS' train appear,
> Disclose[2] the long-expecting flowers,
> And wake the purple year!
> The Attic warbler pours her throat,
> Responsive to the cuckow's note,
> The untaught harmony of spring:
> While whisp'ring pleasure as they fly,
> Cool Zephyrs thro' the clear blue sky
> Their gather'd fragrance fling.

I have suggested that the first four lines of this stanza, which
begin with a bang and continue in the ballad metre, were
designed to be read quickly. They are the equivalent of a
bow to the ode-form. What follows in the rest of the stanza also
goes fast. Because the rhythm is spry, Gray expected us to see
that his real business was not the posing and describing of
tableaux. Not that anything in the opening *tableau* is scamped.
Unlike Collins, who used scholarly materials for his lovely
lyrics, but whose scholarship could not stand the strain, Gray
is always impeccably learned. And although this was his first
published poem, it already showed him to be a fine metrist—
all told, he stands with Milton, Coleridge, Tennyson and Mr
Eliot as our finest. Nor is there any scamping discernible in the
matter. To be sure, it is mainly second-hand. But to be second-
hand was to be sound: Gray was not exhibiting the new things

---

[1] p. 139 above.
[2] =open. Gray is recalling Shakespeare, sonnet 54, l. 8:
> When sommers breath their masked buds discloses;
and *Hamlet*, I. iii. 39 f;
> The canker galls the infants of the spring
> Too oft before their buttons be disclos'd.

he had discovered in the spring, as Wordsworth was to do; he was reminding us of the spring already known to ourselves and mankind generally. And for the same reason he borrowed only what was agreed to be best. As his commentators were soon able to show, much of his matter takes its rise from classical mythology according to the ancient poets, and to modern English poets who were coming to seem of like status with the ancients. The same is true of its expression. 'Lo!' is the 'ecce' of Virgil in the *Georgics*. 'Rosy-bosom'd Hours' is Milton's very phrase, recalling ancient poetry—it probably denotes 'having a bosom filled with roses' (cf. Sidney's 'rosy garland' at p. 82 above).

The use of 'purple year' has also a history behind it. Virgil fixed the epithet *purpureum* to *ver* in his *Eclogues* (ix. 40), and Dryden was so bold as to lift it into his translation with the minimum change. His 'purple spring' can have been fully successful only for those readers who, knowing the Latin text, remembered that they were reading of an Italian spring. Even so, *purple* is violent, and *purpureum* must, I think, have had some violence also for the Romans. Lexicographers have tried not to think so, and so have failed to do justice to the word as used here by Virgil. They have robbed it of much of its violence by robbing it of most of its colour. I have quoted above[1] War-burton's explanation of it as denoting not purple but 'the brightest, most vivid colouring in general', and the lexicographers have gone further and explained it as denoting a colourless or indefinitely coloured 'splendid' or 'lustrous'. But a word that is often applied to dyed garments and to the blood of wounded epic heroes cannot have shed much of its purple when applied to spring. Plainly lexicographers have failed to see it as metaphorical. Even when applied to an Italian spring it is, I grant, violent, but violence is expected from great poets, and we know in general how jealously Virgil loved colour. And surely we may also invoke a principle more general still—that a great poet does not use a word unless his readers can be expected to think it happy. Virgil expected his readers to agree that an Italian spring is gorgeous enough to warrant so warm a compliment. The Roman connotations persist in the English *purple*,

[1] p. 35.

but with certain modifications that prove fatal to it. In English the metaphor is too violent. Blood is always blood and its colour constant, but purple garments usually mean for Englishmen ceremonial garments, and ceremonies for Englishmen are usually indoors; nor is our spring so gorgeous as the Italian. For such reasons *purple* can be made to characterize our English spring only on one supposition—that the English season takes second place to Virgil. The literary principle by virtue of which *purple* was acceptable for spring was strongly favoured in Dryden's time and later, and, literature being books, there is a firm logic behind it—Johnson said that poets drew most of their material from their predecessors. This principle by itself accounts for Dryden's retention of *purple*, but for him there was the further plea that he was translating. Accordingly it was Pope's step that was the crucial one. Writing his pastoral 'Spring', which had its scene laid in England, he bejewelled it with the phrase 'the purple year' (that is, the spring, the year in its purple phase). It will not do for his English spring, but is in place as homage to Virgil and also to Dryden. Gray followed suit, lifting Pope's very words, inappropriately for our months of March to June but appropriately for honouring all three of his great predecessors. Meeting 'purple year' in his ode to the spring, we see that it belongs to that category of literary pleasures to which belong *enamelled* flowers and *velvet* lawns, objects consecrated to literature and if also to the external world to that world as it exists brilliant in sunnier climes. Later in the eighteenth century and increasingly in the nineteenth, English painters and scientists were making a particular point of observing the external world as it existed in England, closely with their own unaided eyes. Johnson—who was almost as much an indication of the literature to come as a fulfilment of the literature of Dryden and Pope—believed that 'An epithet or metaphor drawn from Nature ennobles Art; an epithet or metaphor drawn from Art degrades Nature',[1] and the poets were beginning to agree with him, observing the external world with all the freshness and closeness of their own eyes and without reference to previous poetry. Accordingly there is no purple in the spring of any poet after Gray.

[1] *Lives of the Poets,* iii. 437.

The rest of Gray's first stanza shows a further debt to Milton and from the same context as one of those I have already specified: Milton had already made brilliant use of 'fling' for describing the action of a breeze on fragrance:

> Along the crisped shades and bowres
> Revels the spruce and jocond Spring,
> The Graces, and the rosie-boosom'd Howres,
> Thither all their bounties bring,
> There eternal Summer dwels,
> And West winds, with musky wing
> About the cedar'n alleys fling
> *Nard*, and *Cassia*'s balmy smels.[1]

Milton's words also persist in the periphrasis for nightingale: 'Attic warbler' was Gray's gathering from scattered passages in Milton, who for 'Attic', as applied to the nightingale, had himself gone to the ancients. 'Pours her throat' came straight from *An Essay on Man*, published only a few years earlier in 1733—a brilliantly expressive phrase that derives its verb from Milton. Gray's borrowings, made from two supreme masters of verbal economy among the English poets, help to give the opening stanza formality. For all its speed the bow had not to seem a wriggle.

Then, on a plane other than the strictly literary, Gray's borrowings accorded with the way man in general regarded the external world, and was to go on doing so till the idea of evolution culminated in the *Origin of Species*. External nature was by definition nature external to man, and the line dividing the human from the non-human was accepted as absolute. Later in the poem, as I shall show, Gray availed himself of a principle of thought that spread the human over the rest of the creation, planting over it a terminology that we should now call scientific—an anthropomorphic principle that warmed up, as it were, the rest of the creation by representing it as man in mimicry. Even here, in the first stanza, the anthropomorphic showed itself in the application of 'long-expecting' to flowers, but 'Attic warbler' expressed the fact of the concrete difference. In the next century Hazlitt was to investigate man's consciousness of

[1] *Comus*, ll. 984 ff.

this difference and it is to an article by Dr Janet Spens that I am indebted for my knowledge of his important contribution, her 'Study of Keats's "Ode to a Nightingale".'[1] When examining Keats's thought in his penultimate stanza—

> Thou wast not born for death, immortal Bird!
> No hungry generations tread thee down;
> The voice I hear this passing night was heard
> In ancient days by emperor and clown:
> Perhaps the self-same song. . . .

—she shows how Keats is indebted for it to Hazlitt's lecture on Thomson and Cowper, later to be published in his *Lectures on the English Poets*:

In this lecture Hazlitt lays down that what distinguishes the interest in Nature from others is its *'abstractedness.* The interest we feel in human nature is exclusive, and confined to the individual, the interest we feel in external nature is common, and transferable from one object to all others of the same class.' Further 'there is generally speaking the same foundation for our love of Nature as for our habitual attachments, namely associations of ideas'. But the peculiar quality of this attachment is the 'transferable nature of our feelings with respect to physical objects' so that 'if we have once associated strong feelings of delight with the objects of natural scenery . . . we shall ever after feel the same delight in other objects of the same sort'. He goes on:

If we have once enjoyed the cool shade of a tree, and been lulled into a deep repose by the sound of a brook running at its foot, we are sure that wherever we can find a shady stream, we can enjoy the same pleasure again, so that when we imagine these objects, we can easily form a mystic personification of the friendly power that inhabits them, Dryad or Naiad, offering its cool fountain or its tempting shade. Hence the origin of Grecian mythology. All the objects of the same kind being the same, not only in their appearance, but in their practical uses, we habitually confound them together under the same general idea.

Thus, he goes on to explain, all the associations with all the individuals of a species known to us, come together to enrich each, and each becomes the symbol of a whole complex of emotions. After illustrating his thesis from his own and from Rousseau's experience, Hazlitt ends his lecture with these words: 'The cuckoo, "that wand-

---

[1] *The Review of English Studies*, N.S.III, xi. 1952 pp. 234 ff.

ering voice" that comes and goes with the spring, mocks our ears with one note from youth to age; and the lapwing, screaming round the traveller's path, repeats forever the same sad story of Tereus and Philomel!'[1]

It is because of this that Gray's 'Attic warbler', which repeats a borrowing Milton had himself made from the ancient poets, is Keats's stanza in little.

When poets were dwelling on this abstractedness of the things and creatures of the outer world, and regarding them, species by species, as unchanged and identical, it was inevitable that they should speak in generalizations. In the lines I have quoted from *Comus* there is generalization to a high degree, and since there is personification, and the bestowing of epithets on the resultant 'person', generalization in the highest degree of all. Milton entrusts the nature of all springs to two epithets— 'spruce' and 'jocund'. As it happens, both epithets are original. Nevertheless both are intended to ring true to everybody's experience of any spring that behaves itself properly. Generalization to the point of personification is appropriately promised by Gray's title. Not until we reach the poet himself do we get anything particular, and not until the last stanza does the poet become very particular—when he is scorned as 'A solitary fly'. In the first stanza of the poem even the nightingale and cuckoo are generalizations, stretching far back into the remotest past —the earth was founded, it was still believed, in 4,004 BC, when cuckoos and nightingales were created once for all. And completer still is the generalization 'flowers', though if I am right in my interpretation of 'rosy-bosomed' we have already had one named species.

In this first stanza not everything, I repeat, is borrowed. There is invention in the metre, and the way it is used, and also in the epithets. 'Long-expecting' is a surprise—too much a surprise for certain readers: it was meddlesomely 'corrected' to read 'long-expected' in several editions;[2] 'untaught' was quite new as applied to the duet of the birds, and 'gathered' as applied to fragrance. Though there is speed and much that is grandly familiar, it is quite plain that the reader cannot skip.

---

[1] op. cit., p. 237.
[2] See *The Poems of Thomas Gray*, ed. John Mitford, 1814, p. 2.

Generalization persists in the description immediately following.
We meet the poet not in one particular spot so much as in any
spot where the same conditions obtain:

> Where'er the oak's thick branches stretch
> A broader browner shade;
> Where'er the rude and moss-grown beech
> O'er-canopies the glade,
> Beside some water's rushy brink
> With me the Muse shall sit, and think
> (At ease reclin'd in rustic state) . . .

In 'some' place of this sort—a sort furnished by any and
every spring in plenty—the poet is shown thinking in company
with the muse (or in other words in metre) and his thoughts are
about men or, to be more exact, about those many men who,
unlike himself, are gregarious or proud or merely in great
place:

> With me the Muse shall sit, and think
> (At ease reclin'd in rustic state)
> How vain the ardour of the Crowd,
> How low, how little are the Proud,
> How indigent the Great!

The scene is conducive to thoughts and to thoughts on such a
subject, because

> Still is the toiling hand of Care:
> The panting herds repose:

but the connexion of men and the scene, which had been one of
contrast, now becomes one of parallel—for the scene becomes
animated:

> Yet hark, how thro' the peopled air
> The busy murmur glows!
> The insect youth are on the wing,
> Eager to taste the honied spring,
> And float amid the liquid noon:
> Some lightly o'er the current skim,
> Some shew their gayly-gilded trim
> Quick-glancing to the sun.

The kinds of insects are not specified for there is no point in specification, though there is to be later. Their function is that of prompting the poet to extend his thought to include all men, whether low or great:

> To Contemplation's sober eye
> Such is the race of Man:
> And they that creep, and they that fly,
> Shall end where they began.
> Alike the Busy and the Gay
> But flutter thro' life's little day,
> In fortune's varying colours drest:
> Brush'd by the hand of rough Mischance,
> Or chill'd by age, their airy dance
> They leave, in dust to rest.

And now the latent uneasiness of the poet's mind asserts itself. He had said he was *at ease* reclined in rustic *state*, scorning from that unworldly coign of vantage the gregarious and proud and great. That is what he *said*. Everybody knows—and, as it turns out, Gray relies on our using the knowledge—that scorn of this sort is seldom without its taint of envy. That the poet's was no exception is attested by the last stanza when he receives the taunts of those who see him not so much as a country gentleman taking his ease but as a social outcast:

> Methinks I hear in accents low
> The sportive kind reply:
> Poor moralist! and what art thou?
> A solitary fly!
> Thy joys no glittering female meets,
> No hive hast thou of hoarded sweets,
> No painted plumage to display:
> On hasty wings thy youth is flown;
> Thy sun is set, thy spring is gone—
> We frolick, while 'tis May.

The poem is finished—except for the thought the reader is left to supply, the judgment with which he is left to crown the poem (I have spoken of this on a former occasion).[1]

I have had no difficulty in making my explanation of the whole. Being a good poem, it contains or suggests within itself everything we need to know about it. In 1742 indeed there was

[1] See above, p. 141.

no means of knowing more, and writing it then Gray cannot have imagined that any reader, apart from his immediate friends, would discern that it was a personal document, a point of autobiography, as well as a poem to be presented to the great roaring public. The poem was published in 1748, and the fame that followed the publication of the 'Elegy' three years later brought biographers; and the latest and best of them is now able to write of the last stanza of the poem as follows:

The insects in their turn reply to the poet. They justify their joyful mating in the sunshine, the gathering of their stores of honey, the vivid iridescence of their wings. They are at least more fortunate than the lonely celibate moralist who has been reflecting upon their vain and brief existence, and who has himself neither mate, nor riches, nor brilliance of any kind. . . . It is a most revealing stanza, in which Gray contrived to sum up in a few seemingly artless lines his loneliness, his obscurity, the desolating sense of time passing and nothing achieved which Milton had felt at twenty-three and he himself was feeling at twenty-five.[1]

But, as I say, we do not need to know this, though we cannot now help knowing it, and finding the poem more poignant accordingly.

3

Mr Ketton-Cremer rightly sees the 'turn of thought in the concluding stanza' as 'original and unexpected'. But though it is unexpected it has been prepared for, and that because Gray has taken advantage of the poetic diction available to him. It is this procedure that knits so closely the structure of his little piece. The poet has been thinking of man as he lay on the banks of the stream, and when the insects appear they are described according to Augustan diction: the air they fly in is 'the peopled air' and they are 'the insect youth'. The latter phrase was suggested to Gray by a passage from the poem he acknowledged as his main source, Matthew Green's 'Grotto'.[2] This poem had

[1] R. W. Ketton-Cremer, *Thomas Gray*, Cambridge, 1955, p. 61.

[2] 'The thought on which my ['Ode on the Spring'] turns is manifestly stole from [Green's 'Grotto']:—not that I knew it at the time, but having seen this many Years before, to be sure it imprinted itself on my Memory, & forgetting the Author, I took it for my own [whereupon follows a lengthy passage transcribed from the poem, and from which I quote in the text] (*Correspondence*, i. 299 f.).

described the famous grotto of Queen Caroline, furnished with its busts of Newton, Locke, Wollaston, Clarke and Boyle, and proceeded:

> The thinking Sculpture helps to raise
> Deep Thoughts, the Genii of the Place:
> To the Mind's Ear, & inward Sight,
> There Silence speaks, & shade gives Light:
> While Insects from the Threshold preach,
> And Minds disposed to Musing teach;
> Proud of strong Limbs & painted Hues
> They perish by the slightest Bruise
> Or Maladies begun within
> Destroy more slow Life's frail Machine:
> From Maggot-Youth thro' Change of State
> They feel like us the Turns of Fate;
> Some born to creep have lived to fly,
> And changed Earth's Cells for Dwellings high;
> And some, that did their six Wings keep,
> Before they died, been forced to creep.
> They Politicks, like ours, profess:
> The greater prey upon the less.
> Some strain on Foot huge Loads to bring,
> Some toil incessant on the Wing:
> Nor from their vigorous Schemes desist
> Till Death; & then are never mist.
> Some frolick, toil, marry, increase,
> Are sick & well, have War & Peace,
> And broke with Age in half a Day
> Yield to Successors, & away.

Gray's 'insect youth', then, was suggested by Green's 'Maggot-Youth'. It is a constituent in a scheme of language, of which 'peopled air' and 'sportive kind', which come later, are the other instances, a scheme that accords with the anthropo-morphic principle I have spoken of. From the dawn of liter-ature, animals, birds and insects had been grouped under terms that were also terms for man. *People* is one of them, and Mr Arthos lists twenty-one in English, including *tribe* and *train*, most of which have their equivalent in other languages ancient and modern.[1] So common is the use of them that Pope

[1] Arthos, *The Language of Natural Description in Eighteenth-century Poetry*, Ann Arbor, 1949, pp. 271 ff.

can write adjectivally of 'the green myriads in the peopled grass',[1] and Gray follow suit with 'peopled air'. When meeting these terms we feel we are nearer to man than when, as in common nineteenth-century usage, we drop them for the specific *bees, ants, butterflies,* which invite a degree of visualization that removes them from man decisively. It is because of this scheme of language that the word 'youth' is acceptable. Gray took it from Green, and Green took it from Thomson, in whose 'Spring' we read:

> And now the feathered youth their former bounds,
> Ardent, disdain; and, weighing oft their wings,
> Demand the free possession of the sky.
> But this glad office more, and then dissolves
> Parental love at once, for needless grown,
> Unlavish Wisdom never works in vain.
> 'Tis on some evening, sunny, grateful, mild,
> When nought but balm is breathing through the woods
> With yellow lustre bright, that the new tribes
> Visit the spacious heavens, and look abroad
> On Nature's common, far as they can see
> Or wing, their range and pasture. O'er the boughs
> Dancing about, still at the giddy verge
> Their resolution fails; their pinions still,
> In loose libration stretched, the void abrupt
> Trembling refuse—till down before them fly
> The parent-guides, and chide, exhort, command,
> Or push them off. The surging air receives
> The plumy burden; and their self-taught wings
> Winnow the waving element. On ground
> Alighted, bolder up again they lead,
> Farther and farther on, the lengthening flight;
> Till, vanished every fear, and every power
> Roused into life and action, in the void
> The exoner'd parents see their soaring race,
> And, once rejoicing, never know them more.[2]

As applied to the young of non-human creatures, the word 'youth' is, on the face of it, surprising. The obvious word would

---

[1] *Essay on Man,* i. 210.

[2] op. cit., ll. 729 ff. in the final version of 1746: the text given here is that of 1728 which remained unrevised till 1738 (see the Oxford edition, ed. J. Logie Robertson, 1908).

be 'young', which I myself have just used. Indeed the only user of 'youth' (in the sense concerned) who is cited in the *OED* is Gray in this ode—Thomson and Green are overlooked. And yet how natural the odd term reads in its context in all three poems. It is drawn magnetically into their scheme, for all three poems show the anthropomorphising process at its busiest. Thomson's account of the birds, for all its evidence of a close and indeed brilliant observation, is almost equally an account of members of a human family. And something like this is true of the other two. Green takes advantage of the anthropo-morphic 'Maggot-Youth' to represent his insects as near to man, and so near that he makes them 'preach'. Gray comes a step closer still, and gives them spoken words. Green's 'preach' is no more than a metaphor. Gray's further step into fantasy, into Æsopian fantasy, is made in the interests of man, and is all the better prepared for because the English language still allowed him the use of the old group words. He could not have taken the step so easily in the nineteenth century. In the eighteenth external nature was still mainly valued as it helped to point a moral and adorn a tale about man. For 'hive' we understand bank balance, for 'painted plumage' we understand fine clothes; and 'glittering female' does as well for insects or man—Pope had called his Pamela 'glittering', and any bride can be so called. Because he has called the insects by the names of man-kind, what they say is the more human. Their taunts are those that the poet has feared on the lips of other young men.

Gray's use of the old diction is a further instance of the way it helped Augustan poets towards expressing their meaning and constructing their poems.

X

GRAY'S 'ODE ON THE DEATH OF A FAVOURITE CAT, DROWNED IN A TUB OF GOLD FISHES'

GRAY'S ODE is one of those poems that make allusions to other poems, and that expect the reader to catch them. We all know how the *Rape of the Lock* depends for the tone of its narrative and meaning on contrasts with the great epics, and the same is true in smaller compass of Gray's poem.

Nowadays, if a poet announced such a subject as the death of a cat, we should expect him to treat it seriously. But in 1742 the title allowed of comic treatment as an alternative, and Gray's choice was declared at once by the relationship of the title with the first line of the text:

'Twas on a lofty vase's side.

We now know that the receptacle in which the Strawberry Hill goldfish swam was a china bowl or vase.[1] Knowing this, we see that the word *tub* is Gray's deliberate alteration of the fact. There is a big difference between the two things, and was in 1742: Johnson's Dictionary, thirteen years later, defined the one as 'a large open vessel of wood', and the other as 'a vessel; generally a vessel rather for show than use'. Gray's *tub* is a deliberate lowering because he wants *vase* to be a heightening. When the poem was published in 1748 the reader, who knew nothing of the incident behind the poem except as the poem itself presented it—it was of course all he needed to know—noted the discrepancy and inferred the mock-heroic. That small stroke was an earnest of more of the same sort:

'Twas on a lofty vase's side,
Where China's gayest art had dy'd
The azure flowers, that blow;

[1] It is now in the possession of Lord Derby, and appears as plate 71 of Mr Randolph Churchill's *Fifteen Famous Houses*, 1954.

Demurest[1] of the tabby kind,[2]
The pensive Selima reclin'd,
　　Gazed on the lake below.

Her conscious[3] tail her joy declar'd;
The fair round face, the snowy beard,
　　The velvet of her paws,
Her coat, that with the tortoise vies,
Her ears of jet, and emerald eyes,
　　She saw; and purr'd applause.

Still had she gaz'd; but 'midst the tide
Two angel forms were seen to glide,
　　The Genii of the stream:
Their scaly armour's Tyrian hue
Thro' richest purple to the view
　　Betray'd a golden gleam.

For the modern reader the clues are not perhaps obvious. *Tub* for *vase*, *armour* for *scales*—perhaps these are the only straws visible in the wind. But for the reader Gray had in mind, the cultivated reader of 1742, the wind was strong, and some of the straws, as we shall see, the size of forest-trees.

Almost as famous as Gray's poem is Johnson's comment on it in his Life of Gray, and the odd thing is that it shows him to have mistaken Gray's intentions—or at least to have ignored their point. And if so, with the wilfulness prompted by an imperfect sympathy. Johnson had little liking for Gray and for much of his work, the dislike of the writings being prompted in part at least by the dislike of the man.

---

[1] By Gray's time *demure* had become a sort of Homeric epithet for a cat, whether male or female but more usually the latter. Bacon's essay 'Of Nature in Men' had referred to one of the Æsopian fables in the following terms: 'Like as it was with *Æsopes Damosell*, turned from a Catt to a Woman; who sate very demurely, at the Boards End, till a Mouse ranne before her.' L'Estrange retained the term when translating another of the cat fables (*Fables, of Æsop*, 1669, third ed., p. 287): 'they spy'd a *Cat* upon a Shelf; that lay and look'd . . . Demurely.' Dryden used the epithet in his reference to one of these fables (I quote from Johnson's Dictionary, s.v. *demure*):
　　So cat, transform'd, sat gravely and demure,
　　'Till mouse appear'd, and thought himself secure.
(Greatly strengthened by Gray's use of it, the epithet recurs in nineteenth-century descriptions of cats: see *Blackwood's Magazine*, Nov. 1846, and the opening of *Through the Looking Glass*).
　　[2] See above, p. 54.　　[3] See above, p. 77.

The prickly relation of Gray and Johnson was much discussed during the half century following the inclusion of the Life of Gray in the *Lives of the Poets,* and all the more earnestly because at this time Gray was having so marked an effect on English poetry. For us, Johnson's Life of Gray is all the more unfortunate because it separates two men who by rights stand side by side. Johnson and Gray are men and writers remarkably alike, for, to put it sharply, if any other writer of 1751 could have written Gray's 'Elegy' that writer was Johnson. They had both attained to the same estimate of human life, and had minds deeply learned, powerful, genial with ripe understanding, and impatient of cheapness. On the surface there were of course striking differences, and between any two actual living acquaintances surface is likely to count for more than inner worth. What they saw and heard of each other's externals gave them prickly grounds for dislike: Gray called Johnson 'ursa major, the great bear', and Johnson thought Gray a finicky exquisite. Left alive to write Gray's life, Johnson was too fair-minded not to salute Gray's solid greatness. Accordingly he praised the 'Elegy' more highly than any other English poem: 'Had Gray written often thus it had been vain to blame, and useless to praise him';[1] and, having Mason's memoir of Gray before him with its ample quotations from the letters, he saw that Gray's 'mind had a large grasp'. But in the rest of his life his homage exists indirectly in the spiritedness of his writing—the Life of Gray is Johnson at his gayest. He is, however, spiritedly unfair. Even where we admit the justice in some of his strictures, we see them to cover too much. Gray's poetry, brief in quantity, is more various line by line than that of any other English poet, and to write, in Quintilian phrase, of his being 'tall by walking on tiptoe', or to discover 'glittering accumulations of ungraceful ornaments' is to ignore magnitude and jewels that are authentic, and to miss so much that is uniquely great.

His criticism of the ode on the cat has, one suspects, the brilliance of the wit who dazzles in order to get by. Johnson either does not recognize, or does not choose to, what is at the basis of the poem—what its kind is, in other words. To see its kind is to see its sense.

[1] *Lives of the Poets,* iii. 442.

Johnson begins his account of the poem in this way:

The poem on the Cat was doubtless by its author considered as a trifle, but it is not a happy trifle. In the first stanza 'the azure flowers that blow' shew resolutely a rhyme is sometimes made when it cannot easily be found.[1]

It almost seems that the *look* of the poem on the page, with its four- and three-foot lines, was enough to put him off, for he disliked ballads on principle, and so was disqualified for meeting any particular ballad, or ballad-like poem. If Gray's ode had, like the *Rape of the Lock*, been in heroic couplets, Johnson might have been fairer to it. He might then have read it closely enough to catch those references to epic that are the main-spring of the mock-epic method. It is because he disliked ballads that he did not see the point of the third line of the poem. What he disliked in that line cannot have been the actual word that rimed, for *blow* was then the ordinary prose word for a plant's act of flowering: it occurs in Gray's letters and in Johnson's Dictionary, and that the whole phrase has nothing would-be 'poetical' about it is shown by Wordsworth's having borrowed it for the quiet ending of one of his greatest poems:

> To me the meanest flower that blows can give
> Thoughts that do often lie too deep for tears.

What Johnson objected to was the redundancy of 'that blow', forgetting that redundancies of this cheerful jingling sort are part of the method of a true ballad, and so a grace in a mock-ballad. Looking for faults, he missed virtues. Blind to the pointed veering from *tub* to *vase*, he missed later on a more particular example of the mock-heroic method, an omission that explains the rest of what he objects to:

Selima, the Cat, is called a nymph, with some violence both to language and sense; but there is good use made of it when it is done; for of the two lines,
> 'What female heart can gold despise?
> What cat's averse to fish?'
the first relates merely to the nymph, and the second only to the cat. The sixth stanza contains a melancholy truth, that 'a favourite

[1] id., iii. 434.

has no friend,' but the last ends in a pointed sentence of no relation to the purpose; if what glistered had been 'gold' the cat would not have gone into the water; and, if she had, would not less have been drowned.[1]

'Selima, the Cat', writes Johnson, and had he been attentive he would have seen that that collocation is the key to the poem. The grand name that Walpole chose for his Persian was that of the heroine of Rowe's *Tamerlane*, a much acted play in the eighteenth century: she was the captive daughter of the Turk Bajazeth. (In a few years' time, as it happened, Walpole was to write an epilogue for the play.) Naming a cat after a princess, Walpole was himself inaugurating the mock-heroic. Gray crowned the proceeding first in little—by the heightening of *tub* to *vase*—and then grandly by referring the cat to the heroine of a famous play, and then to the heroine of the *Iliad* itself.

In the 'Argument' before the third Book in Pope's translation we read:

The Armies being ready to engage, a single Combate is agreed upon between *Menelaus* and *Paris* (by the Intervention of *Hector*) for the Determination of the War. *Iris* is sent to call *Helena* to behold the Fight. She leads her to the Walls of *Troy*, where *Priam* sate with his Counsellors observing the *Grœcian* Leaders on the Plain below, to whom *Helen* gives an Account of the chief of them.

And in the text itself:

> Within the Lines they[2] drew their Steeds around,
> And from their Chariots issu'd on the Ground:
> Next all unbuckling the rich Mail they wore,
> Lay'd their bright Arms along the sable Shore.

Helen is summoned by Iris to

> Approach, and view the wondrous Scene below.

In the description that follows she is accorded a 'fair Face',[3]

---

[1] id., iii. 434.　　　[2] The Greeks and Trojans.

[3] The brilliant description of the cat's face comes from Pope: 'fair round Face' occurs in his version of 'The Wife of Bath, her Prologue' (and has no source in Chaucer). The description amusingly overlaps with the description of Helen's face. A contribution to the definition of 'fair' in these contexts comes from James's *Portrait of a Lady*, ch. 1, where we read that Mr Touchet has a face 'with evenly-distributed features'.

over which she throws a 'snowy' veil, and in the conversation she holds with Priam about the Greek heroes, occur other words of Gray: she speaks of her 'conscious' shame, and he of the Sangaris that ran 'purple' with blood. We then hear of heralds who bring 'rich' wine and 'golden' goblets, and later on of 'Azure Armour' and 'purple' cuishes. More pointedly still we come on this:

> Meantime the brightest of the Female Kind,
> The matchless *Helen* o'er the Walls reclin'd.

The cat in her setting is so like Helen in hers that the poem at this point may be said to have a double subject. Of course the subject cannot be double throughout: Helen does not fall off the walls of Troy to be left to die. Nevertheless, having been given a strong sense of the woman in the cat, we take the cat story, *mutatis mutandis*, as also a story about woman, *in posse* if not *in esse*, and by analogy if not in fact. Nor as the poem proceeds does Gray let us forget the woman:

> The hapless Nymph with wonder saw:
> A whisker first and then a claw,
>   With many an ardent wish,
> She stretch'd in vain to reach the prize.
> What female heart can gold despise?
>   What Cat's averse to fish?
>
> Presumptuous Maid! with looks intent
> Again she stretch'd, again she bent,
>   Nor knew the gulf between.
> (Malignant Fate sat by, and smil'd)
> The slipp'ry verge her feet beguil'd,
>   She tumbled headlong in.
>
> Eight times emerging from the flood
> She mew'd to ev'ry watry God,
>   Some speedy aid to send.
> No Dolphin came, no Nereid stirr'd:
> Nor cruel *Tom*, nor *Susan* heard.
>   A Fav'rite has no friend!

The cat is called a 'Nymph', and when she stretches after the fish we get not only a rhetorical question about cats but one about cupidinous woman, which comes in with special neatness because, as it happens, the fish are 'Gold Fishes' (goldfish had only lately been brought to England,[1] and this added piquancy to the poem in 1748, justifying its long description of the fishes on the score of informativeness as well as art). Furthermore the cat is apostrophized in womanly terms as 'Presumptuous Maid!' and when the disaster is completing itself, the absence of help and the comment it prompts are applicable both to cats and human beings: 'No Dolphin came', as one did come to help Arion, 'no Nereid stirr'd', as they had stirred when Hylas fell into the stream, 'Nor cruel *Tom*', the footman, 'nor *Susan*', the maidservant, heard, for it is a universal truth that 'A fav'rite has no friend!'

Johnson's objection that no good use is made of the doubling of cat and woman (for his 'good use' is of course ironic) shows that he had missed the thoroughness with which the doubling proceeds. And his final thrust—'if what glistered had been "gold", the cat would not have gone into the water; and, if she had, would not less have been drowned', shows that he failed to see how the poem ends. Here is the last stanza that follows on the line just quoted:

> From hence, ye Beauties, undeceiv'd,
> Know, one false step is ne'er retriev'd,
>   And be with caution bold.
> Not all that tempts your wand'ring eyes
> And heedless hearts, is lawful prize;
>   Nor all, that glisters, gold.

At the end of his cat-poem Gray comes to his moral in accordance with the practice of all fablers.[2] 'From hence' detaches what is now on the way from what went before, and 'ye Beauties' tells us that what is on the way is addressed to women. Johnson, missing this transition, criticizes the moral in vain: for the gold in the last line is as distinct from the golden colour of the fishes as 'ye Beauties' is from cats. The fable, in which a cat snatched fatally at some beautiful fish, is now over, and we are left with

---

[1] See A. R. Humphreys, 'Lords of Tartary', *Cambridge Journal*, III (1949), i.

[2] It is worth noting that one of Æsop's fables (no. 61 in L'Estrange's translation) recounts how Venus changed a beloved cat into a woman for the greater pleasure of a young man who admired her.

the human counsel it has suggested, and suggested all the more vividly because behind it lurked, and at times almost obtruded, the feminine in its human form. The moral is the better for the literary form, the mock-heroic, of what precedes it. We can detach the last stanza from the cat and attach it more readily to 'ye Beauties' just because Helen has stood behind the cat throughout the poem, Helen who did not control her wandering eyes, who did take a false step, and who did have too much boldness—a moral quality that Gray is not for disallowing to women completely![1] Homer, we recall, did not condemn Helen.

Johnson's treatment of Gray's poem has often been thought an act of elephantine ineptitude, but not always an unsuccessful one. I have heard it credited with having broken a butterfly upon a wheel. To liken Gray's ode to a butterfly is to insult its strength and pungency; to liken Johnson's method of criticism to a wheel is more felicitous, but the wheel, on the present occasion, rolls round without grazing the integrity of Gray's little masterpiece.

[1] One of the phrases of the 'moral' may be intended to refer pointedly to a couplet in the English translation of Ovid's *Ars Amandi*, where the common phrase 'lawful prize' is given an amorous sense: 'But that a Mistress may be lawful Prize,/None, but her Keeper, I am sure, denies.' (*Ovid's Art of Love . . . By Several Eminent Hands*, 1709, p. 223.)

XI

JOHNSON'S DICTIONARY

FOR MOST of us Johnson exists as he exists in the pages of Boswell's *Life*. In those pages he provides, of course, a magnificent spectacle. And yet Boswell's account of him is lopsided. Granted that it well represents Johnson as a personality and also as a moral being, it does not fully represent him as an intellectual being. The most adequate representation that Boswell gives of him in that capacity, he gives in the writings he quotes—that is, mainly in Johnson's letters. Otherwise Johnson's mind in Boswell's pages is often a mind at play. When Johnson was on the right side of dinner and among delightful companions he displayed his mental powers rather for the sake of display. On these occasions the object of his thinking was not so much truth as victory. It is in his writings that we find his mind responsibly concerned with truth, which for him was mainly truth about man as a public and private person—in Boswell's words 'true, evident and actual wisdom'.[1] It is in his writings that Johnson's intellect is at its greatest. And the *Dictionary* stands among those writings.

There are two pieces of extended writing connected with the *Dictionary*. The body of the *Dictionary* could not, in its very nature, be more than a series of short items, but as usual Johnson took the opportunity to deliver himself at large on the principles of the work he was concerned in doing. Eight years before the *Dictionary* was published, he brought out his 'Plan of an English Dictionary', and when the work was completed he affixed to it a Preface. The Plan is enough to show that Johnson had been conscious of the nature of English words long before there had been any question of his making a dictionary. It shows a magnificent grasp of what lay ahead. When the time came for him to write his Preface he did not need to supersede the Plan at any important point. Plan and Preface together are

---

[1] *Life*, iv. 28.

two of the most remarkable writings we have about the matters they treat of. STET !

The Plan and the Preface show that Johnson saw his work as concerned not so much with words as with language. That is one of the supreme merits of the *Dictionary*. It is possible for a dictionary-maker to do his work quite happily on a much lower plane. He is paid to take the words of the language, to arrange them in alphabetical order and to give us an account—some account—of their meaning. And this had been what dictionary-makers up to that time had felt to be all that was expected of them. But Johnson came to see that to isolate a word in dictionary fashion was to destroy something essential in its nature. He saw English words as things belonging to what he called 'a living tongue', and he saw that the advantage of belonging to a living tongue was that words were themselves alive in the sense that their meaning depended upon the various places they had occupied, or were occupying, among their fellows. He saw words as gregarious things, as things, as it were, that had faces which lit up only when in company. There are no more interesting passages in his Plan and Preface than those which deal with the subtleties that words owe to their successive contexts.

'Names,' he said, 'have often many ideas.' And again:

When the construction of a word is explained, it is necessary to pursue it through its train of phraseology, through those forms where it is used in a manner peculiar to our language, or in senses not to be comprised in the general explanations.

And these are some of the phrases he uses: 'exuberance of signification', 'nice and subtle ramifications of meaning', and— a phrase now common which he seems to have invented— 'shades of meaning'. He despaired of seizing these distinctions, but he saw that we could discern them by noting words in their place in the living language, especially when it is written or spoken by those who understand 'the genius of the tongue'— again the phrase is his and again he seems to have invented it. In the Plan of the *Dictionary* he gave the idea this modern turn:

The signification of adjectives may be often ascertained [i.e., pinned down] by uniting them to substantives; as, *simple swain*, *simple sheep*. Sometimes the sense of a substantive may be elucidated by the epithets annexed to it in good authors; as, the *boundless ocean,* the *open lawns.*

Now it had been the dream of some of Johnson's contemporaries and some of his immediate predecessors, that English could become fixed in a changeless state. Johnson himself had begun with hoping that he might make that dream come true.

We can understand why in the eighteenth century there was a wish to see English fixed. The literary ideal of its great writers was the ideal of correctness. And that was an ideal partly, sometimes mainly, dependent on the means of expression, on language. Prose writers often had new thoughts and so needed to have them understood. Poets had old thoughts mainly, and so looked to expression to justify their expressing them once again. And yet they saw that English had proved itself a broken reed. It had been a language so given to change that the writings of one age had become progressively unintelligible to later ages. If it was still possible to discern that Chaucer was a great poet, that was because this greatness had proved too lively to be quite extinguished by its medium. And not only Chaucer. Atterbury, the friend of Pope, said that much of Shakespeare was unintelligible at that date.[1] Did it not follow that the same doom was awaiting the would-be correct writings of Swift, Addison and Pope? Pope certainly thought so:

> And such as Chaucer is shall Dryden be.[2]

This feeling about the transience of English was sharpened by the admiration these men felt for the comparative fixity of Latin—what survived of Latin literature made use of a language that, beside English, appeared beautifully stable. Pope

[1] The whole passage deserves to be quoted: 'I have found time to read some parts of Shakespear which I was least acquainted with. I protest to you, in an hundred places I cannot construe him, I dont understand him. The hardest part of Chaucer is more intillegible to me than some of those Scenes, not merely thro the faults of the Edition, but the Obscurity of the Writer: for Obscure he is, & a little (not a little) enclin'd now & then to Bombast whatever Apology you may have contriv'd on that head for him. There are Allusions in him to an hundred things, of which I knew nothing, & can guess nothing. And yet without some competent knowledge of those matters there's no understanding him. I protest Æschylus does not want a Comment to me, more than he does . . .' (Pope, *Correspondence*, ii. 78 f.).

[2] *Essay on Criticism*, l. 483.

himself purposed to help in a formal way the fixing of English. He had the idea of making a dictionary which should draw its words from the best English writers of the sixteenth and seventeenth centuries.[1] And it was Pope's plan apparently that was passed on to Johnson, who speaks of Pope's solicitude 'for the success of this work'.[2] Johnson came to see that nobody could fix a living language any more than King Canute could fix the sea. Even so he did something towards saving it from unnecessary change. Along with other great writers he worked, both as writer and lexicographer, in the spirit of that exhortation in his Preface: 'We have long preserved our constitution, let us make some struggles for our language.'

Because of the outcome of the struggles we can still read the writing of Swift and Pope—I mean skim along the surface, of course—almost as effortlessly as their first readers.

And so to my third point. Johnson complained, when speaking of those subtle verbs *get*, *take*, and so on, that in English we had too many of them. Modern linguists will resent that complaint. But Johnson himself knew it was an idle one. He saw his office as that of 'registering' not 'forming' the language. We can see how wise he was when we think of the vain endeavours that Robert Bridges, say, engaged himself in. Bridges assumed that language could be shaped according to the desires of those interested in shaping it. What a pity he did not read Johnson's Preface which proclaims that 'to enchain syllables and to lash the wind, are equally the undertakings of pride, unwilling to measure its desires by its strength'.

My final point brings me back to what I said about Johnson and truth. Everybody knows that when, half-way through his vast *Dictionary*, he arrived at the word 'lexicographer' he allowed himself the pleasure of intruding into his definition the phrase 'a harmless drudge', but he did so because he himself was as incapable of the mindlessness of drudgery as of the inanity of harmlessness. 'I am not yet so lost in lexicography,' he assures us in the Preface, 'as to forget that *words are the daughters of earth, and that things are the sons of heaven*. Language is only the instrument of science [i.e., knowledge], and words are but

---

[1] Spence, *Anecdotes*, p. 310.
[2] 'Plan of *an English* Dictionary', para: 'It has been asked . . .'.

the signs of ideas.' He was not so lost as to forget to make of his *Dictionary* more than a dictionary. He made of it the occasion for a long series of inlets into great literature. For Johnson great literature embodied truth. He had a passion for 'true, evident and actual wisdom'. All his writings were means of honouring it. Even his *Dictionary* honours it. For when he chose to show words actively alive in his exhibits, he chose to show them so in exhibits worth reading on their own account. We of the twentieth century with our weakness for snippets can think of each dozen pages of his *Dictionary*—and there are about 3,000 pages—as offering us a tear-off calendar of great thoughts! As well as everything else, his *Dictionary* is an anthology of 'beauties'. Of course, they could only be brief beauties, but it is interesting to learn that their number had to be reduced on revision, and it is amusing to see the amplitude of some of those that were retained. So interesting are these examples as pieces of truth that the *Dictionary* comes near to defeating its own ends. It is a dictionary that can be read, and in practice we find ourselves reading it. In other words, it is made to serve the ends that are served by *The Rambler*, *Rasselas* and the *Lives of the Poets*. When Anna Seward said that all Johnson's writings were poetry —that is, writings that added delight to instruction—she made an exception of his orthographical works. But she need not have done so.

XII

RASSELAS

The History of Rasselas, Prince of Abissinia is a sizeable story, consisting of chapters which, though brief, amount to forty-nine in all, the whole thing occupying some 120 pages of 350 words apiece. It tells the story of Rasselas and his friends, who escape from the Happy Valley in quest of a happiness solid and permanent, such as no man has found in the Valley, and who return at length to their native country wiser because informed.

Better known, perhaps, than the story of the book is Boswell's story of its composition:

1759: ÆTAT. 50]—In 1759, in the month of January, his mother died at the great age of ninety, an event which deeply affected him; not that 'his mind had acquired no firmness by the contemplation of mortality', but that his reverential affection for her was not abated by years, as indeed he retained all his tender feelings even to the latest period of his life. I have been told that he regretted much his not having gone to visit his mother for several years, previous to her death. But he was constantly engaged in literary labours which confined him to London; and though he had not the comfort of seeing his aged parent, he contributed liberally to her support.

Soon after this event, he wrote his 'RASSELAS, PRINCE OF ABYSSINIA'; concerning the publication of which Sir John Hawkins guesses vaguely and idly, instead of having taken the trouble to inform himself with authentick precision. Not to trouble my readers with a repetition of the Knight's reveries, I have to mention, that the late Mr. Strahan the printer told me, that Johnson wrote it, that with the profits he might defray the expence of his mother's funeral, and pay some little debts which she had left. He told Sir Joshua Reynolds that he composed it in the evenings of one week, sent it to the press in portions as it was written, and had never since read it over. Mr. Strahan, Mr. Johnston, and Mr. Dodsley purchased it for a hundred pounds, but afterwards paid him twenty-five pounds more, when it came to a second edition.[1]

[1] *Life*, i. 339 ff.

A note in Malone's edition of the *Life* qualifies one of these statements:

Finding [a copy of *Rasselas*] accidentally in a chaise with Mr Boswell, Johnson read it eagerly. This was doubtless long after the declaration to Sir Joshua Reynolds.

This note is welcome, and the fact it records must have been particularly so to Boswell, who read *Rasselas* once every year. The rate of composition, granted that we are dealing with the powers of genius, offers no difficulty. Johnson was always a fast writer, and as it happens, we know the rate at which he wrote his other sizeable narrative, 'The Vision of Theodore' —Thomas Tyers records that it took him 'one night . . . after finishing an evening in Holborn'.[1] 'The Vision of Theodore' is one seventh the length of *Rasselas*, and 'the evenings of a week' may be taken as seven times as long as 'one night'. Before sitting down to write the story of Theodore, Johnson may have had the outline of it in his head. And this may also have been true of the story of *Rasselas*, for an outline existed, as a hint or suggestion, in a book we know him to have been acquainted with, the *Persian Tales*.[2] If he had some sort of prepossession of his tale we may be sure he took no pleasure in anticipating the committal of it to paper. He did not relish any sort of writing in prospect, whatever authorial pleasures the process of writing or its completion can have given him; and he can have had least pleasure of all in the prospect of writing a narrative. In the event the writing of *Rasselas* was in response to a spur. The logic of the business was plain but painful—a work of fiction would exact the largest possible sum from a publisher, but to write it would be to do what Johnson did not approve. Not, at least, in theory. He has left on record his disapproval of kinds and instances of narrative. As I have said,[3] he read through *Amelia* at a sitting, not so much because he was enthralled as because he did not wish to take longer over it. If he admitted the greatness of Richardson's novels, it was mainly

[1] id., i. 192 *n*.
[2] See my '*Rasselas* and the *Persian Tales*' in *Essays in Criticism and Research*, Cambridge, 1942, pp. 111 ff.
[3] See above, p. 133.

because they offered a treasury of practical wisdom; he advises Richardson as follows:

I wish you would add an *Index Rerum*, that when the reader recollects any incident he may easily find it, which at present he cannot do, unless he knows in which volume it is told; For Clarissa is not a performance to be read with eagerness and laid aside for ever, but will be occasionally consulted by the busy, the aged, and the studious, and therefore I beg that this Edition by which I suppose Posterity is to abide, may want nothing that can facilitate its use.[1]

And yet, on the other hand, he himself loved reading stories of a primitive sort:

'when a boy he was immoderately fond of reading romances of chivalry, and he retained his fondness for them through life; so that (adds his Lordship[2]) spending part of a summer at my parsonage-house in the country, he chose for his regular reading the old Spanish romance of FELIXMARTE OF HIRCANIA, in folio, which he read quite through. Yet I have heard him attribute to these extravagant fictions that unsettled turn of mind which prevented his ever fixing in any profession.'[3]

But though *Rasselas* contained no Guy of Warwick or Don Bellianis, Johnson himself, as we have seen, read it with the eagerness of approval when he lighted on it again by chance. The explanation of his split mind is, I think, that while narratives were poor things in themselves, they were a necessary concession to man in his weakness. When he himself read them with delight it was because his mind was at the ebb, at such times and seasons as that memorably recorded by Boswell:

[1] *Letters*, i. 35 f. [2] *sc.* Bishop Percy.

[3] Boswell's *Life*, i. 49. Johnson would have sympathised with the young Jane Eyre: 'I saw a girl sitting on a stone bench near; she was bent over a book, on the perusal of which she seemed intent: from where I stood I could see the title—it was "Rasselas"; a name that struck me as strange, and consequently attractive. In turning a leaf she happened to look up, and I said to her directly:—

"Is your book interesting?" I had already formed the intention of asking her to lend it to me some day.

"I like it," she answered, after a pause of a second or two, during which she examined me.

"What is it about?" I continued. I hardly know where I found the hardihood thus to open a conversation with a stranger; the step was contrary to my nature and habits: but I think her occupation touched a chord of sympathy somewhere; for I too liked reading, though of a frivolous and childish kind; I could not digest or comprehend the serious or substantial' (op. cit., ch. v).

once, when Johnson was ill, and unable to exert himself as much as usual without fatigue, Mr Burke having been mentioned, he said, 'That fellow calls forth all my powers. Were I to see Burke now, it would kill me.'[1]

Man was often at his weakest. At the top of his strength, he might be equal to receiving truth as a direct impact, in the way that the Houyhnhnms received it habitually:

Neither is reason among them a point problematical as with us, where men can argue with plausibility on both sides of a question; but strikes you with immediate conviction, as it must needs do where it is not mingled, obscured or discoloured by passion and interest.[2]

Once or twice in a lifetime perhaps each man attains to the Houyhnhnms' power of receiving truth, but mainly he receives it fumbling among his preoccupations, and when at his feeblest can only take it watered down, and sweetened up. Narrative had that much to be said for it—assuming, of course, that it did in fact contain truth. It shared in its inferior way the usefulness that Johnson accorded poetry, which on one occasion he described as 'the art of uniting pleasure with truth, by calling imagination to the help of reason'.[3] By 'imagination' he meant the power of creating or receiving mental images, pictures still or in motion—the picture, for instance, in a 'character' or a narrative. And by 'truth' he meant matter that comes home to men's business and bosoms. For Johnson, as for Pope, the matter 'proper' for poetry was 'what oft was thought', because thoughts that recurred to all men without ever seeming false were likely to be true. Man, of course, was not first of all a reading, but an acting animal. And when he made the inevitable pauses from action, the 'proper' occupation for his mind was thinking. In the nature of things, however, thinking was a strenuous occupation—in *Rasselas*, as it happens, Johnson had occasion to remark that 'the labour of excogitation is too violent to last long' (ch. xliv). When not excogitating, man might be idle, or, less reprehensibly, might read the thought of others— the thought of philosophers, or of the poets who combine their

---

[1] Boswell's *Life*, ii. 450.   [2] Swift, *Gulliver's Travels*, IV, ch. viii.
[3] *Lives of the Poets*, i. 170.

thinking with imagery and sometimes identify the two, or of story-tellers who sometimes give us thinking pure and simple, but who usually identify it with narrative. Narrative in verse— unless the verse takes the childish form of ballad metre—is likely to prove more taxing to men than narrative in prose. A tale or novel, therefore, came low in the scale of literature, but, things being what they are, was not to be despised—man, alas, is often capable of nothing more strenuous. After all, in its humble way, prose narrative fulfilled the function of poetry, uniting pleasure with truth by calling the imagination to the help of reason.

In practice Johnson was sometimes satisfied with truth, or rather with a relationship to it, in a form that satisfies children, or men very much at leisure. To read romances, in a pause from action, was merely to acknowledge the inescapable truth that to act, as the hero acts in a story, is a necessity to man (when fully himself), whether he finds it pleasant or not. Then again, Johnson's love of argument acknowledged another item of truth. When arguing, he was not seeking to establish truth, but merely to prove the superiority of his own brain-machine over that of his opponents; he was attesting one particular truth, attested also by animals, that might, whether of brawn or brain, is right—that as Mrs Battle held, 'Man is a gaming animal. He must always be getting the better of something or other.'[1] This holds, however much certain men may be ashamed of the way they themselves exemplify it. This sort of activity Johnson knew to be inferior to the thinking he put into his writings, for all his writings were done as if on oath, the thinking being as good as he could make it. There was never, therefore, any fear that when he turned to write a long work of fiction, the 'truth' and 'reason' of literature would be omitted or skimped. In the event, as Boswell saw, *Rasselas* contained 'a fund of thinking'.[2]

Much of the thinking it contains is all the better for being re-thinking. A favourite theme of Johnson is the contrast between how things are expected to turn out and how they turn out indeed. The shortest instance is his maxim, 'Nothing is

---

[1] Lamb, *Essays of Elia*, 'Mrs. Battle's Opinions on Whist'.
[2] *Life*, i. 342.

more hopeless than a scheme of merriment'.[1] And in his *Account of the Life of Mr. Richard Savage*, written sixteen years before *Rasselas*, he had pleased himself, as he was to do later in his essays, with enlarging on a common instance of disillusion:

As he was ready to entertain himself with future pleasures, he had planned out a scheme of life for the country, of which he had no knowledge but from pastorals and songs. He imagined that he should be transported to scenes of flowery felicity, like those which one poet has reflected to another; and had projected a perpetual round of innocent pleasures, of which he suspected no interruption from pride, or ignorance, or brutality.

With these expectations he was so enchanted, that when he was once gently reproached by a friend for submitting to live upon a subscription, and advised rather by a resolute exertion of his abilities to support himself, he could not bear to debar himself from the happiness which was to be found in the calm of a cottage, or lose the opportunity of listening without intermission to the melody of the nightingale, which he believed was to be heard from every bramble, and which he did not fail to mention as a very important part of the happiness of a country life.[2]

Another favourite theme of his was the related one of happiness, and the chances of it for man. That same *Life of Savage* had opened with a paragraph that might have introduced *Rasselas* itself:

It has been observed in all ages that the advantages of nature or of fortune have contributed very little to the promotion of happiness; and that those whom the splendour of their rank or the extent of their capacity have placed upon the summits of human life, have not often given any just occasion to envy in those who look up to them from a lower station: whether it be that apparent superiority incites great designs, and great designs are naturally liable to fatal miscarriages; or that the general lot of mankind is misery, and the misfortunes of those whose eminence drew upon them an universal attention have been more carefully recorded, because they were more generally observed, and have in reality been only more conspicuous than those of others, not more frequent, or more severe.

[1] *Idler*, no. 58; cf. *Letters*, ii. 410.
[2] *Lives of the Poets*, ii. 410.

That affluence and power, advantages extrinsick and adventitious, and therefore easily separable from those by whom they are possessed, should very often flatter the mind with expectations of felicity which they cannot give, raises no astonishment: but it seems rational to hope that intellectual greatness should produce better effects; that minds qualified for great attainments should first endeavour their own benefit; and that they who are most able to teach others the way to happiness should with most certainty follow it themselves.

But this expectation, however plausible, has been very frequently disappointed.[1]

Moreover, Johnson was likely to be the better story-teller because he was not invariably the moralist, or rather was not invariably the confident moralist. One of the best instances of his pausing comes in the same *Life* where he subjects actors, whom he never liked as a class, to his cool observation, and is unable to do more than observe them, though as far as observation goes it is devastatingly complete:

He [Savage] was now again abandoned to fortune without any other friend than Mr. Wilks, a man who, whatever were his abilities or skill as an actor, deserves at least to be remembered for his virtues, which are not often to be found in the world, and perhaps less often in his profession than in others. To be humane, generous, and candid is a very high degree of merit in any case, but those qualities deserve still greater praise when they are found in that condition which makes almost every other man, for whatever reason, contemptuous, insolent, petulant, selfish, and brutal.[2]

'For whatever reason'—Johnson admits to bafflement as a psychologist and a biographer, and therefore as a moralist, and such an attitude augured well for him as the teller of a long tale. On the other hand, the *Life of Savage* well exemplifies how far he could go in the sure-footed examination of a complex character and personality. Here is part of his account of the zigzag of pleased and vexed self-deceiving that Savage acted out before the intense gaze of his biographer:

The sale of this poem [*The Bastard*] was always mentioned by Savage with the utmost elevation of heart, and referred to by him as an incontestable proof of a general acknowledgement of his abilities. It was indeed the only production of which he could justly boast a general reception.

[1] id., ii. 321. [2] ibid., p. 334.

But though he did not lose the opportunity which success gave him, of setting a high rate on his abilities, but paid due deference to the suffrages of mankind when they were given in his favour, he did not suffer his esteem of himself to depend upon others, nor found any thing sacred in the voice of the people when they were inclined to censure him; he then readily shewed the folly of expecting that the publick should judge right, observed how slowly poetical merit had often forced its way into the world: he contented himself with the applause of men of judgement, and was somewhat disposed to exclude all those from the character of men of judgement who did not applaud him.

But he was at other times more favourable to mankind than to think them blind to the beauties of his works, and imputed the slowness of their sale to other causes; either they were published at a time when the town was empty, or when the attention of the publick was engrossed by some struggle in the parliament, or some other object of general concern; or they were by the neglect of the publisher not diligently dispersed, or by his avarice not advertised with sufficient frequency. Address, or industry, or liberality, was always wanting; and the blame was laid rather on any person than the author . . . He proceeded throughout his life to tread the same steps on the same circle; always applauding his past conduct, or at least forgetting it, to amuse himself with phantoms of happiness which were dancing before him, and willingly turned his eyes from the light of reason, when it would have discovered the illusion and shewn him, what he never wished to see, his real state.

He is even accused, after having lulled his imagination with those ideal opiates, of having tried the same experiment upon his conscience; and, having accustomed himself to impute all deviations from the right to foreign causes, it is certain that he was upon every occasion too easily reconciled to himself, and that he appeared very little to regret those practices which had impaired his reputation. The reigning error of his life was, that he mistook the love for the practice of virtue, and was indeed not so much a good man as the friend of goodness.[1]

This surely is a high-water mark in biographical writing, and the powers it evinced augured well for Johnson's story. And indeed a few months before writing *Rasselas* he had already sketched something of its theme unwittingly in the letter he sent his young friend Bennet Langton, who had just gone up to Oxford:

[1] id., ii. 378 ff.

Dear Sir

Though I might have expected to hear from you upon your entrance into a new state of life at a new place, yet recollecting, (not without some degree of shame), that I owe you a letter upon an old account, I think it my part to write first. This indeed I do not only from complaisance but from interest, for living on in the old way I am very glad of a correspondent so capable as yourself to diversify the hours. You have at present too many novelties about you to need any help from me to drive along your time.

I know not any thing more pleasant or more instructive than to compare experience with expectation, or to register from time to time the difference between Idea and Reality. It is by this kind of observation that we grow daily less liable to be disappointed. You, who are very capable of anticipating futurity, and raising phantoms before your own eyes must often have imaged to yourself an academical life, and have conceived what would be the manners, the views, and the conversation of men devoted to letters, how they would chuse their companions, how they would direct their studies, and how they would regulate their lives. Let me know what you expected and what you have found.[1]

In general, from all that I have quoted, it will be seen how much interest Johnson had in the stuff of narratives, whether tales or novels. The truth he sought was mainly human truth, which is as much matter for stories as for moral disquisition. In a word, his remark about a scheme of merriment might have come from Jane Austen, who admired him so much, and so much from fellow-feeling: we can imagine it introducing or closing a sadly laughable chapter in one of the novels.

Johnson, then, possessed the sort of matter no story-teller can do without. Nor was there any fear on that other score he provided for in his definition of poetry—the score of the 'imagination', the authorial faculty that for the more vivid expression of the poet's 'truth' created 'images'. For Johnson was interested as much in images as in ideas. Or, to put it more exactly, he was never happy, when truth came to the point of expression, to express it without an illustrative accompaniment of material particulars. If he did not think in images, as certain writers do, he did not express thought without their aid. That is why Anna Seward was able to see, as I have noted above,[2]

---

[1] *Letters*, i. 109 f.   [2] See above, pp. 125 and 228.

that, whatever his verbal medium, he was always a poet. He loved the abstract, and also the concrete. The evidence is everywhere in his writings early and late, and also in his sayings. Notable, among the writings that precede *Rasselas*, are the periodical essays, which are sown with 'images' in the form of fictional situations and anecdotes. Among them come the essays that are frankly stories, and among these the oriental tales that Percy, a connoisseur of fiction, held to be 'not the least striking products of his pen'.[1]

Johnson, then, may be said to have been in full possession of the matter for his tale, both in its 'truth' and 'images', if we allow that some of it was in a general rather than a particular form.

Before we look into his performance, however, it would be well to observe the form of fiction he was undertaking to fill. He was not setting out to write a novel, but a work in a much stricter form. A novel for him came lower down the scale of practical usefulness than a tale, for a novel found room in itself for what he considered to be accidentals. The set of his mind, so far as thinking went, was towards generality. He thought most about man, and his 'Vision of Theodore', his favourite work, is a story about man. But a story-teller cannot write many such stories without repeating himself, and so he comes to write about men. Johnson had studied all the men he had ever met, but not altogether for their own sakes. He constantly compared one with another so as to relate them to man, even if they exemplified mainly types of men. Stories could not begin till they had men, till they had personages, but the more they aspired towards generality, the better for Johnson the stories—his praise for the personages of Shakespeare's stories is that 'an individual . . . is commonly a species'.[2] He did not approve of stories that found much space for what he held to be mere accidentals—such as the rather big chin that Fielding gave to Sophia Western. Now we know that in a great novel what to a cursory glance might look like accidentals are microscopic parts of the body of the story. We have had the benefit of Henry James's discovery that there are no superfluities in a great novel:

[1] Boswell's *Life*, i. 537.   [2] Preface to Shakespeare.

I cannot . . . conceive, in any novel worth discussing at all, of a passage of description that is not in its intention narrative, a passage of dialogue that is not in its intention descriptive, a touch of truth of any sort that does not partake of the nature of incident, or an incident that derives its interest from any other source than the general and only source of the success of a work of art—that of being illustrative.[1]

This, I think, would have been news to Johnson. He would have seen that it perfectly described the tale—say the ending of his own incident of the disillusioned hermit:

They heard his resolution ['to return into the world to morrow'] with surprise, but, after a short pause, offered to conduct him to Cairo. He dug up a considerable treasure which he had hid among the rocks, and accompanied them to the city, on which, as he approached it, he gazed with rapture. (ch. xxi).

Or this from Pekuah's account of her adventures among the Arabs:

The diversions of the women . . . were only childish play, by which the mind accustomed to stonger operations could not be kept busy. I could do all which they delighted in doing by powers merely sensitive, while my intellectual faculties were flown to Cairo. They ran from room to room as a bird hops from wire to wire in his cage. They danced for the sake of motion, as lambs frisk in a meadow. One sometimes pretended to be hurt that the rest might be alarmed, or hid herself that another might seek her. Part of their time passed in watching the progress of light bodies that floated on the river, and part in marking the various forms into which clouds broke in the sky. (ch. xxxix).

These are examples of how the matter of stories was dealt with in a tale, which could not spare room for anything not illustrative patently and pointedly. It would have surprised Johnson to find the same sort of claim being made for the matter of a novel. *Rasselas* does not tell us anything about the person of Nekayah—the size of her chin or the colour of her eyes. All we know is that she is sensitive to experience and capable (not all at once but in the end) of drawing conclusions from it for the purpose of living more wisely. We shall agree that Johnson's

[1] 'The Art of Fiction.'

particulars are more thoroughly illustrative than most of the particulars in a novel. If the difference between a novel and a tale is one of degree rather than of kind, then the difference of degree is wide.

Rasselas is a tale, and its 'images' accordingly depend on the 'truth' for the sake of which the tale has come to be. Johnson's task, in the first place at least, was to show Rasselas and his friends what human life, as far as happiness goes, is like for all the various types of human beings engaged in living their own portion of it, and from the total evidence to draw a conclusion how best to live it—a conclusion that shall be applicable to everybody. The evidence had to be adequate or there would be room for an appeal to what remained unexamined.

And so to the story itself, the fulfilment of the project. The nature of the material forecast for the experiments is of great interest to Rasselas, Nekayah and Pekuah her maid because all the material is new to them. For Imlac, however, the experiments are all the same, and their conclusions all foregone: he undertakes the role of guide, philosopher and friend, being replete with the experience that has been denied to the rest of the party. And, to detach ourselves from the story, we as readers are in the same position as Imlac: we also know in advance how the experiments will turn out. The danger implicit in the story, therefore, is that the reader will find it boring. Johnson was particularly alive to dangers of this sort—he recoiled from boredom with almost a physical shudder. In the _Life of Dryden_ he was to write:

> Works of imagination excel by their allurement and delight; by their power of attracting and detaining the attention. That book is good in vain which the reader throws away.[1]

It was Johnson's main task as an artist to defeat any tedious expectation. By the time the experiments begin in chapter xvii he could count on a store of good will in his reader. By that point he had shown the life in the Happy Valley, the process by which Rasselas determined to escape from it, the futile attempt to escape by means of a flying-machine; and in addition Imlac had found occasion to tell the party the history of a life mainly spent in the world beyond the valley, in the course

---

[1] _Lives of the Poets_, i. 454.

of which he had given his own brilliant account of what is needed by a man setting up to be a great poet. All this, and the account of the successful escape and the journey into Egypt where the experiments are to begin, had all been made solidly and vividly interesting for the reader.[1] But could the interest be maintained among experiments which, as forecast, are all at bottom the same? Rasselas thinks that peasants will be happy if fast young men in Cairo are not, that rulers will be happy if subjects are not, that the married will be happy if the single are not, that a philosopher holding one sort of world-view will be happy if a philosopher holding another sort is not. To some extent Johnson can count on the interest that the variety of mere surface affords. The material for the experiments is after all human material, and as such interesting in itself. All the same the use to which the material is to be put is, from the reader's point of view, identical, and therefore at bottom likely to be boring—and especially so since the experimenters, apart from Imlac, are inevitably enthusiastic. In the event Rasselas is not too glowingly enthusiastic but rather buoyant, fresh and vigorous, having something of the gay brightness that we discern below the sables of Hamlet; and the personalities of Nekayah and Pekuah are discreetly vivid and distinct. But at the point where boredom seems likely to set in we do not yet fully know they will all prove so delightful. What neither Rasselas nor ourselves foresee is that the plan of the experiments is soon to look foolish. Rasselas starts on the assumption, common to youth, that life can be controlled. Indeed Johnson at one stage considered calling his story 'The Choice of Life', and the phrase recurs in the text, where it is usually given italics. Rasselas plans his experiments on the assumption that man can *choice* choose his life at will, though he soon comes to see that the possession of money makes a great difference to this power. What he neither foresees, nor comes to learn quickly, and what the reader *as a reader* also fails to foresee, is that any power of choice an individual person may possess is subject to accident

---

[1] There is, however, some deficiency in ch. iv., where Rasselas acts violently, having deliberately 'impressed upon his mind' the 'image' of a maiden in distress. His action accords with the philosophy touched on in ch. xliv, 'Dangerous Prevalence of the Imagination', but the way Johnson manages the narration is clumsy.

beyond his control. And the triumph of Johnson as an artist shaping a story is that he so arranges the course of the experiments that the royal party and ourselves become increasingly aware of how little it matters, comparatively, whether man can choose or not. This course of enlightenment proceeds along with the course of the experiments, which produce results not forecast by the experimenters. They produce what is always considered precious by Englishmen, and what we express in the word that is so odd because so laconic, 'experience'. Johnson arranges that the experiments shall be transformed by the addition of a variety of material that could not be allowed for, and which accordingly alters the course of the story and the composition of the 'truth' as both these things had been foreseen. Under Johnson's hands what was proposed as an academic course of study has turned into an education in life and the nature of things.

The first experiments are tried on the least complex materials. Is a fast young man happy?—by the way, we must distinguish happiness from pleasure: the name of the Happy Valley is ironic: it comes to be named more accurately in Imlac's description of it as 'the prison of pleasures' (ch. xlvii). Is a peasant happy? a ruler? The answer is that they are unhappy as soon as the variegated surface is pierced. We shrug our shoulders, noting privately that the life of a rake, for example, is all told a foolish life, that the life of a peasant might be improved a little if he migrated to a town, but not enough to give him happiness; and so on. And that is the whole answer so far as we are encouraged to think. But among these early experiments is one that takes man beyond the accidents of his trade.

The experiment that comes second in the series shows that not everything in life is within the power of a man's choice, for any happiness the philosopher may have been enjoying is cut off by the death of his daughter from fever. Johnson makes nothing of this beyond its result in terms of the experiment, and this is true to the narrative because Rasselas is not yet worn down into thinking outside the terms he has set himself. It is enough for the narrative and its 'truth' that the second experiment has come to grief as an experiment. But it warns us how the experiments are going to be made to look foolish. When, later

242

on, the party visits the pyramids, another accident happens and happens to them, the experimenters themselves being subjected to an experiment they did not bargain for. This time it is not an accident in the form of a bacterial germ, causing fever and death, but is wholly contrived by man—a troop of Arabs carry off Pekuah. Interference with the happiness of any individual is, then, at the mercy of other men. Nekayah is desolated, and at last comes to the point of a thought. She is well capable of thinking, and indeed much of the truth of the story is discovered by her. She had already been entrusted with the summary that concludes the chapter 'Disquisition upon Greatness':

'Whether perfect happiness would be procured by perfect goodness, said Nekayah, this world will never afford an opportunity of deciding. But this, at least, may be maintained, that we do not always find visible happiness in proportion to visible virtue. All natural and almost all political evils, are incident alike to the bad and good: they are confounded in the misery of a famine, and not much distinguished in the fury of a faction; they sink together in a tempest, and are driven together from their country by invaders. All that virtue can afford is quietness of conscience, and a steady prospect of a happier state; this may enable us to endure calamity with patience; but remember that patience must suppose pain.' (ch. xxvii.)

And now the loss of Pekuah prompts her to see a new aspect of the truth that is being found, if it cannot quite be said that it is being sought:

'Yet what, said [Nekayah], is to be expected from our persuit of happiness, when we find the state of life to be such, that happiness itself [in this instance her happiness in Pekuah] is the cause of misery?'

A later experiment is tried on a learned man, an astronomer, but for him happiness of any sort or duration is ruled out absolutely:

'Hear, Imlac, what thou wilt not without difficulty credit. I have possessed for five years the regulation of weather, and the distribution of the seasons: the sun has listened to my dictates, and passed from tropick to tropick by my direction; the clouds, at my call, have poured their waters, and the Nile has overflowed at my command; I have restrained the rage of the dog-star, and mitigated the fervours of the crab. The winds alone, of all the elemental powers, have hitherto refused my authority, and multitudes have perished by equinoctial tempests which I found myself unable to prohibit or restrain. I have administered this great office with exact justice, and made to the different nations of the earth an impartial dividend of rain and sunshine. What must have been the misery of half the globe, if I had limited the clouds to particular regions, or confined the sun to either side of the equator?'

And so to the conclusion drawn by Imlac:

'Of the uncertainties of our present state, the most dreadful and alarming is the uncertain continuance of reason.'

Nothing is said of happiness—to mention it at such a juncture would be farcical. The next chapter, 'The Dangerous Prevalence of Imagination', begins with a startling generalization that again confounds the experimenters, though they cannot be said to be unprepared for it:

'Disorders of intellect, answered Imlac, happen much more often than superficial observers will easily believe. Perhaps, if we speak with rigorous exactness, no human mind is in its right state.'

Imlac and the rest try to cure the deluded astronomer, and leave him with Imlac's encouragement: 'Your learning and virtue may justly give you hopes.' In Johnson's view, hope is necessary to man if he is to stay the course of life; the first sentence of his story—I quote it below, at p. 250—speaks with indulgent contempt of 'phantoms of hope' and their pursuit, but the astronomer's hopes are more than these, being raised *justly* on the solidity of learning and virtue, for Johnson counts learning high among human virtues and benefits, and his prose is never more roundly contemptuous than when he refers to brute ignorance, which, 'when it is voluntary, is criminal' (ch. xxx).[1]

The visit to the pyramids, which takes place about mid-way in the story, was to some extent to the discredit of the experiments. Imlac bullies the party into making the excursion on the general grounds that ocular experience of long-surviving monu-

---

[1] For an instance of his contemptuous phrasing, see below, p. 246, *n*. 1.

ments is a good in itself, and it is only after much general discussion on things such as 'the hunger of the imagination that
preys on life' that he is able to reassure them that this excursion
also has contributed to their scheme:

'Whoever thou art, that, not content with a moderate condition,
imaginest happiness in royal magnificence, and dreamest that
command or riches can feed the appetite of novelty with perpetual
gratifications, survey the pyramids, and confess thy folly!'

We feel that the experiments are discredited a little when this is
all they can show—Rasselas already knew such a truth sufficiently from this confinement in the Happy Valley. But it is a later
excursion that shows up most sharply the triviality of their
quest, at least in its original form. For the catacombs lead to
the matter of the penultimate chapter, 'Imlac discourses on the
Nature of the Soul'. Again the wording of their further progress
in 'truth' is left to Nekayah:

'To me . . . the choice of life is become less important; I hope hereafter to think only on the choice of eternity.'

core

That contains Johnson's own answer, and carried for him the
implications of Christianity. In modified form of course it
applies, and was intended to apply to everybody, whether
Christian or not—plainly any life is less miserable if what is
given is accepted, for whatever reason, and if what is un-
avoidable and of small importance not fretted over. In the last
chapter of all the party turns back towards Abyssinia,
foregoing any choice of life they themselves might have the
power to make. Circling back to the beginning, we have all
come a long way, through the gathering solemnity and
deepening shade. The way has been in accordance with
Johnson's disclosure of the 'truth', but if we have come smoothly,
it is because of his art.

I might have paused on the way to remark the simpler *narrative*
arrangements that defeat the effect of monotony where materials *tech.*
are discernible as sameish at bottom—the varying of the experiments in length, and in the length of the talking they
prompt, the punctuating of one experiment by another, the
splitting up of the party to make experiments separately—

especially when Pekuah is snatched away to make further experiments much against her will. There is one experiment, however, that evinces an art less straightforward. It seems quite separate from the experiment that precedes it, but points to a truth lying between them, which is more alarming than that of either. The former of these experiments is the one made by Rasselas on the young men of Cairo. He finds them engaged on pleasure of the sort he is ashamed of:

Their mirth was without images,[1] their laughter without motive; their pleasures were gross and sensual, in which the mind had no part. . . .

He sees them as 'sad or cheerful only by chance', and cries that 'Happiness . . . must be something solid and permanent, without fear and without uncertainty'. Johnson proceeds:

But his young companions had gained so much of his regard by their frankness and courtesy, that he could not leave them without warning and remonstrance. 'My friends, said he, I have seriously considered our manners and our prospects, and find that we have mistaken our own interest. The first years of man must make provision for the last. He that never thinks never can be wise. Perpetual levity must end in ignorance; and intemperance, though it may fire the spirits for an hour, will make life short or miserable. Let us consider that youth is of no long duration, and that in maturer age, when the enchantments of fancy shall cease, and phantoms of delight dance no more about us, we shall have no comforts but the esteem of wise men, and the means of doing good. Let us, therefore, stop, while to stop is in our power: let us live as men who are sometime to grow old, and to whom it will be the most dreadful of all evils not to count their past years but by follies, and to be reminded of their former luxuriance of health only by the maladies which riot has produced.'

They stared a while in silence one upon another, and, at last, drove him away by a general chorus of continued laughter.

[1] 'images' is sufficiently explained by the conclusion of the sentence in which it occurs. Imlac had already remarked, in ch. xii, that 'I am less unhappy than the rest [of the 'prisoners' in the Happy Valley], because I have a mind replete with images, which I can vary and combine at pleasure. I can amuse my solitude by the renovation of the knowledge which begins to fade from my memory, and by recollection of the accidents of my past life. Yet all this ends in the sorrowful consideration, that my acquirements are now useless, and that none of my pleasures can be again enjoyed. The rest, whose minds have no impression but of the present moment, are either corroded by malignant passions, or sit stupid in the gloom of perpetual vacancy.'

The consciousness that his sentiments were just, and his intentions kind, was scarcely sufficient to support him against the horrour of derision. But he recovered his tranquillity, and persued his search.

And so to his next experiment. He finds a 'wise and happy man' as he supposes, a philosopher who lectures on happiness with the utmost conviction that it is within man's reach:

He then communicated the various precepts given from time to time for the conquest of passion, and displayed the happiness of those who had obtained the important victory, after which man is no longer the slave of fear, nor the fool of hope; is no more emaciated by envy, inflamed by anger, emasculated by tenderness, or depressed by grief; but walks on calmly through the tumults or the privacies of life, as the sun persues alike his course through the calm or the stormy sky.

Rasselas is enraptured, according him 'the veneration due to the instructions of a superior being':

'I have found, said the Prince, at his return to Imlac, a man who can teach all that is necessary to be known, who, from the un-shaken throne of rational fortitude, looks down on the scenes of life changing beneath him. He speaks, and attention watches his lips. He reasons, and conviction closes his periods. This man shall be my future guide: I will learn his doctrines, and imitate his life.'

The shock comes a few days later, when he makes his way into the home of the philosopher, whom he found

in a room half darkened, with his eyes misty, and his face pale. 'Sir, said he, you are come at a time when all human friendship is useless; what I suffer cannot be remedied, what I have lost cannot be supplied. My daughter, my only daughter, from whose tenderness I expected all the comforts of my age, died last night of a fever. My views, my purposes, my hopes are at an end: I am now a lonely being disunited from society.'

'Sir, said the Prince, mortality is an event by which a wise man can never be surprised: we know that death is always near, and it should therefore always be expected.' 'Young man, answered the philosopher, you speak like one that has never felt the pangs of separation.' 'Have you then forgot the precepts, said Rasselas, which you so powerfully enforced? Has wisdom no strength to arm the heart against calamity? Consider, that external things are naturally variable, but truth and reason are always the same.' 'What comfort, said the mourner, can truth and reason afford me?

of what effect are they now, but to tell me, that my daughter will not be restored?'

Rasselas draws the moral for himself:

The Prince, whose humanity would not suffer him to insult misery with reproof, went away convinced of the emptiness of rhetorical sound, and the inefficacy of polished periods and studied sentences.

All that Rasselas sees in this second experiment is that a lecturer on philosophy, quite sure of himself while on the platform, is not proof against an 'act of God'. To show this any accident would have done: Shakespeare had already remarked that

> . . . there was never yet philosopher
> That could endure the toothache patiently.

But Johnson gives the philosopher the particular sort of accident that Rasselas, in his concluding speech to the young men of Cairo, had confidently provided against: 'The first years of man must make provision for the last.' The philosopher had indeed made provision, as far as man can. A 'truth', then, is implicit in the two experiments that Johnson shows Rasselas to be incapable of drawing out, at this stage at least of his experience.

The making of two points simultaneously is not characteristic of Johnson, for he liked to be explicit, and liked others to be so too. One of the defects of his greatness as a critic of Shakespeare is that he wanted him to be more explicit about the philosophy on which the plays stood firmly; he was not content to see that the play was the thing, that its philosophy is the play, and that any formulation of it in any other way injures and diminishes its meaning.[1] I have not noted any further instances of the implicit on this scale in *Rasselas*, but it is a story which, read and reread, discloses more and more cross-references within itself. Like any great work of art, its parts are minutely interconnected, and, again like any great work of art, it proceeds by cumulation.

[1] Cf. D. C. Tovey, *Essays in Musical Analysis*, 1936, iii. 125: 'And now we have the finale [of Brahms's piano concerto in B♭]. What tremendous triumph shall it express? Brahms's answer is such as only the greatest of artists can find; there are no adequate words for it (there never are for any art that is not itself words—and then there are only its own words).'

XIII

TIME IN *RASSELAS*

THERE IS an obvious danger when we re-read a work of literature and are on the look-out for examples of one particular thing in it—the danger that we see nothing else. All of us have noted this danger besetting the critics who read Shakespeare for his images. Nevertheless, I suggest that on at least one occasion when *Rasselas* is being read again the reader should mark its notifications of time. There is no end of them, and their presence in plenty is part of the meaning of the story.

To say that in *Rasselas* time is more important than place may not be saying much. No doubt it is so in every story, even in stories so deeply localized as *Wuthering Heights* and *The Return of the Native* and *To the Lighthouse*. But there is an unusual, perhaps a unique, significance for *Rasselas* in clock and calendar. Its events are arranged in temporal sequence (as in any story), and the passage of time has an effect (as in certain stories) on the minds and characters and personalities of the people represented. But in *Rasselas*, perhaps uniquely, time is seen as a prime condition governing human life—indeed as *the* prime condition, for the worth of human life is to be measured, as Johnson sees it, by how time has been used. He would have respected the earnest calculations that Ruskin made at the age of 37:

There is a Sunday meditation in his diary (of 7 Sept. 1856) which reveals some of the inner currents of Ruskin's life. He makes a numerical 'calculation of the number of days which under perfect term of human life I might have to live'. He works the sum out to 11,795, and for some years onward the days in his diary are noted by the diminishing numbers.[1]

Place, as I shall show later, is for Johnson a condition of human life that is to be ignored as much as possible. But time is given us to be 'redeemed', to be saved from being lost. The story of *Rasselas* unfolds to the chime of clocks and to the rapidly

[1] *Works*, VII. xxiii.

turning leaves of the calendar, and beyond the reach of their functions stretches eternity, because the soul is immortal (ch. xlviii).

It would be pleasant to re-tell the story of *Rasselas* pointing out its recurrent notices of time, but I shall refer only to a selection of them. The result of this procedure—for which I apologize—will be to represent as scrappy what is in fact smoothly ordered.

At the outset the future is opposed to the present with all the power of Johnson's most menacing music:

> Ye who listen with credulity to the whispers of fancy, and persue with eagerness the phantoms of hope; who expect that age will perform the promises of youth, and that the deficiencies of the present day will be supplied by the morrow; attend to the history of Rasselas prince of Abissinia.

This kind of opposition, or rather interconnexion, between present and future (or between present and past) is constantly recurring in the story, and I shall note one or two further instances later on. It is with what I may call temporal particulars that I shall be concerned most, however, and especially with those that specify numbers. Rasselas—who is introduced as an item in a dynastic process according to which he must wait in the Happy Valley 'till the order of succession should call him to the throne' (ch. i)—Rasselas and the rest of the Emperor's children have the duty of entertaining their father on his annual visits, when

> during eight days every one that resided in the valley was required to propose whatever might contribute to make seclusion pleasant, to fill up the vacancies of attention, and lessen the tediousness of time (ch. i).

During the rest of the year 'revelry and merriment was the business of every hour from the dawn of morning to the close of even' (ch. ii). And so, not surprisingly for the hero of a story, Rasselas suffers repletion, and his age, which we are now given, is in itself an explanation: he is 'in the twenty-sixth year of his age' (ch. ii). A quarter of a century, then, has gone by of his perfect term of life, his three score years and ten. He has entered on the period of maturity during which the mind, if it exists substantially, claims an increasing part in life: 'pleasure' is no longer enough; 'I have already enjoyed too much; give me something to desire' (ch. iii). What he seeks, as well, or instead, is that finer, more mental thing, happiness, those 'peculiar enjoyments'—that is, those enjoyments proper to man as distinct from the other animals—which surely must balance the 'peculiar sufferings' that fall to man's lot, and especially perhaps to the lot of men who, like Rasselas, have enough mind to be 'burdened' with themselves (ch. ii). Rasselas has recourse to his old tutor, whose lectures by the way 'pleased only while they were new' (ch. iii), and it is he who suggests that Rasselas makes what come to be called 'experiments upon life' (ch.xvii), and that he seeks out the miseries of the world so as to 'know how to value [his] present state' (ch. iii). Rasselas 'had been before terrified at the length of life which nature promised him, because he considered that in a long time much must be endured; he now rejoiced in his youth, because in many years much might be done' (ch. iv). Whereupon, in this anticipatory state of mind, 'amidst hourly preparations for the various incidents of human affairs', 'passed twenty months of the life of Rasselas' (ch. iv). After this protracted and merely 'visionary bustle' there comes the inevitable reaction:

'How long is it that my hopes and wishes have flown beyond this boundary of my life, which yet I never have attempted to surmount!'

'Struck with this reflection', Rasselas stops his bustling, and sits down 'to muse'. He then 'remembered' that 'since he first resolved to escape from his confinement, the sun had passed twice over him in his annual course. . . . He compared twenty months with the life of man'. And hereupon follows a sketch of the map of human life, as Johnson saw it.

'In life, said he, is not to be counted the ignorance of infancy, or imbecility of age. We are long before we are able to think, and we soon cease from the power of acting. The true period of human existence may be reasonably estimated as forty years, of which I have mused away the four and twentieth part [i.e., 20 months]. What I have lost was certain, for I have certainly possessed it; but of twenty months to come who can assure me?'

251

More follows to the same effect—only to be followed itself by the discovery that in the process of 'resolving to lose no more time in idle resolves' four more months have flown. These passages are amongst the most important in the story because they bear on the prime question at issue, whether happiness is indeed discoverable in human life. Happiness is possible if at all only during the forty years that lie between ignorant infancy and imbecile old age. Infancy, which lasts twenty years may well be a time of enjoyment, but that is because it is ignorant. When knowledge comes, it is followed by thought, and it is Johnson's contention that anybody who thinks—and any rational being must—cannot be happy. Happiness of the kind that Rasselas is on the look-out for—which 'must be something solid and permanent, without fear and without uncertainty' (ch. xvii)—is out of the question in so far as a person thinks. To such a thinking person the state of man on earth cannot but be fraught with fears and uncertainties—let alone miseries—both his own and those of others. To be happy men must surrender their claim to be rational—as Swift and others had implied in defining happiness as 'a perpetual possession of being well deceived'. At last Rasselas resolves to escape in earnest, only to find that the ways of escape are so difficult that 'in these fruitless searches he spent ten months' (ch. v).

The means of escape that first suggests itself is by air, but it takes the inventor 'a year' to build his aircraft, and when the trial flight is made the machine drops in to the lake 'in an instant'. A whole year gone by in inflating, so to speak, a balloon that burst! It is now that Rasselas hears the life story of the poet-philosopher Imlac, an account studded with references to time. After which the means of escape are sought with supreme earnestness: 'no time was now lost' (ch. xiii). Escape is at last effected and the journey is begun, but time is still insisting on its rights:

By degrees the royal wanderers were taught to understand that they had for a time laid aside their dignity, and were to expect only such regard as liberality and courtesy could procure. And Imlac, having, by many admonitions, prepared them to endure the tumults of a port, and the ruggedness of the commercial race, brought them down to the sea-coast.

The prince and his sister, to whom every thing was new, were gratified equally at all places, and therefore remained for some months at the port without any inclination to pass further. Imlac was content with their stay, because he did not think it safe to expose them, unpractised in the world, to the hazards of a foreign country.

At last he begun to fear lest they should be discovered, and proposed to fix a day for their departure. They had no pretensions to judge for themselves, and referred the whole scheme to his direction. He therefore took passage in a ship to Suez; and, when the time came, with great difficulty prevailed on the princess to enter the vessel. They had a quick and prosperous voyage, and from Suez travelled by land to Cairo (ch. xv).

In Cairo Rasselas mingles with the 'young men of spirit and gaiety', and of course discovers that they have made no plans for the wise laying out of time: they do not 'live as men who are sometime to grow old'. And so the story proceeds with its 'experiments', and with the adventures the experimenters meet with. When we are hearing evidence as to the happiness of this and that state of life, the plotting of each human life in time is not lost sight of. Just before the end, after Imlac has taken occasion to discourse on the nature of the soul, we come on the last explicit piece of reasoning in the story: the experimenters and Imlac their mentor are on the point of turning away from the catacombs:

'But the Being, said Nekayah, whom I fear to name, the Being which made the soul, can destroy it.'

'He, surely, can destroy it, answered Imlac, since, however unperishable, it receives from a superiour nature its power of duration. That it will not perish by any inherent cause of decay, or principle of corruption, may be shown by philosophy; but philosophy can tell no more. That it will not be annihilated by him that made it, we must humbly learn from higher authority.'

The whole assembly stood a while silent and collected. 'Let us return, said Rasselas, from this scene of mortality. How gloomy would be these mansions of the dead to him who did not know that he shall never die; that what now acts shall continue its agency, and what now thinks shall think on for ever. Those that lie here stretched before us, the wise and the powerful of antient times, warn us to remember the shortness of our present state: they were, perhaps, snatched away while they were busy, like us, in the choice of life.'

'To me, said the princess, the choice of life is become less important; I hope hereafter to think only on the choice of eternity.'

They then hastened out of the caverns, and, under the protection of their guard, returned to Cairo.

With the word eternity, the various points and spans of time fall into place in the total scheme.

The party returns to Abyssinia, sadder and wiser. It is sadder because they now know that solid happiness is not the lot of man, and they are wiser because they now see that there is no solution of human problems that comes of changing place, either geographical or social. When Imlac discoursed on pilgrimages and the benefits that may come of them, he remarked that they were not a *necessary* means to piety or knowledge: 'Long journies in search of truth are not commanded' (ch. xi). Rasselas therefore might well have remained at home in the Happy Valley in accordance with the dynastic custom into which he was born. For in Johnson's view it is a prime duty of man to make the best of the conditions in which he is placed. The experiments that Rasselas made upon life were made in the attempt to choose a life for himself. But if he did not stay and make the best of the Happy Valley, he returns to do what he can. To return to the Happy Valley is not possible—'those, on whom the iron gate [of the Valley] had once closed, were never suffered to return' (ch. i).[1] Rasselas returns to Abyssinia, presumably to wait 'till the order of succession should call him to the throne'. After gaining a great deal of experience (the value of which Johnson would in general be the last to deny) Rasselas does in fact reassume as far as possible the duties from which he had tried to escape. In the end 'nothing is concluded', because he is virtually where he was at the beginning.

It took an urgent occasion to rouse Johnson to write *Rasselas*. We cannot but wish that another as urgent, though less painful, had roused him to write a sequel—a sequel to show how the

---

[1] See G. Sherburn, 'Rasselas Returns—to What?', *Philological Quarterly*, xxxviii, iii, July 1959, pp. 383 f.

much-thinking Rasselas made himself a life he had no cause
to be ashamed of.[1]

[1] According to Hawkins, Johnson did consider writing a sequel: 'Rasselas . . .
was so concluded as to admit of a continuation; and, in fact, Johnson had medi-
tated a second part, in which he meant to marry his hero, and place him in a state
of permanent felicity: but it fared with this resolution as it did with that of Dr.
Young, who, in his estimate of human life, promised, as he had given the dark, so
in a future publication he would display the bright side of his subject; he never did
it, for he had found out that it had no bright side, and Johnson had made much
the same discovery, and that in this state of our existence all our enjoyments are
fugacious, and permanent felicity unattainable.' (Hawkins' *Life of Johnson*, 1787,
pp. 371 f.)
There are two parts to this story: (*a*) the broaching of a sequel, and (*b*) the
suggestion for its theme. Of these (*b*) cannot be taken seriously. If Johnson did
in fact consider a sequel, it could not have treated marriage as a state of permanent
felicity if only for the reason that a truthful eye had already been turned on it in
Rasselas, in those brilliant chapters on parents and children, husband and wife
(xxv-vi, xxviii-ix). Either (*b*) is apocryphal, or Johnson figures in it as an unde-
tected ironist. Ellis Cornelia Knight, however, purported to take both (*a*) and
(*b*) seriously. She quoted Hawkins in the preface to her *Dinarbas*, the sequel to
Rasselas which she wrote six years after Johnson's death. In the event, however,
she accepted the suggestion of sequel without accepting the subject, for her story
about Rasselas and his little group is one of martial—not marital—adventure and
courtship. Only in the last chapter are Rasselas and Nekayah introduced to the
married state. Meanwhile there has been no experience of any permanent happiness—all is wretchedness and uneasiness. The sequel we should have liked from
Johnson would have been that indicated above.

INDEX

Abercrombie, Lascelles, 85
Addison, Joseph, 37n, 39, 156
Æsop, 76, 215, 217n, 222n
'Agenor', 95
Ampleforth Journal, 105n
Arbuthnot, John, 159, 168
Aristotle, 46, 119–20
Arnold, Matthew, 28, 31–2, 35n, 65, 139n; 'The Bishop and the Philosopher', 118n; *On the Study of Celtic Literature*, 29n; 'Thyrsis', 30–2, 60; 'To a Friend', 105
Arthos, John, 67, 108–10, 213
Atterbury, Francis, 119n, 148, 226
Augustus Caesar, 30
Ault, Norman, 147–54, 171n
Austen, Jane, 237

Bach, Johann Sebastian, 89
Bacon, Francis, 116n, 217n
Barfield, Owen, 45
Barstow, Marjorie Latta, 55n, 71–3, 95, 115n
Bartas, Guillaume de Salluste, du. *See* Sylvester, Joshua
Bath, Thomas Henry Thynne, marquess of, 168n, 171n
Beattie, James, 39, 41n
Beaumont, Francis, 74
Beerbohm, Max, 34
Beethoven, Ludwig van, 137n
Benlowes, Edward, 72n
Bergson, Henri, 31
Bible, 33, 43, 89, 91–2, 129
Blackmore, Richard, 44
Blackwood's Magazine, 217n
Blake, William, 23
Blount, Martha, 150
Blount, Teresa, 150
Blunden, Edmund, 62, 63
Boethius, 62
Bolingbroke, Henry St John, viscount, 142n
Boothby, Brooke, 194n

Boswell, James: account of the composition and nature of *Rasselas*, 229, 233; account of Johnson's mind at its ebb, 231–2
Life of Johnson, 99, 125, 127, 133, 135, 136, 224, 229, 230, 231, 232 233, 238; *Life of Johnson* (Malone edn.), 230
Bourke, John, 89
Bowles, William Lisle, 151
Boyle, Robert, 213
Boys, Richard C., 192–3
Braddon (Maxwell), Mary Elizabeth, 62
Bridges, Robert, 35n, 114, 117–18, 145–6, 227
Brontë, Charlotte, 231n
Brontë, Emily, 249
Brooks, H. F., 121n
Broome, William, 19, 156
Brown, Lancelot ('Capability'), 18
Browne, Thomas, 47
Browne, William, 35n, 62, 63
Browning, Robert, 23, 28, 80, 163
Buckinghamshire, John Sheffield, duke of, earl of Mulgrave, 68–9, 143
Bunyan, John, 33–4, 105
Burke, Edmund, 136, 232
Burlington, Dorothy, countess of, 156
Burlington, Richard Boyle, third earl of, 156, 159
Burnet, Thomas, 142n
Butler, Samuel, 36n, 41
Butt, John, 147–54
Byron, George Gordon, Lord, 23, 60, 97

Carlton-House Magazine: or, Annals of Taste, Fashion, and Politeness, 95
Carlyle, Jane, 76
Caroline, queen of Britain (wife of George II), 213
Carroll, Lewis, 217n
Caryll, John, 161
Case, A. E., 147, 193
Chapman, George, 35n, 162–4

R*